W9-AHD-577

DAVID JESUS VIGNOLLI

NEW WORLD

Published by
ARCHAIA.

COLORS BY
LEELA AND DAVID JESUS VIGNOLLI

COVER BY
DAVID JESUS VIGNOLLI

DESIGNER
CHELSEA ROBERTS

EDITOR
CAMERON CHITTOCK

SPECIAL THANKS TO
SIERRA HAHN

Ross Richie CEO & Founder
Joy Huffman CFO
Matt Gagnon Editor-in-Chief
Filip Sablik President, Publishing & Marketing
Stephen Christy President, Development
Lance Kreiter Vice President, Licensing & Merchandising
Arune Singh Vice President, Marketing
Bryce Carlson Vice President, Editorial and Creative Strategy
Scott Newman Manager, Production Design
Kate Henning Manager, Operations
Spencer Simpson Manager, Sales
Sierra Hahn Executive Editor
Jeanine Schaefer Executive Editor
Dafna Pleban Senior Editor
Shannon Watters Senior Editor
Eric Harburn Senior Editor
Chris Rosa Editor
Matthew Levine Editor
Sophie Philips-Roberts Associate Editor
Gavin Gronenthal Assistant Editor
Michael Moccio Assistant Editor

Gwen Waller Assistant Editor
Amanda LaFranco Executive Assistant
Jillian Crab Design Coordinator
Michelle Ankley Design Coordinator
Kara Leopard Production Designer
Marie Krupina Production Designer
Grace Park Production Designer
Chelsea Roberts Production Design Assistant
Samantha Knapp Production Design Assistant
José Meza Live Events Lead
Stephanie Hocutt Digital Marketing Lead
Esther Kim Marketing Coordinator
Cat O'Grady Digital Marketing Coordinator
Amanda Lawson Marketing Assistant
Holly Aitchison Digital Sales Coordinator
Morgan Perry Retail Sales Coordinator
Megan Christopher Operations Coordinator
Rodrigo Hernandez Mailroom Assistant
Zipporah Smith Operations Assistant
Breanna Sarpy Executive Assistant

NEW WORLD, August 2019. Published by Archaia, a division of Boom Entertainment, Inc. New World is ™ & © 2019 David Jesus Vignolli de Mello. All rights reserved. Archaia™ and the Archaia logo are trademarks of Boom Entertainment, Inc., registered in various countries and categories. All characters, events, and institutions depicted herein are fictional. Any similarity between any of the names, characters, persons, events, and/or institutions in this publication to actual names, characters, and persons, whether living or dead, events, and/or institutions is unintended and purely coincidental.

BOOM! Studios, 5670 Wilshire Boulevard, Suite 400, Los Angeles, CA 90036-5679. Printed in China. First Printing.

ISBN: 978-1-68415-398-5, eISBN: 978-1-64144-381-4

MUNDUS NOVUS

I trust your Magnificence will be pleased
to hear of the marvelous things that
I experienced during my voyage.

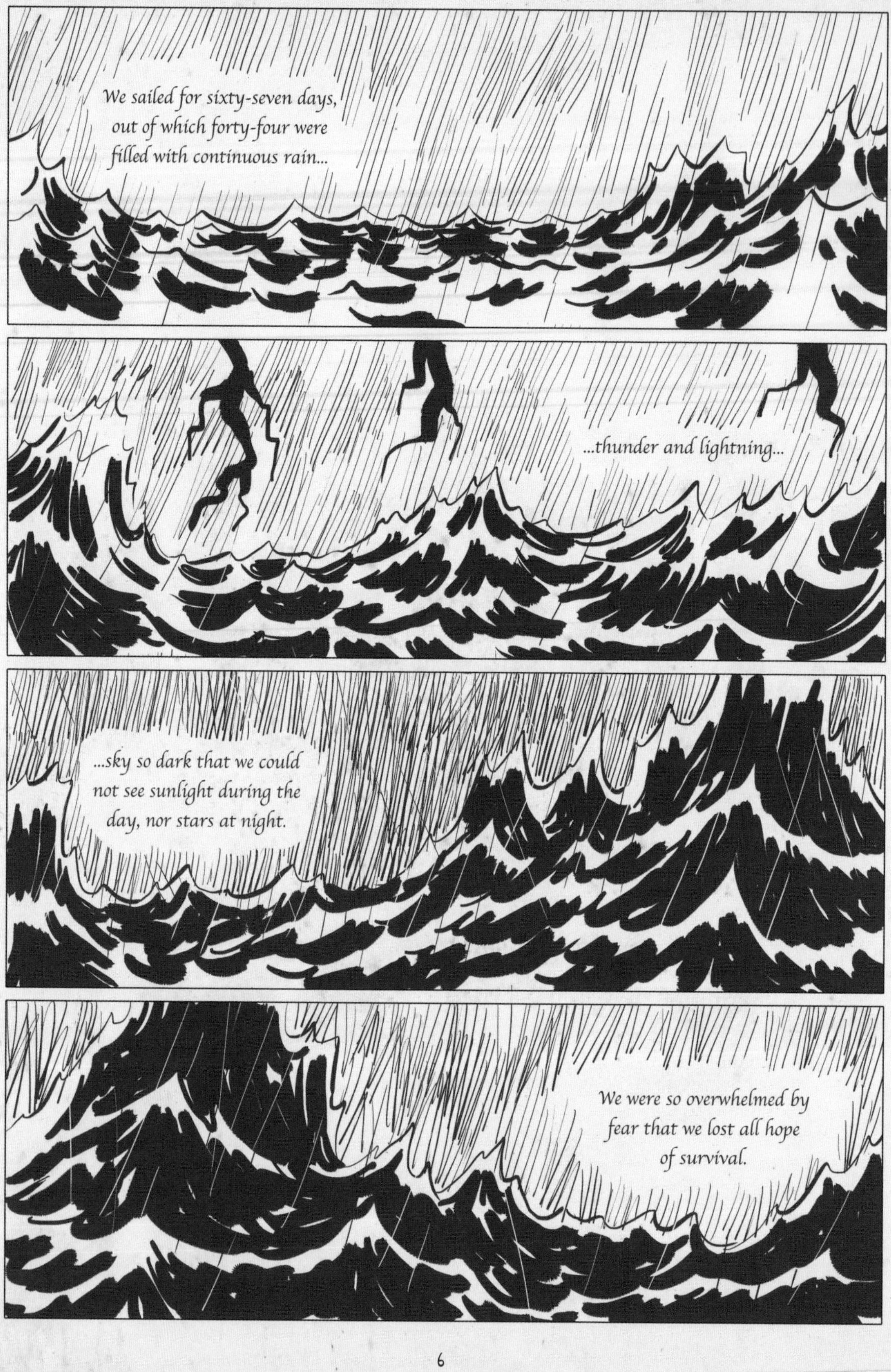
We sailed for sixty-seven days, out of which forty-four were filled with continuous rain...
...thunder and lightning...
...sky so dark that we could not see sunlight during the day, nor stars at night.
We were so overwhelmed by fear that we lost all hope of survival.

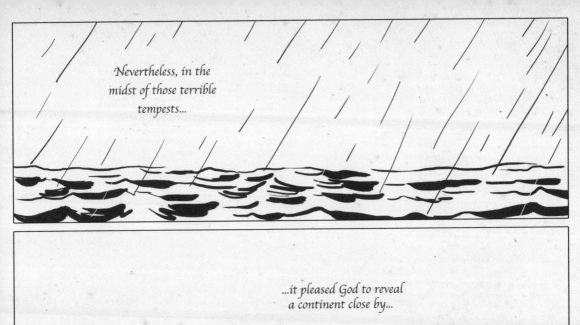

Nevertheless, in the midst of those terrible tempests...

...it pleased God to reveal a continent close by...

...a new region...

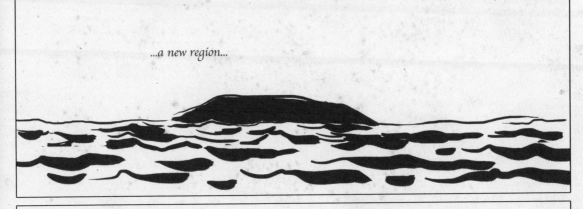

...and an unknown earth.

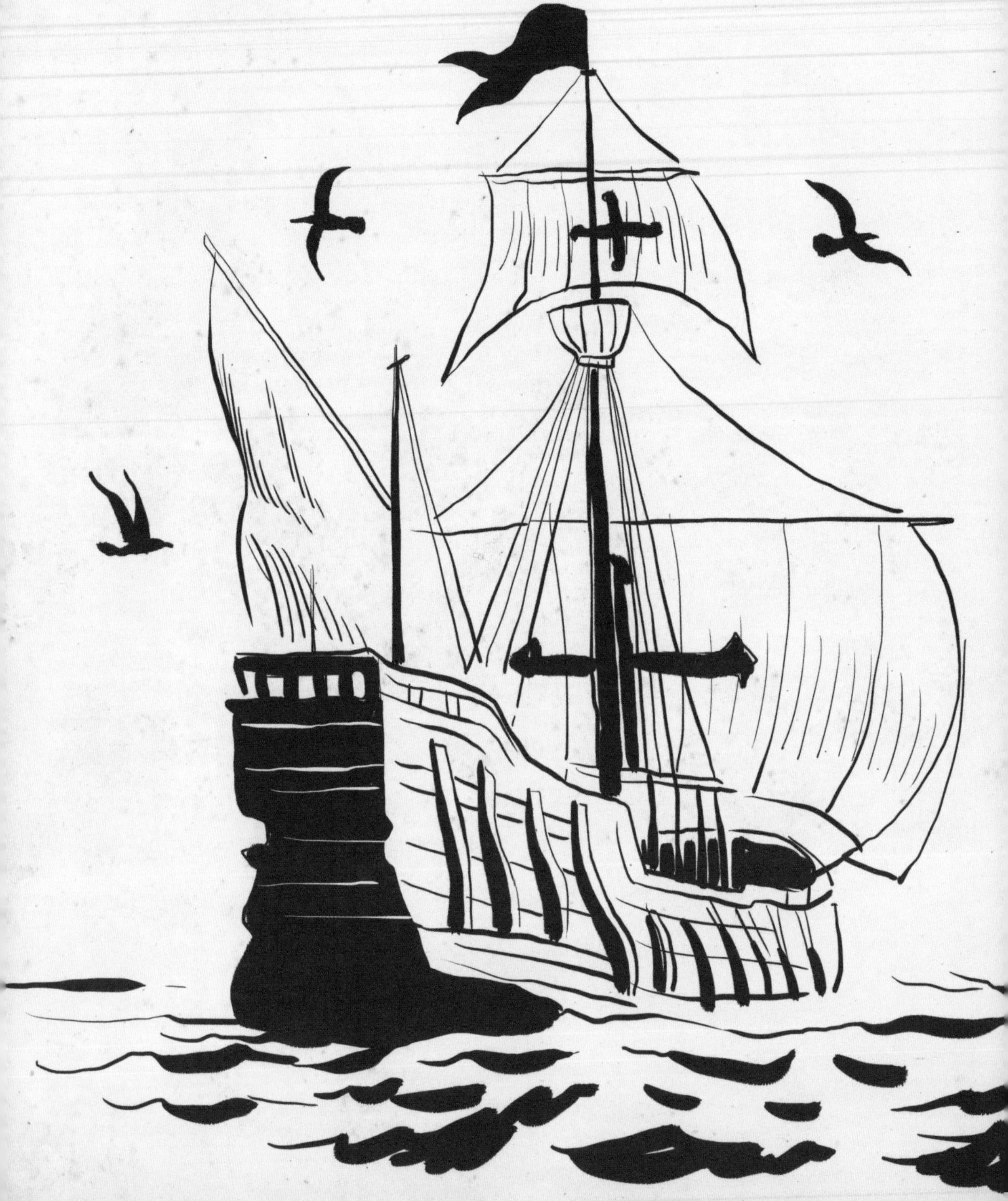

Having seen the land we thanked God, launched the boats...

...and sixteen men strong, landed ashore.

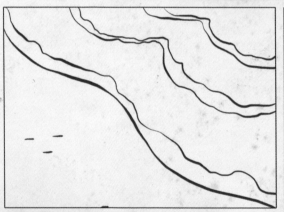

What we witnessed can be only described as an earthly paradise.

I am certain...

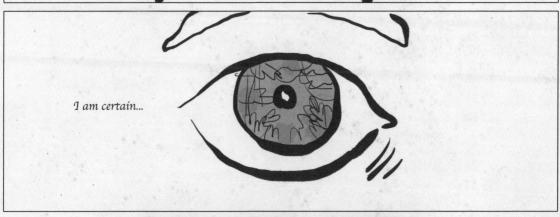

...that we have discovered a...

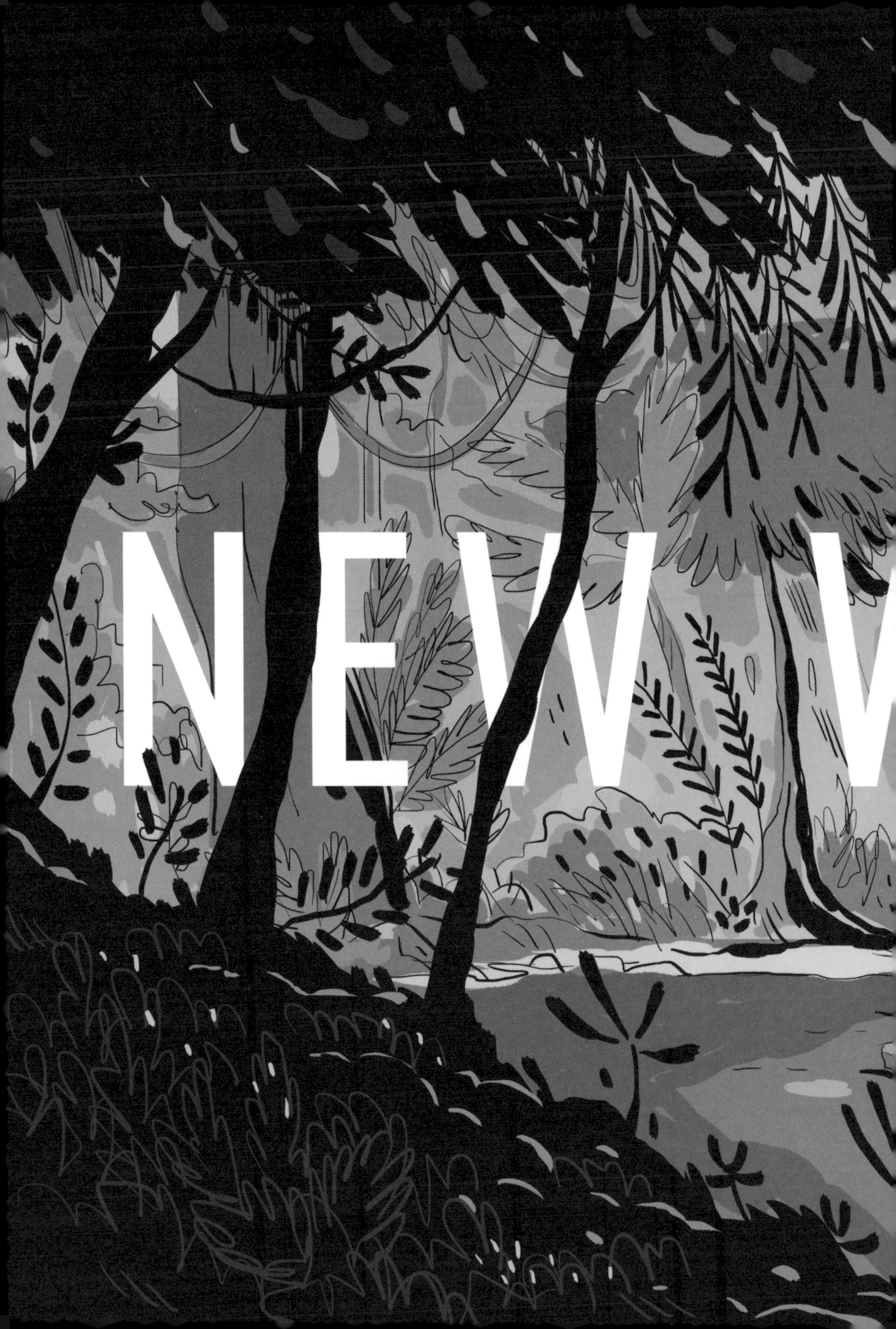
NEW

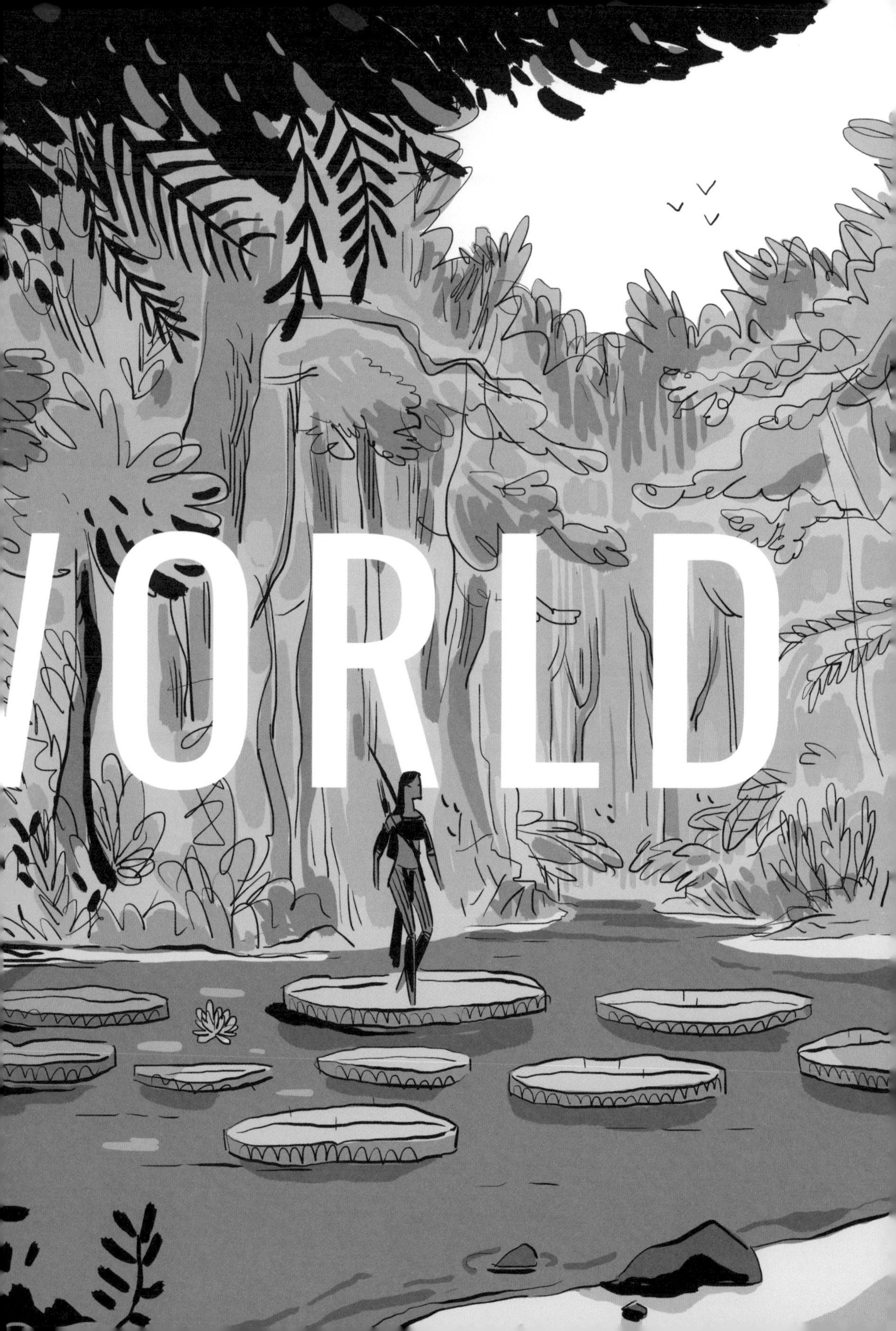
ORLD

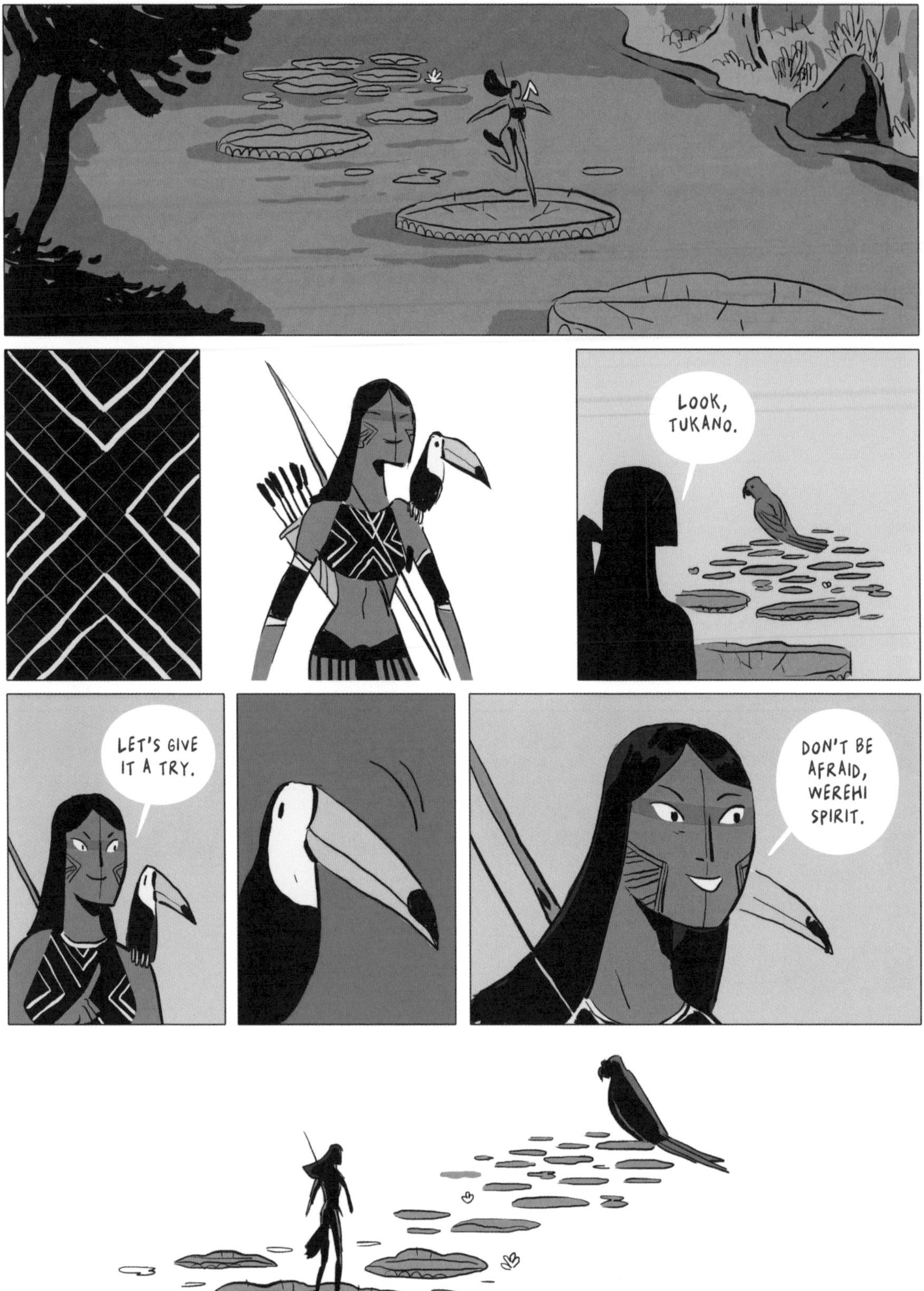
LOOK, TUKANO.
LET'S GIVE IT A TRY.
DON'T BE AFRAID, WEREHI SPIRIT.

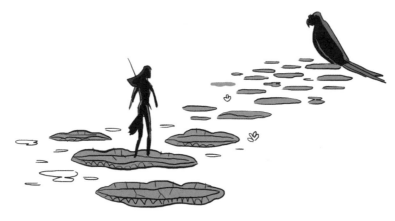

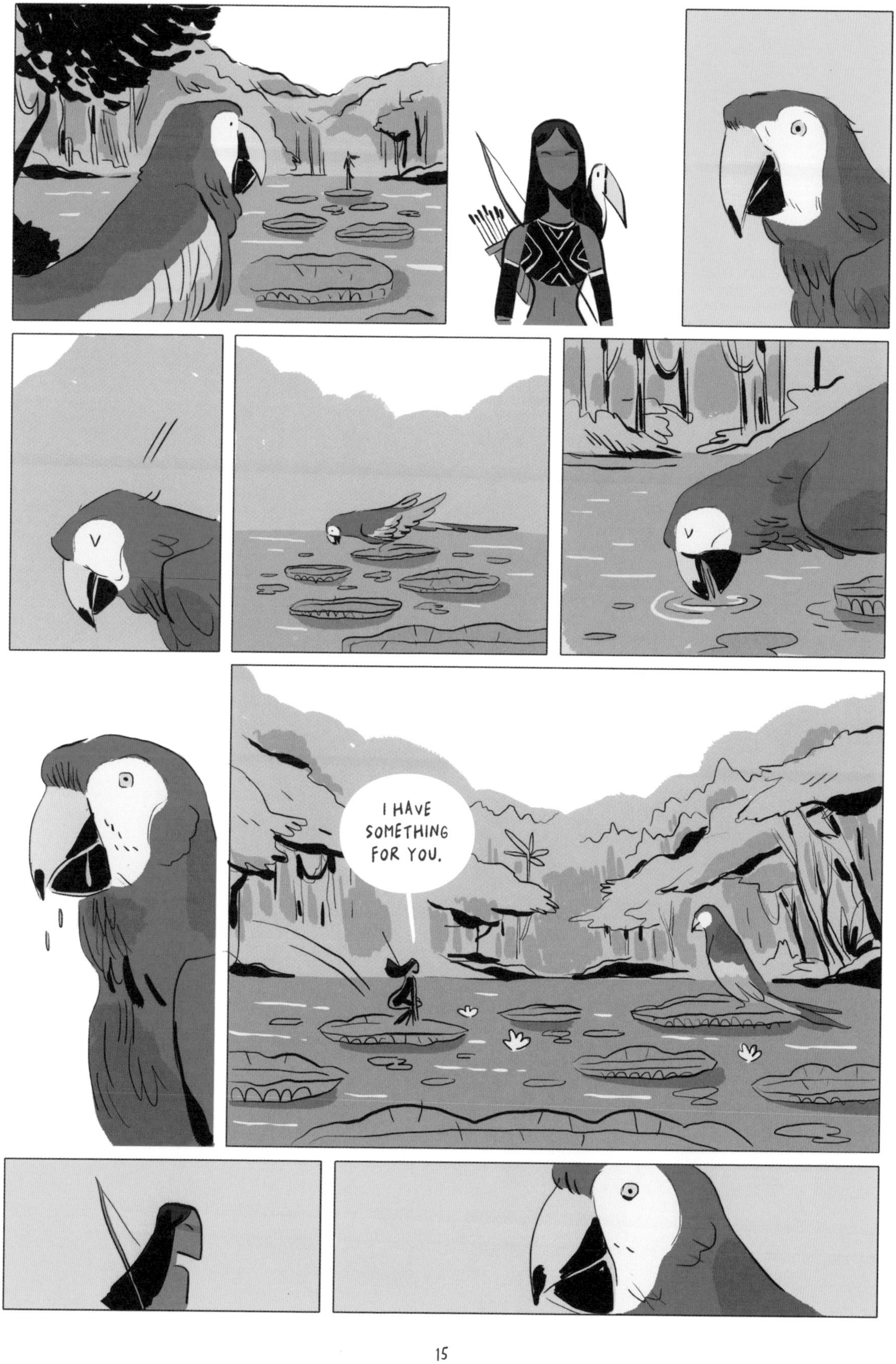
I HAVE SOMETHING FOR YOU.

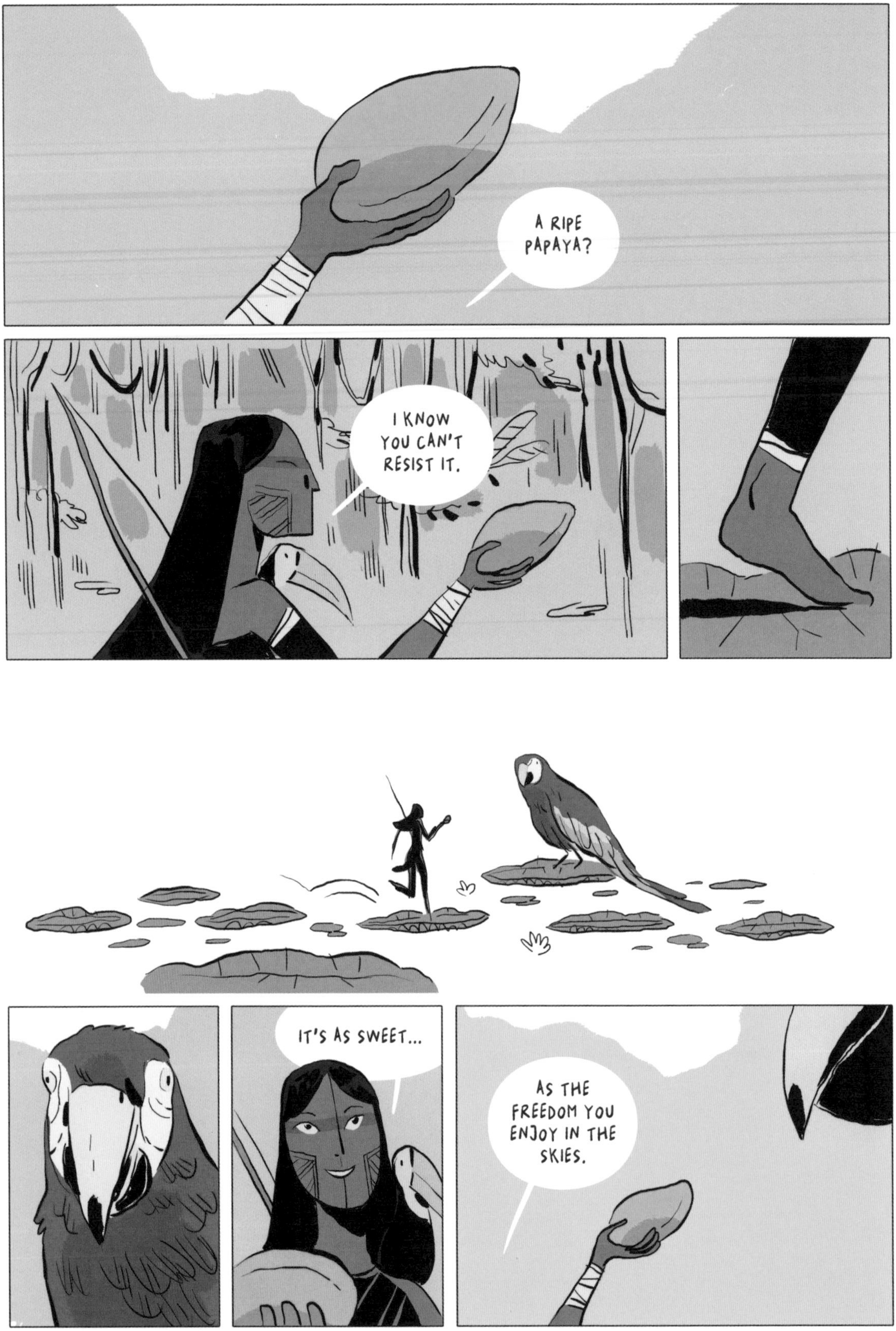
A RIPE PAPAYA?
I KNOW YOU CAN'T RESIST IT.
IT'S AS SWEET...
AS THE FREEDOM YOU ENJOY IN THE SKIES.

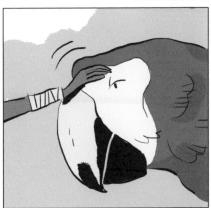

WHERE WILL YOU TAKE ME THIS TIME?

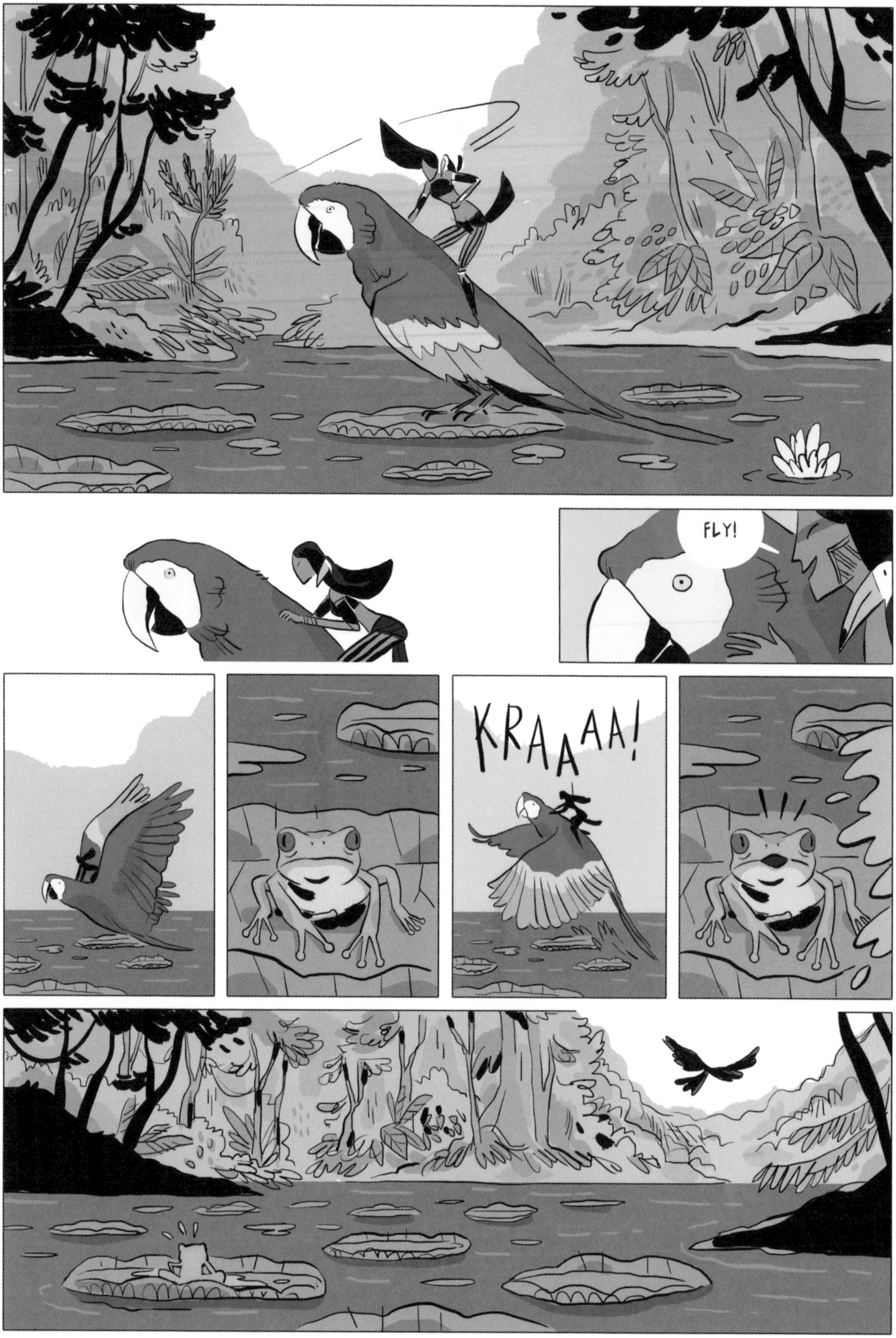
FLY!
KRAAAAA!

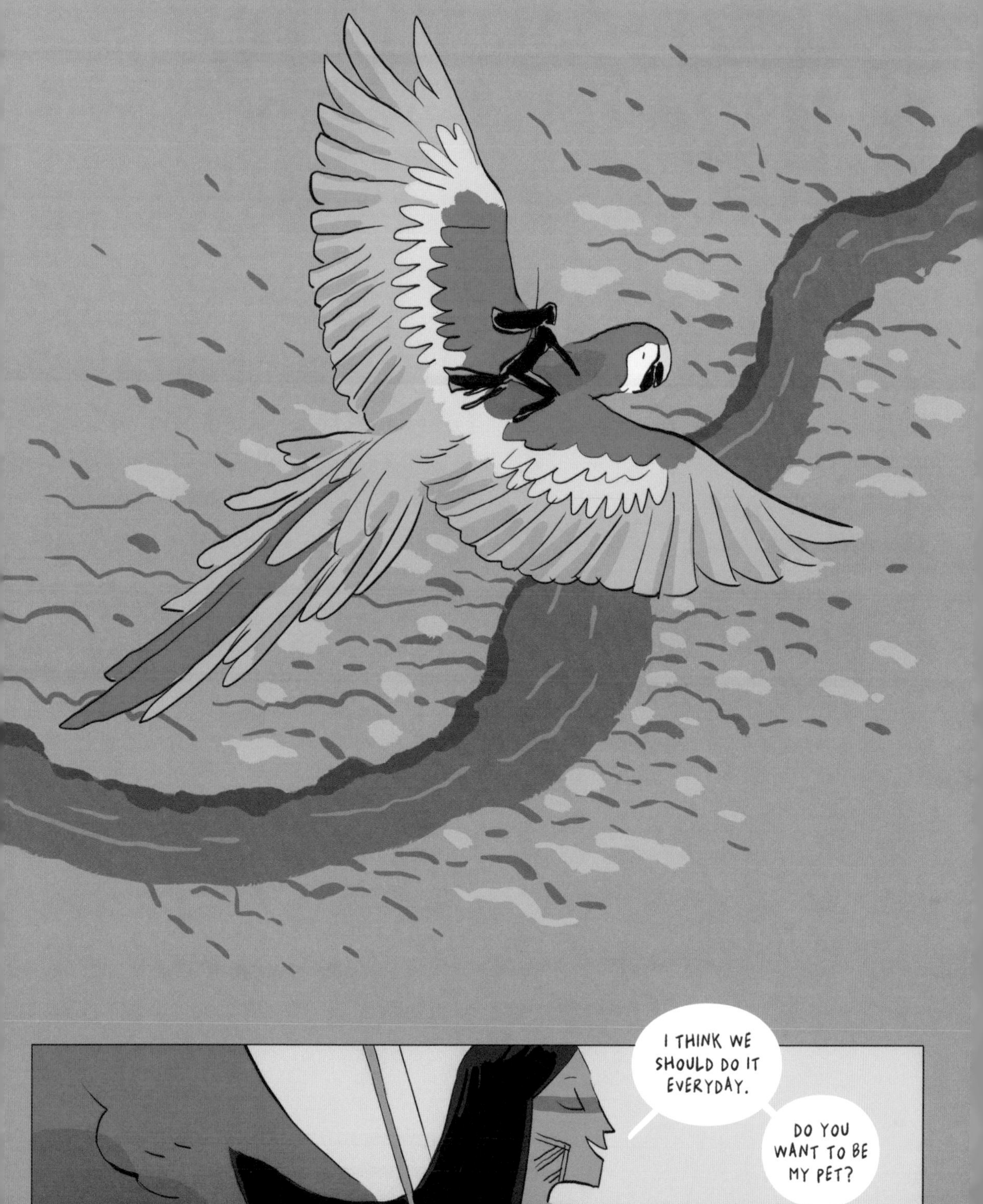
I THINK WE SHOULD DO IT EVERYDAY.
DO YOU WANT TO BE MY PET?

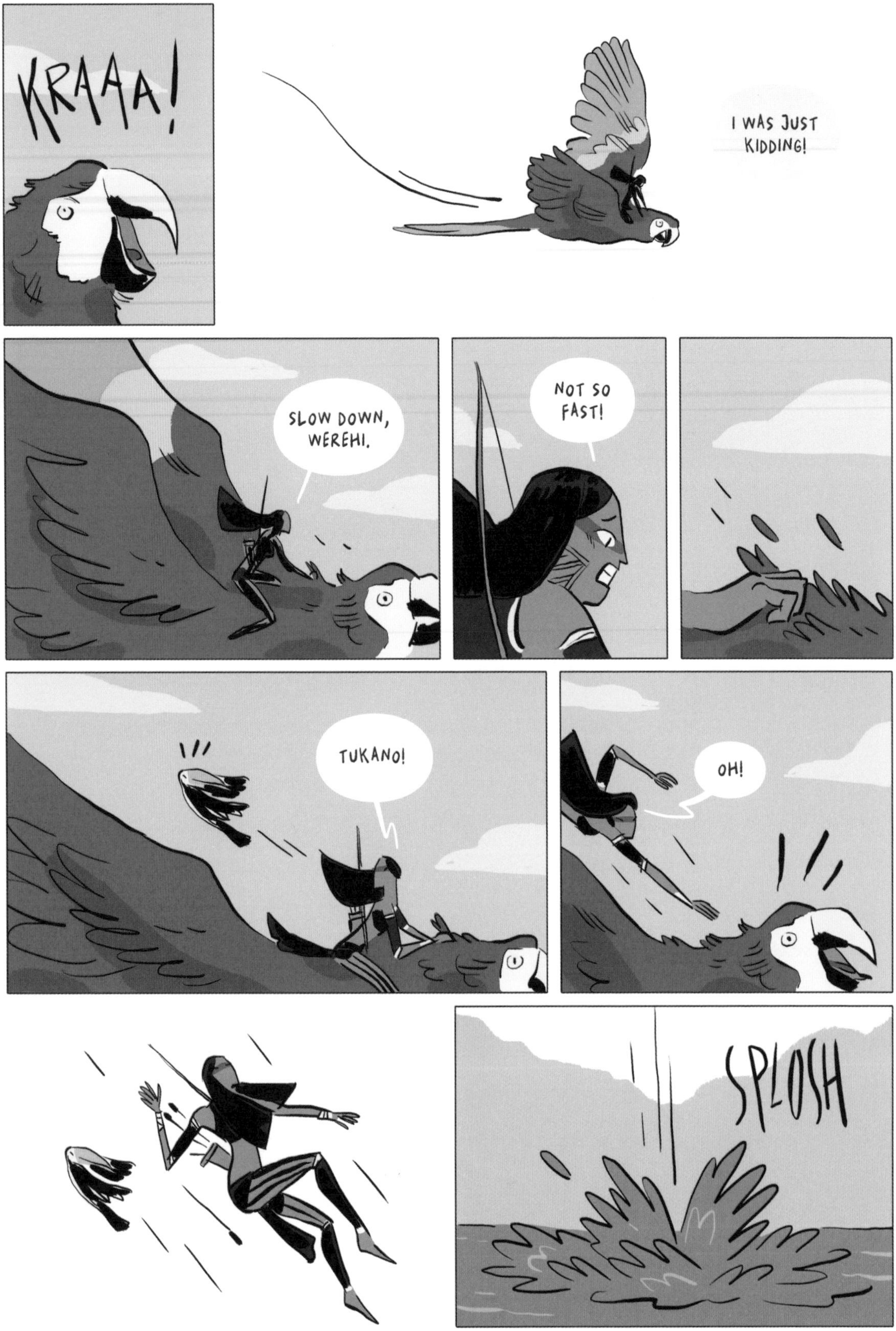
KRAAA!
I WAS JUST KIDDING!
SLOW DOWN, WEREHI.
NOT SO FAST!
TUKANO!
OH!
SPLOSH

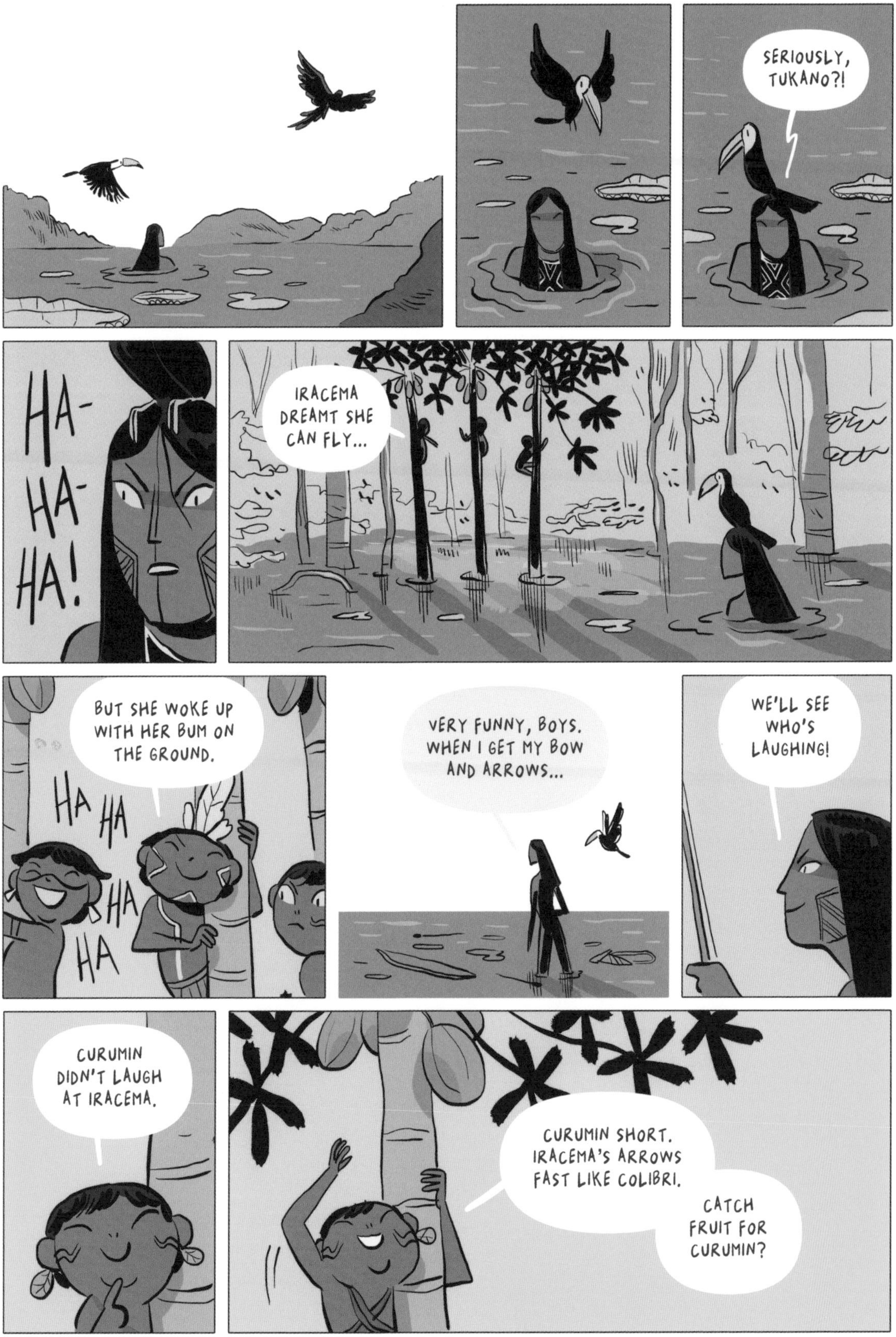
SERIOUSLY, TUKANO?!
HA-HA-HA!
IRACEMA DREAMT SHE CAN FLY...
BUT SHE WOKE UP WITH HER BUM ON THE GROUND.
HA HA HA HA
VERY FUNNY, BOYS. WHEN I GET MY BOW AND ARROWS...
WE'LL SEE WHO'S LAUGHING!
CURUMIN DIDN'T LAUGH AT IRACEMA.
CURUMIN SHORT. IRACEMA'S ARROWS FAST LIKE COLIBRI.
CATCH FRUIT FOR CURUMIN?

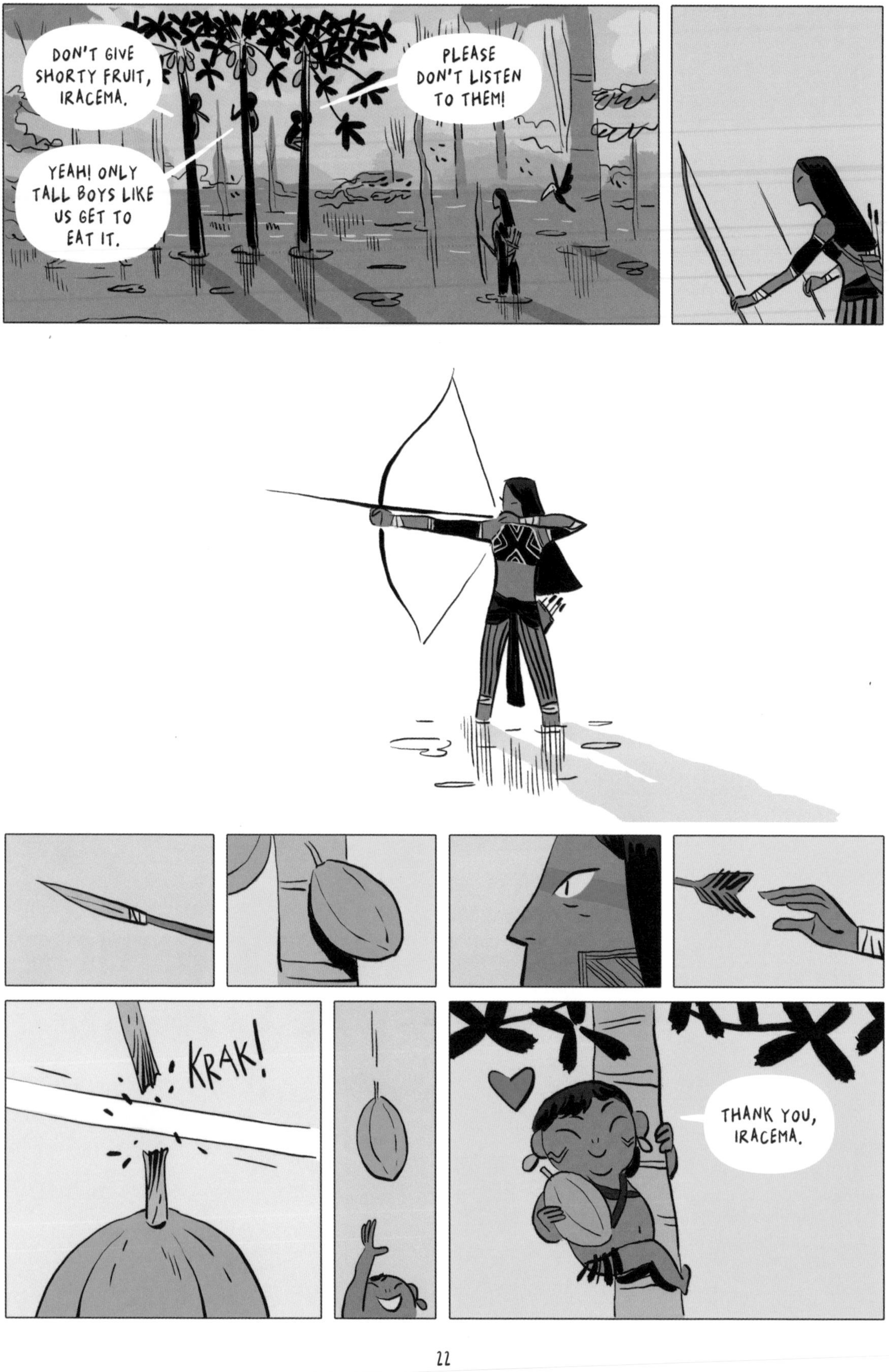
DON'T GIVE SHORTY FRUIT, IRACEMA.
YEAH! ONLY TALL BOYS LIKE US GET TO EAT IT.
PLEASE DON'T LISTEN TO THEM!
KRAK!
THANK YOU, IRACEMA.

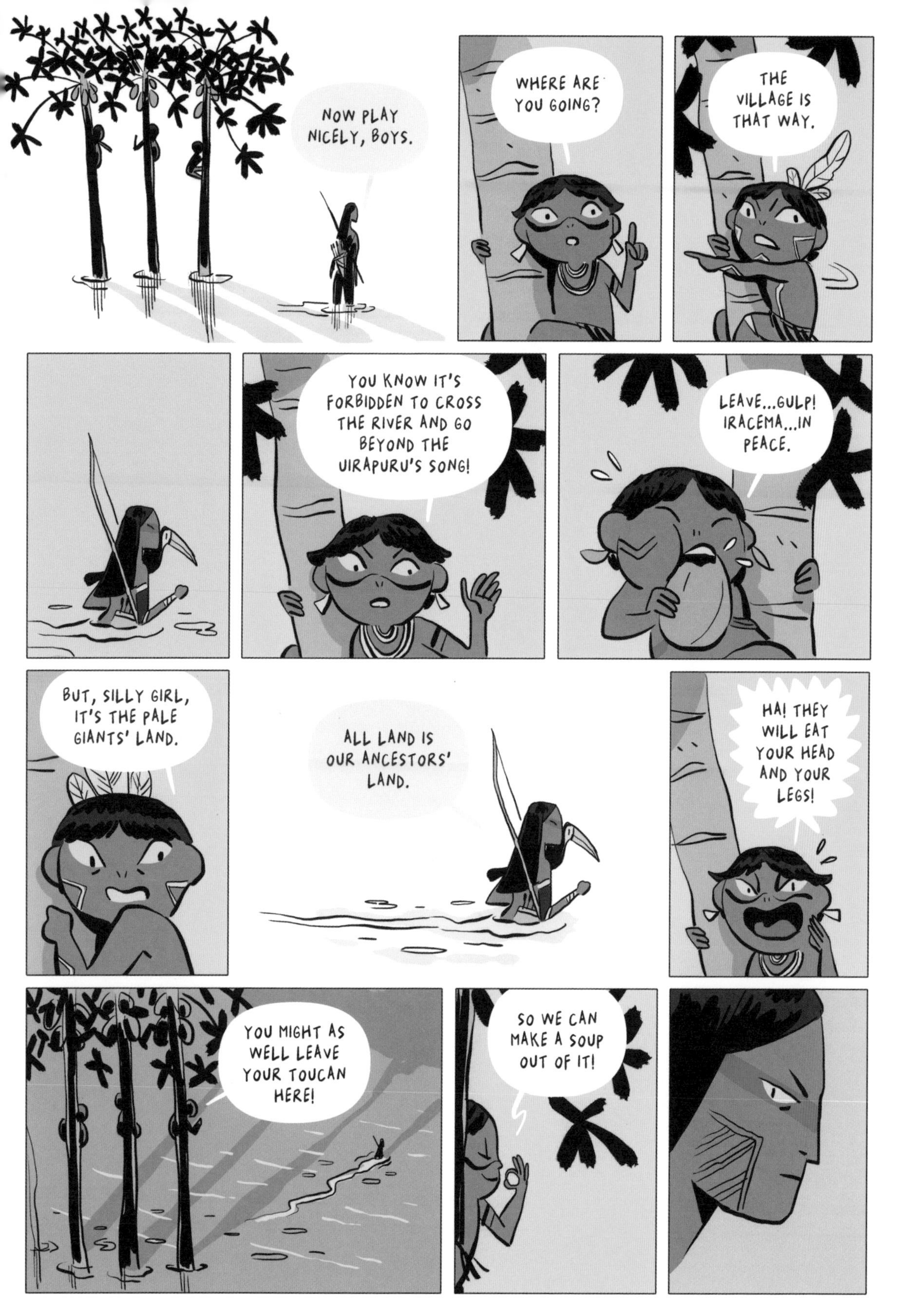

NOW PLAY NICELY, BOYS.
WHERE ARE YOU GOING?
THE VILLAGE IS THAT WAY.
YOU KNOW IT'S FORBIDDEN TO CROSS THE RIVER AND GO BEYOND THE UIRAPURU'S SONG!
LEAVE...GULP! IRACEMA...IN PEACE.
BUT, SILLY GIRL, IT'S THE PALE GIANTS' LAND.
ALL LAND IS OUR ANCESTORS' LAND.
HA! THEY WILL EAT YOUR HEAD AND YOUR LEGS!
YOU MIGHT AS WELL LEAVE YOUR TOUCAN HERE!
SO WE CAN MAKE A SOUP OUT OF IT!

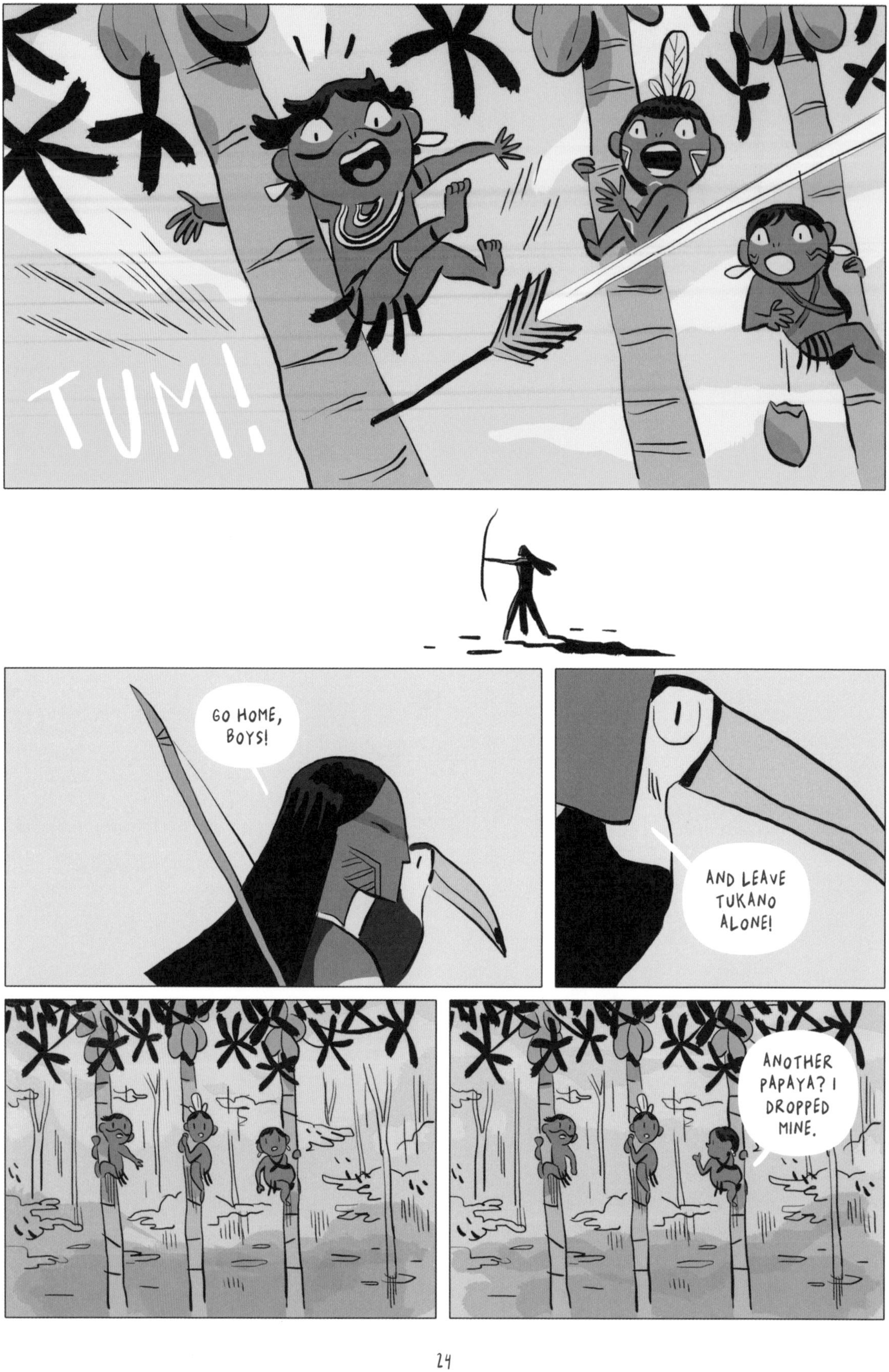
TUM!
GO HOME, BOYS!
AND LEAVE TUKANO ALONE!
ANOTHER PAPAYA? I DROPPED MINE.

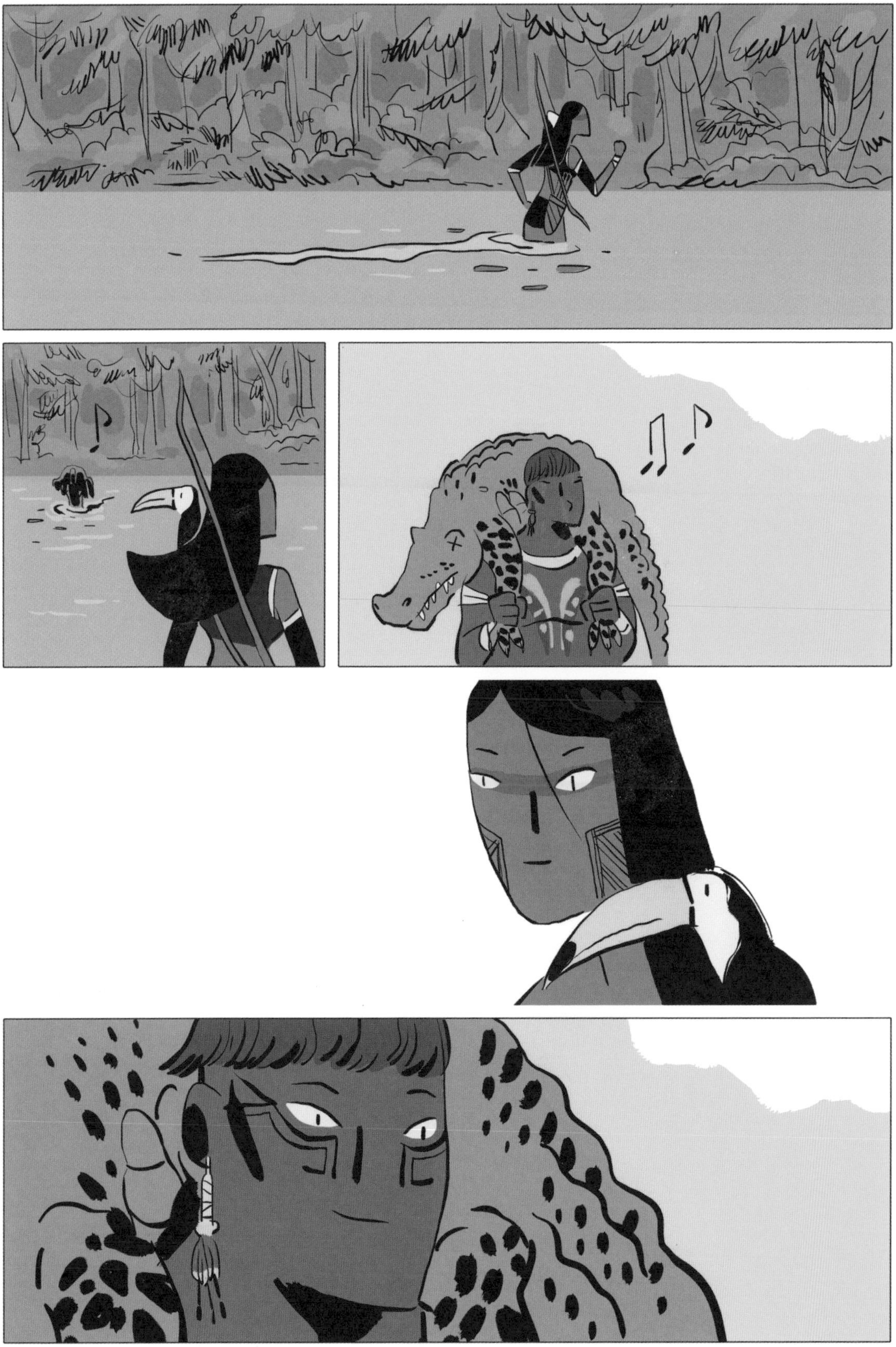

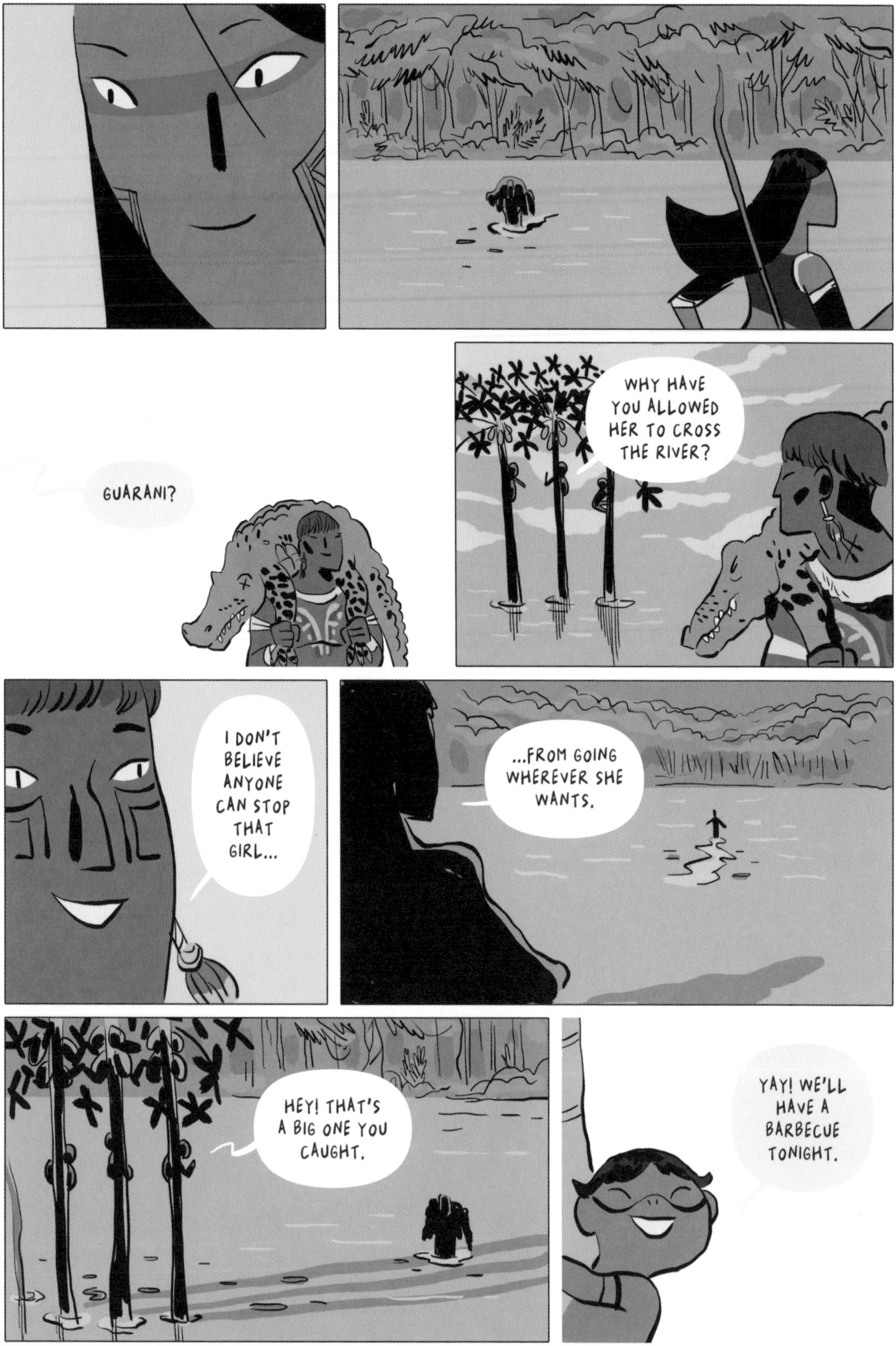
GUARANI?
WHY HAVE YOU ALLOWED HER TO CROSS THE RIVER?
I DON'T BELIEVE ANYONE CAN STOP THAT GIRL...
...FROM GOING WHEREVER SHE WANTS.
HEY! THAT'S A BIG ONE YOU CAUGHT.
YAY! WE'LL HAVE A BARBECUE TONIGHT.

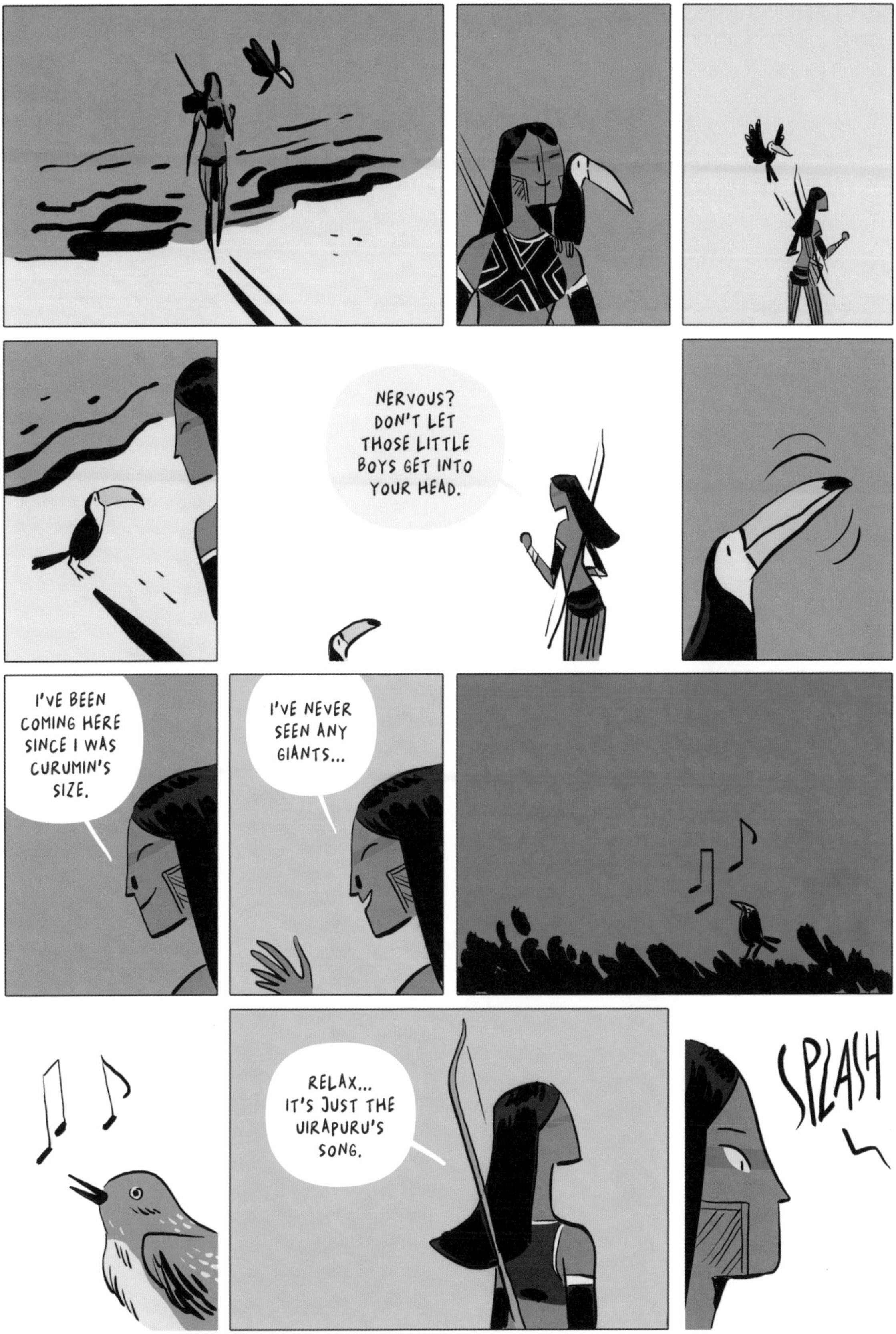
NERVOUS? DON'T LET THOSE LITTLE BOYS GET INTO YOUR HEAD.
I'VE BEEN COMING HERE SINCE I WAS CURUMIN'S SIZE.
I'VE NEVER SEEN ANY GIANTS...
RELAX... IT'S JUST THE UIRAPURU'S SONG.
SPLASH

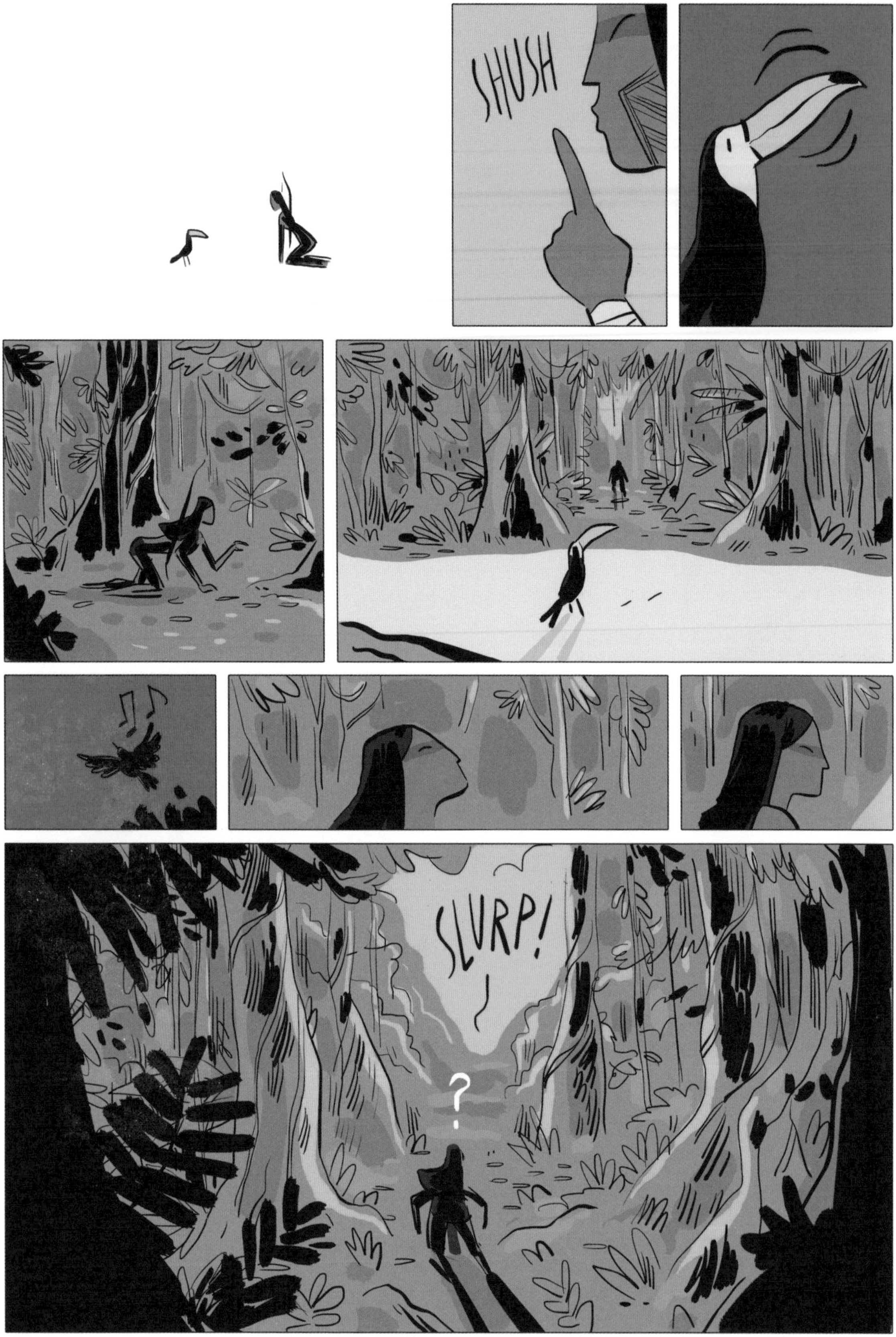
SHUSH
SLURP!
?

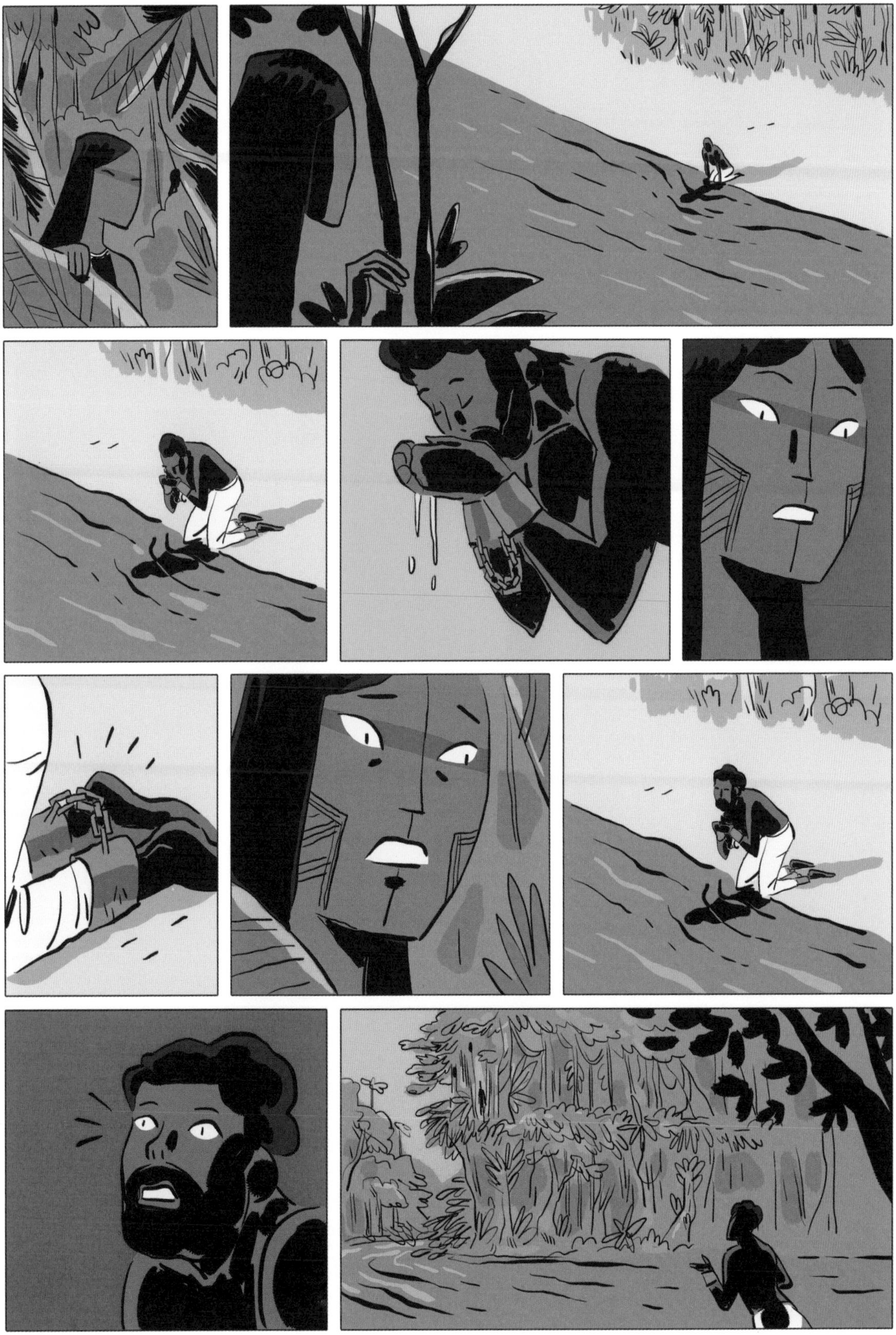

KRAK!

I'M GETTING TIRED OF IT.

WHERE, FOR HEAVEN'S SAKE, YOU ARE TRYING TO ESCAPE TO?

YOU ARE IN THE MIDDLE OF A DAMNED FOREST YOU KNOW NOTHING ABOUT.

IF THE BUGS WON'T KILL YOU, THE SAVAGES WILL.

I'M YOUR BEST BET.

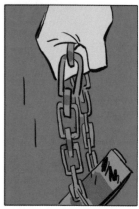

I THINK YOU HAVEN'T THOUGHT YOUR OPTIONS THROUGH.

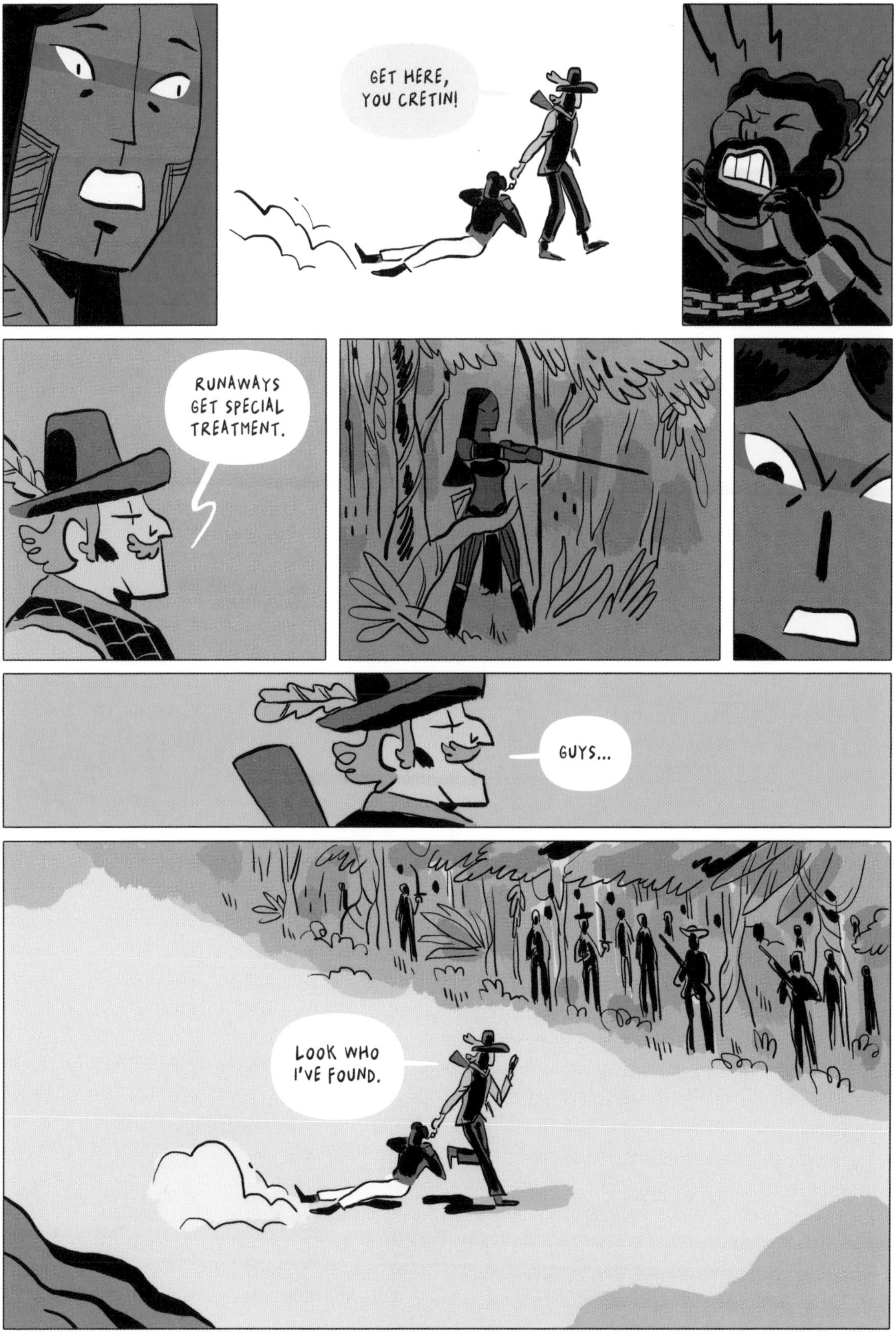
GET HERE,
YOU CRETIN!
RUNAWAYS
GET SPECIAL
TREATMENT.
GUYS...
LOOK WHO
I'VE FOUND.

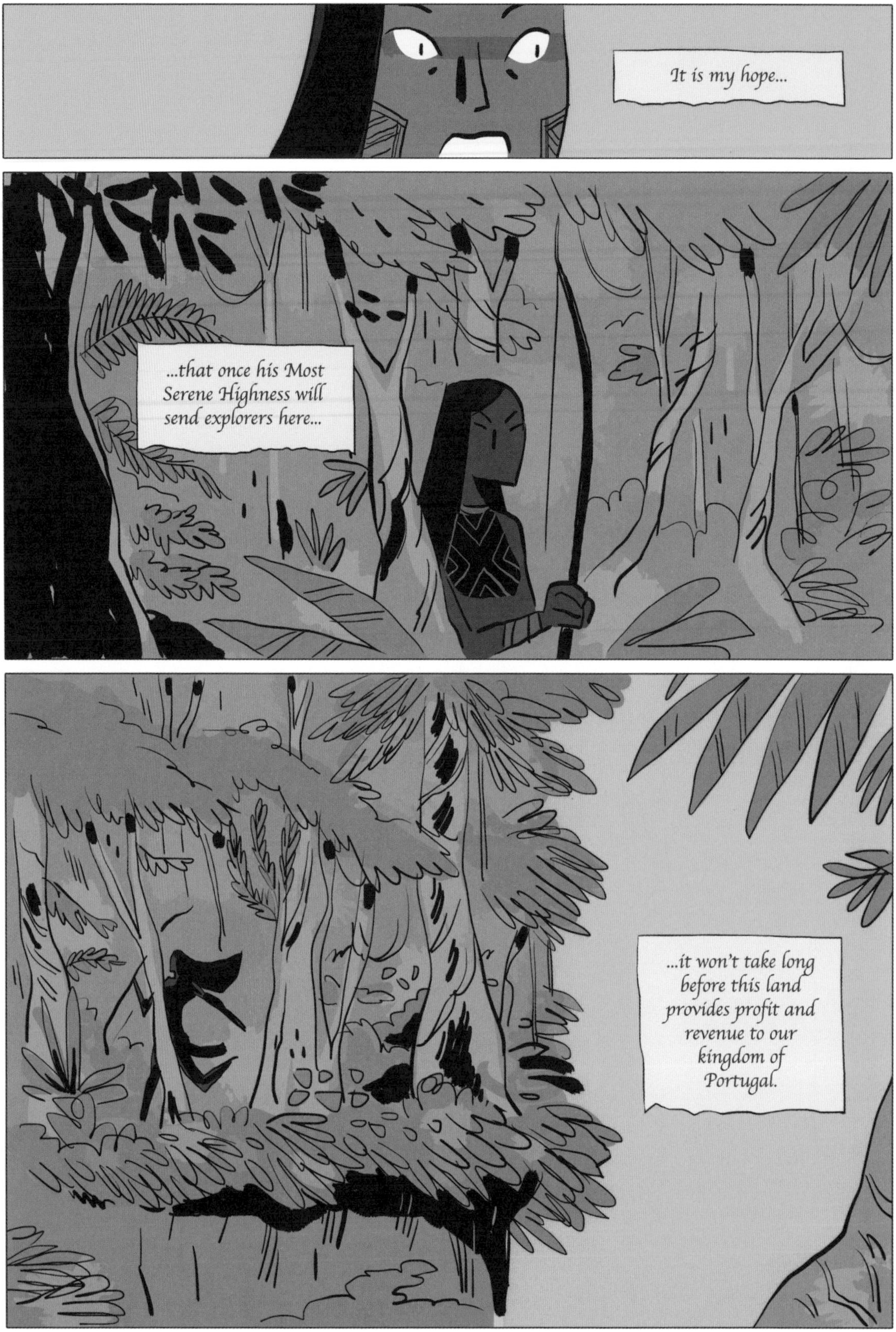
It is my hope...
...that once his Most Serene Highness will send explorers here...
...it won't take long before this land provides profit and revenue to our kingdom of Portugal.

May happen whatever most pleases God and befits
His holy service and the salvation of my soul.

Your Magnificence's humble servant,
Amerigo Vespucci, 18 July 1500

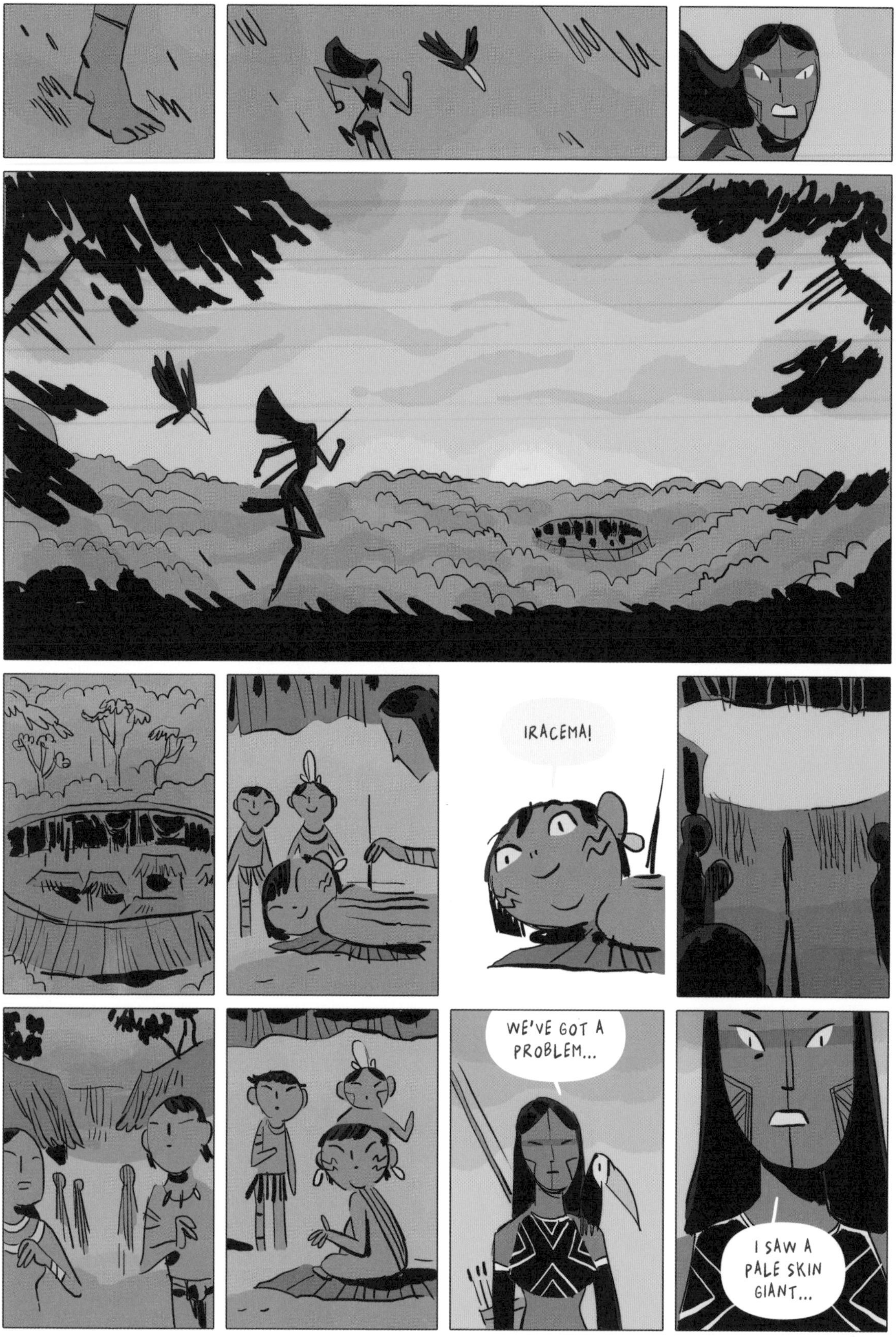
IRACEMA!
WE'VE GOT A PROBLEM...
I SAW A PALE SKIN GIANT...

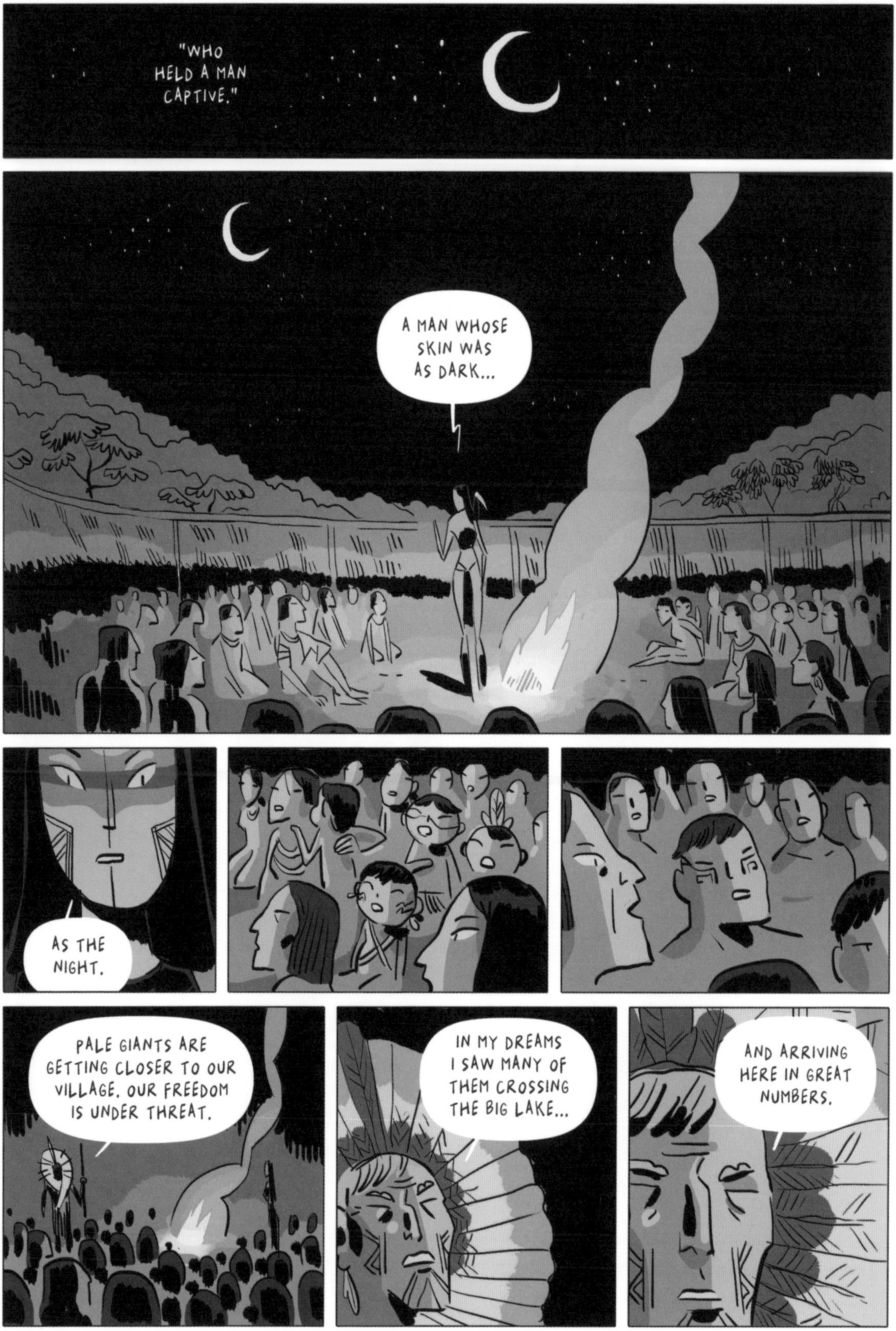
"WHO HELD A MAN CAPTIVE."
A MAN WHOSE SKIN WAS AS DARK...
AS THE NIGHT.
PALE GIANTS ARE GETTING CLOSER TO OUR VILLAGE. OUR FREEDOM IS UNDER THREAT.
IN MY DREAMS I SAW MANY OF THEM CROSSING THE BIG LAKE...
AND ARRIVING HERE IN GREAT NUMBERS.

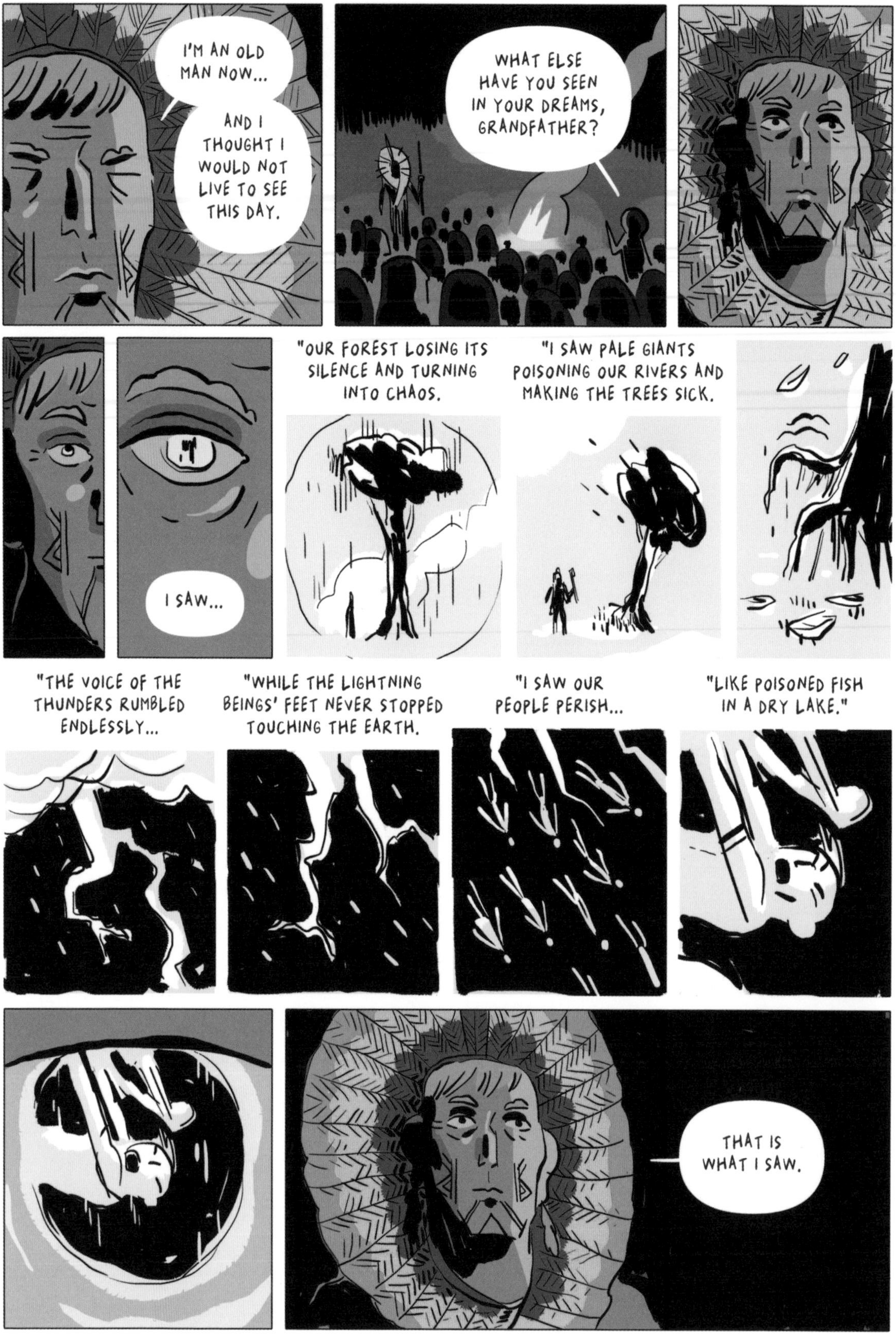
I'M AN OLD MAN NOW...
AND I THOUGHT I WOULD NOT LIVE TO SEE THIS DAY.
WHAT ELSE HAVE YOU SEEN IN YOUR DREAMS, GRANDFATHER?
I SAW...
"OUR FOREST LOSING ITS SILENCE AND TURNING INTO CHAOS.
"I SAW PALE GIANTS POISONING OUR RIVERS AND MAKING THE TREES SICK.
"THE VOICE OF THE THUNDERS RUMBLED ENDLESSLY...
"WHILE THE LIGHTNING BEINGS' FEET NEVER STOPPED TOUCHING THE EARTH.
"I SAW OUR PEOPLE PERISH...
"LIKE POISONED FISH IN A DRY LAKE."
THAT IS WHAT I SAW.

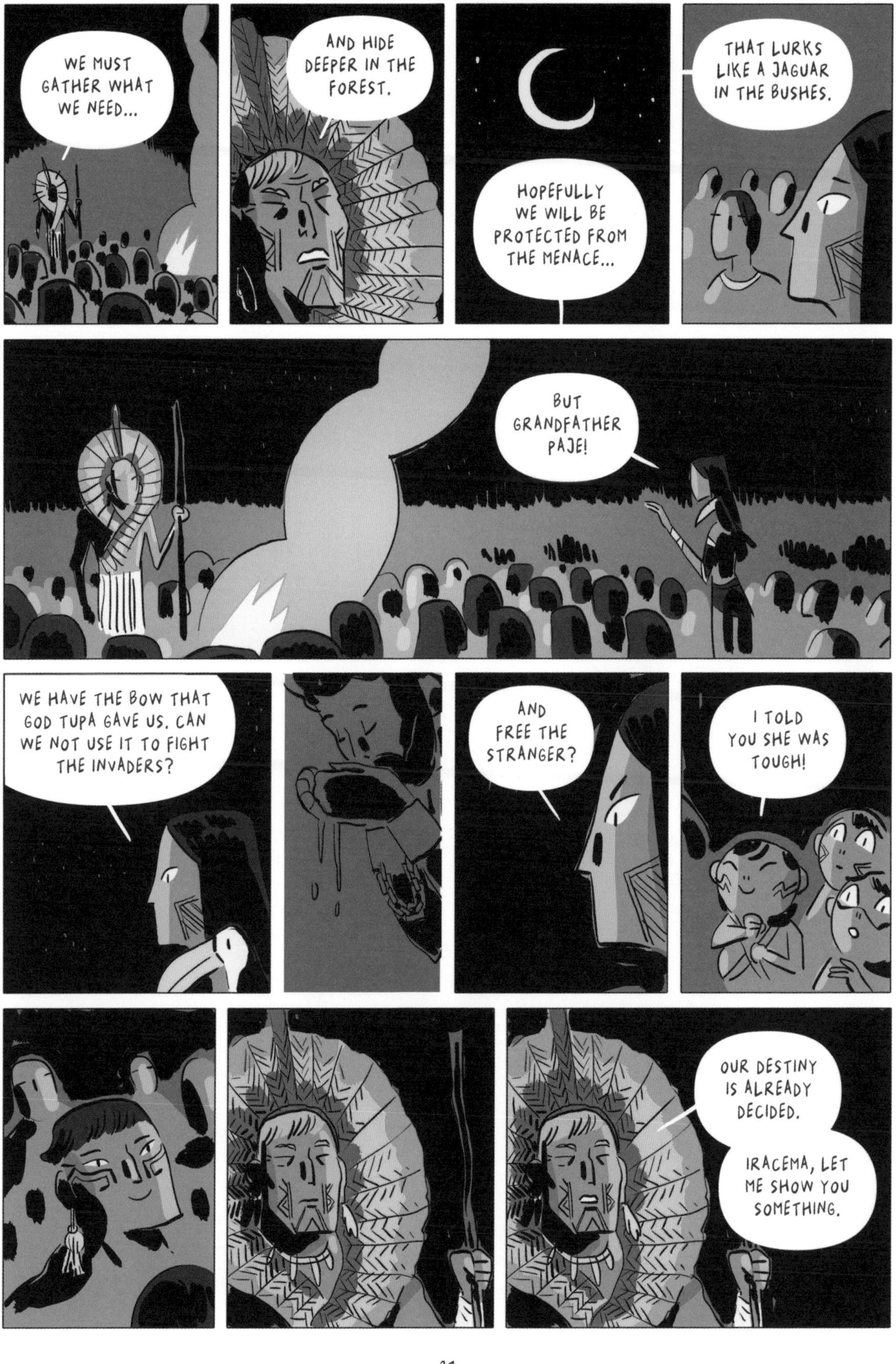
WE MUST GATHER WHAT WE NEED...
AND HIDE DEEPER IN THE FOREST.
HOPEFULLY WE WILL BE PROTECTED FROM THE MENACE...
THAT LURKS LIKE A JAGUAR IN THE BUSHES.
BUT GRANDFATHER PAJE!
WE HAVE THE BOW THAT GOD TUPA GAVE US. CAN WE NOT USE IT TO FIGHT THE INVADERS?
AND FREE THE STRANGER?
I TOLD YOU SHE WAS TOUGH!
OUR DESTINY IS ALREADY DECIDED.
IRACEMA, LET ME SHOW YOU SOMETHING.

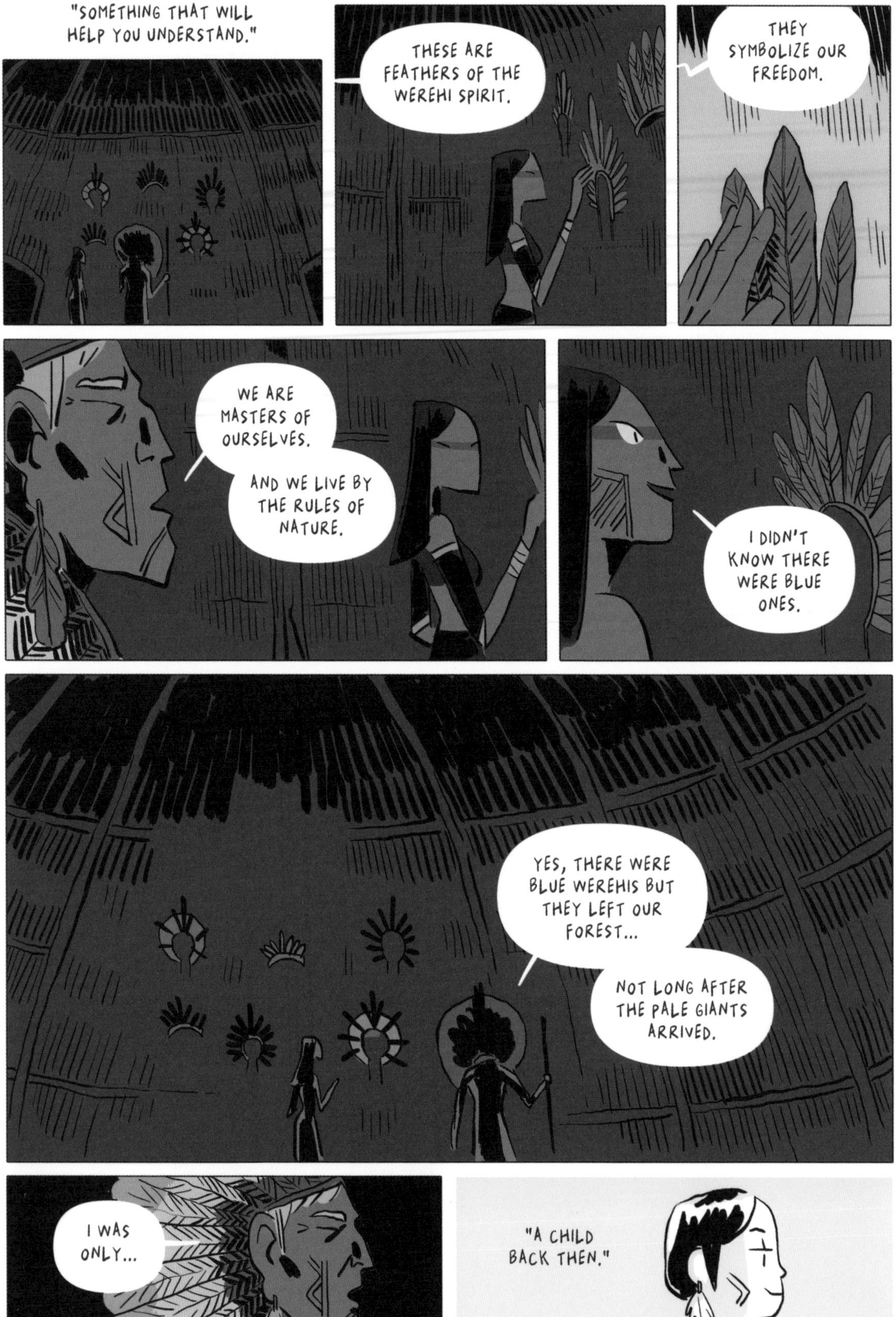
"SOMETHING THAT WILL HELP YOU UNDERSTAND."
THESE ARE FEATHERS OF THE WEREHI SPIRIT.
THEY SYMBOLIZE OUR FREEDOM.
WE ARE MASTERS OF OURSELVES.
AND WE LIVE BY THE RULES OF NATURE.
I DIDN'T KNOW THERE WERE BLUE ONES.
YES, THERE WERE BLUE WEREHIS BUT THEY LEFT OUR FOREST...
NOT LONG AFTER THE PALE GIANTS ARRIVED.
I WAS ONLY...
"A CHILD BACK THEN."

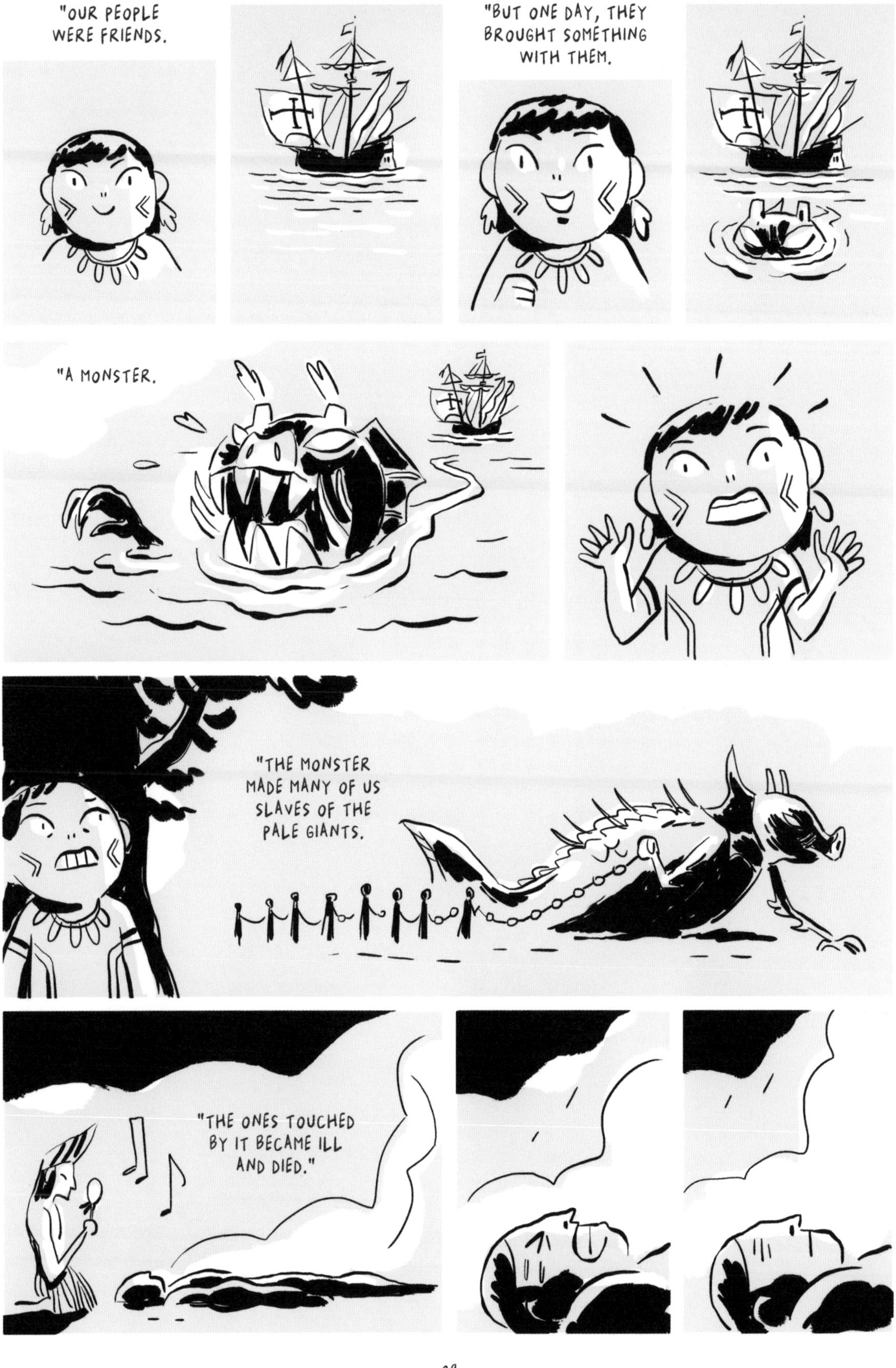

"OUR PEOPLE WERE FRIENDS.
"BUT ONE DAY, THEY BROUGHT SOMETHING WITH THEM.
"A MONSTER.
"THE MONSTER MADE MANY OF US SLAVES OF THE PALE GIANTS.
"THE ONES TOUCHED BY IT BECAME ILL AND DIED."

I LOST MANY OF MY FRIENDS.

IN THE BEGINNING OF TIME, GOD TUPA CREATED US AND GAVE US THE LIGHTNING BOW SO THAT WE...

...COULD PROTECT OURSELVES FROM MONSTERS AND EVIL BEINGS.

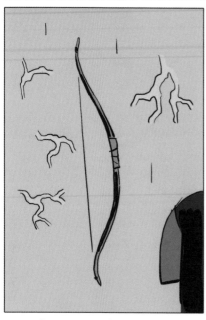

"WE USED IT TO KILL THE MONSTER...

KA-BWOOM!

"AND SPILL ITS BLOOD."

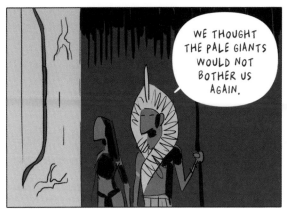

WE THOUGHT THE PALE GIANTS WOULD NOT BOTHER US AGAIN.

BUT ONE DAY I HAD ANOTHER DREAM...

"I SAW THEIR MONSTER LEAVING THE WORLD OF THE DEAD...

"AND REBORN AS A MAN.

"THE BOW IS A DIVINE WEAPON AND GOD TUPA TOLD US TO USE IT ONLY AGAINST MONSTERS BUT NEVER AGAINST OTHER HUMANS.

"IF WE BREAK THIS RULE, OUR TRIBE WILL BE CURSED.

"IT'S SAID, 'ONLY THE MELODY OF A MAGIC FLUTE CAN TRANSFORM THE MAN BACK TO MONSTER.

"ARROW THE CREATURE IN ITS TRUE FORM AND OUR FOREST WILL BE FREE FROM EVIL AGAIN.'

"I HAVE GROWN OLD AND THIS SONG HAS NEVER ECHOED AMONG OUR TREES."

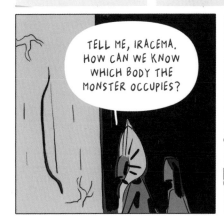

TELL ME, IRACEMA. HOW CAN WE KNOW WHICH BODY THE MONSTER OCCUPIES?

"THE ONLY WAY TO PRESERVE OURSELVES IS TO STAY AWAY FROM THE GIANTS.

"THAT'S WHY WE MUST SEEK REFUGE."

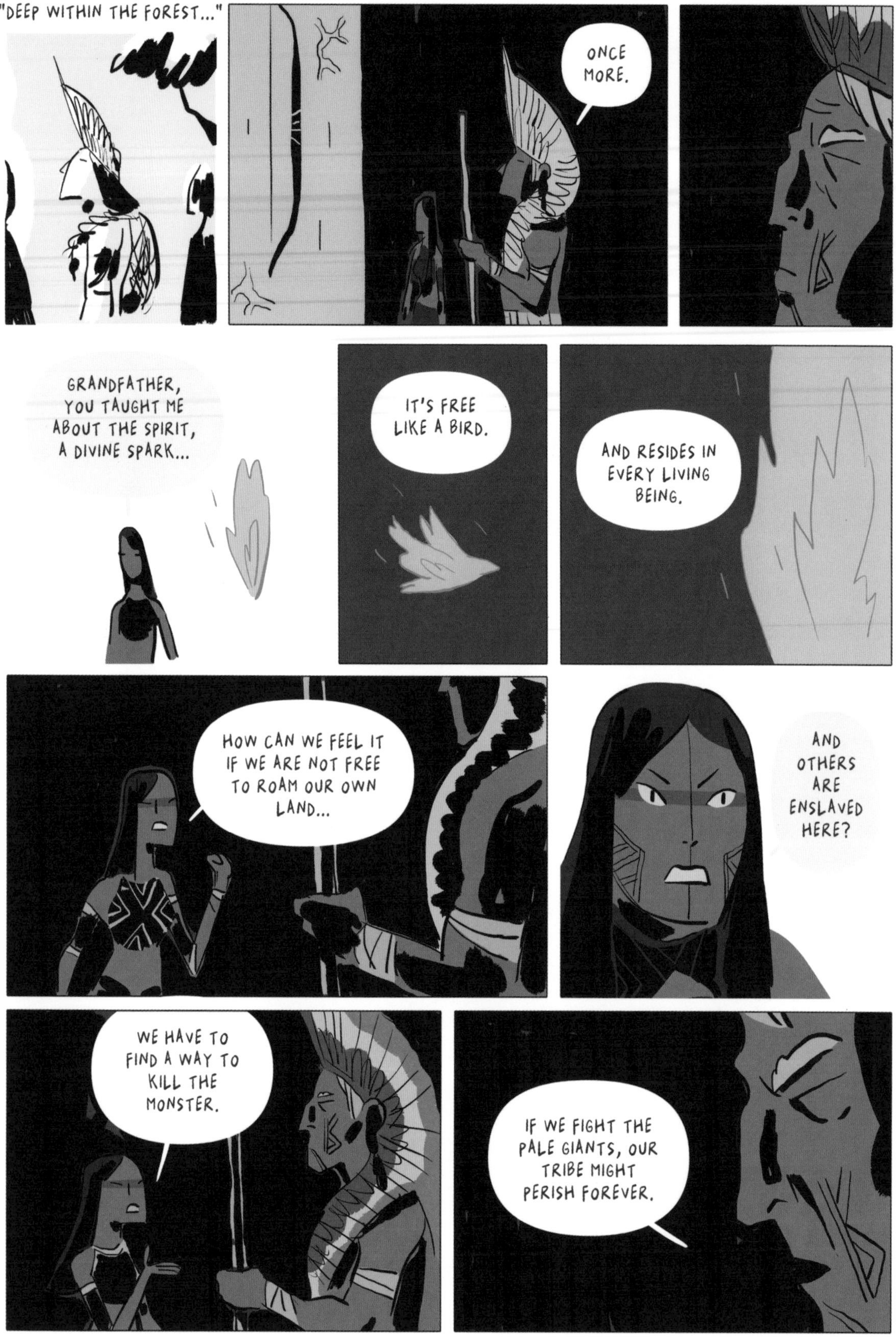
"DEEP WITHIN THE FOREST..."
ONCE MORE.
GRANDFATHER, YOU TAUGHT ME ABOUT THE SPIRIT, A DIVINE SPARK...
IT'S FREE LIKE A BIRD.
AND RESIDES IN EVERY LIVING BEING.
HOW CAN WE FEEL IT IF WE ARE NOT FREE TO ROAM OUR OWN LAND...
AND OTHERS ARE ENSLAVED HERE?
WE HAVE TO FIND A WAY TO KILL THE MONSTER.
IF WE FIGHT THE PALE GIANTS, OUR TRIBE MIGHT PERISH FOREVER.

PERHAPS THE UIRAPURU SPIRIT LED ME TO THE STRANGER TO SHOW ME SOMETHING.

 THERE MUST BE A WAY.

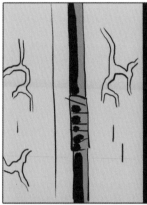

I'M ONE OF OUR BEST ARCHERS. I CAN MANAGE THE BOW.

 IT'S TOO DANGEROUS. YOU WOULD PUT AT RISK NOT ONLY YOURSELF BUT YOUR PEOPLE.

 BUT...

 I HAVE SEEN MORE SUNSETS THAN YOU, DAUGHTER...

 WE ARE GOING DEEPER INTO THE FOREST, AND I SAY THE DAY IS OVER.

 GO TO SLEEP, IRACEMA.

43

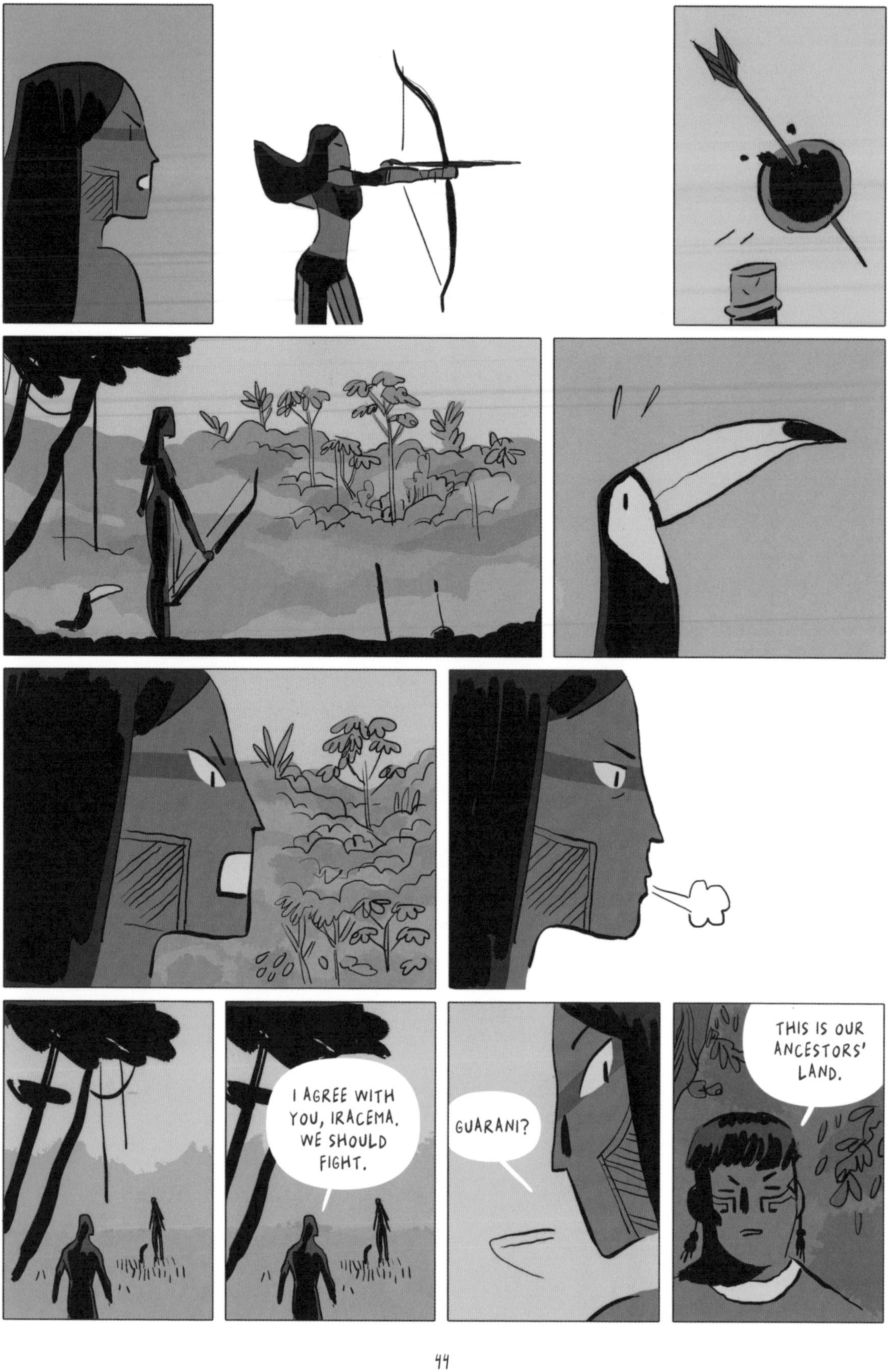
I AGREE WITH YOU, IRACEMA. WE SHOULD FIGHT.
GUARANI?
THIS IS OUR ANCESTORS' LAND.

WE ARE NOT ARMADILLOS.

WE DO NOT HIDE IN THE GROUND.

I WILL FIGHT AT YOUR SIDE.

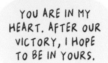

PAJE SAYS IT'S WAY TOO RISKY.

THEY MADE US GO AWAY ONCE. THIS IS NEVER GOING TO END IF WE DON'T ACT NOW.

YOU ARE IN MY HEART. AFTER OUR VICTORY, I HOPE TO BE IN YOURS.

JUST TELL ME WHEN, IRACEMA. I WILL FOLLOW YOU!

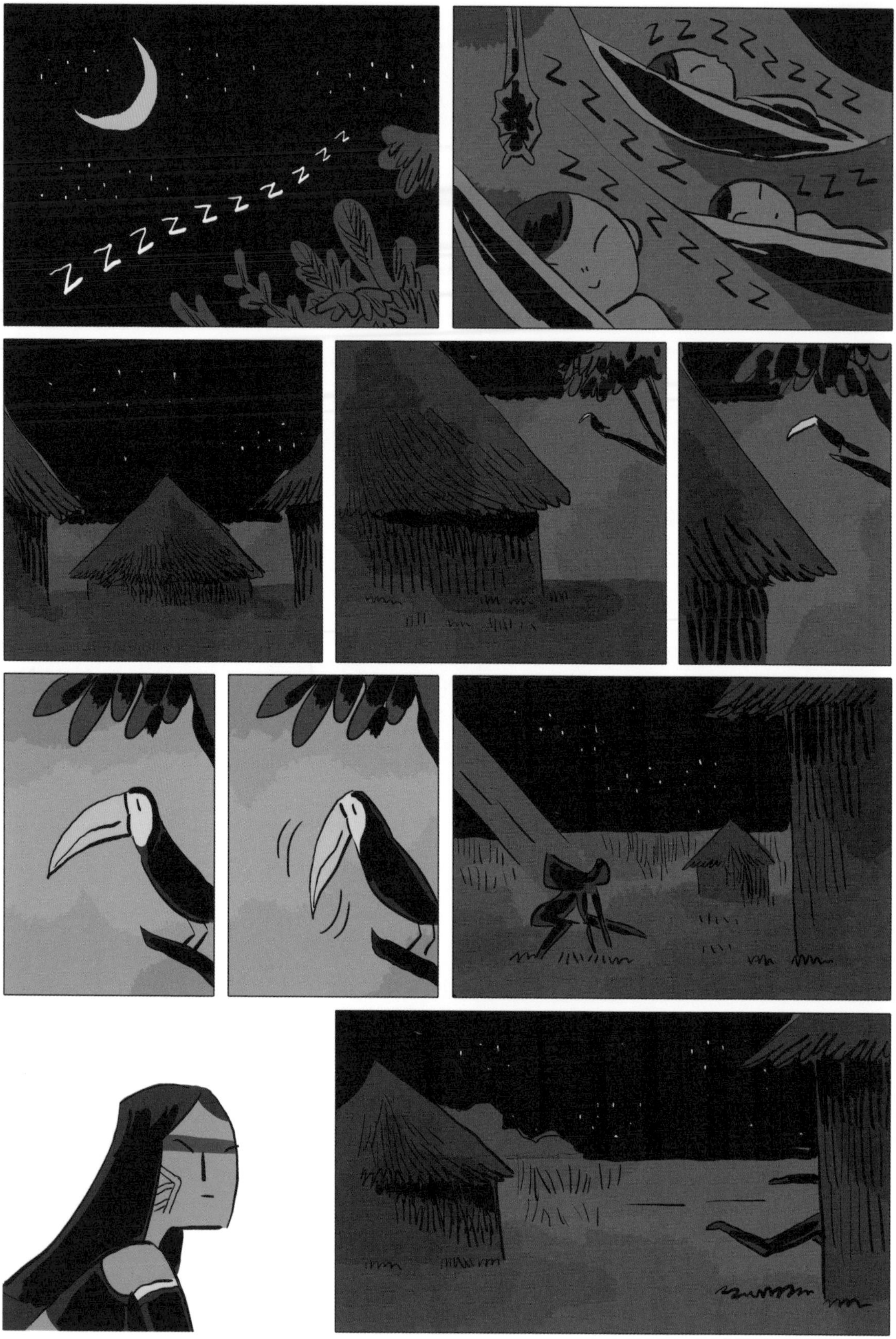
ZZZZZZZZZZZ
ZZZZZZZZZ
ZZZZZZZZZ
ZZZZ

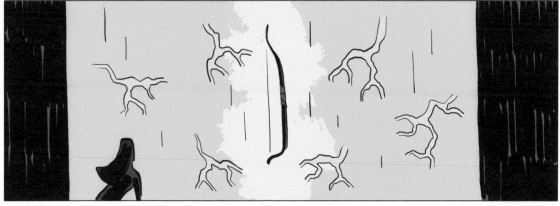

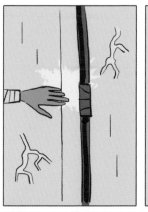

I HOPE WE DID THE RIGHT THING, TUKANO.

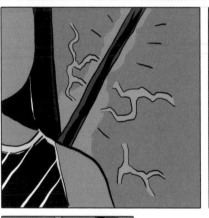

I CANNOT LET MY PEOPLE DOWN.

WE MUST KILL THE MONSTER.

LET'S GO!

WHAT'S THE MATTER?

YOU WORRY TOO MUCH. THE SIGNS WERE CLEAR ENOUGH FOR GUARANI.

HE WILL FIND US.

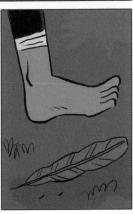

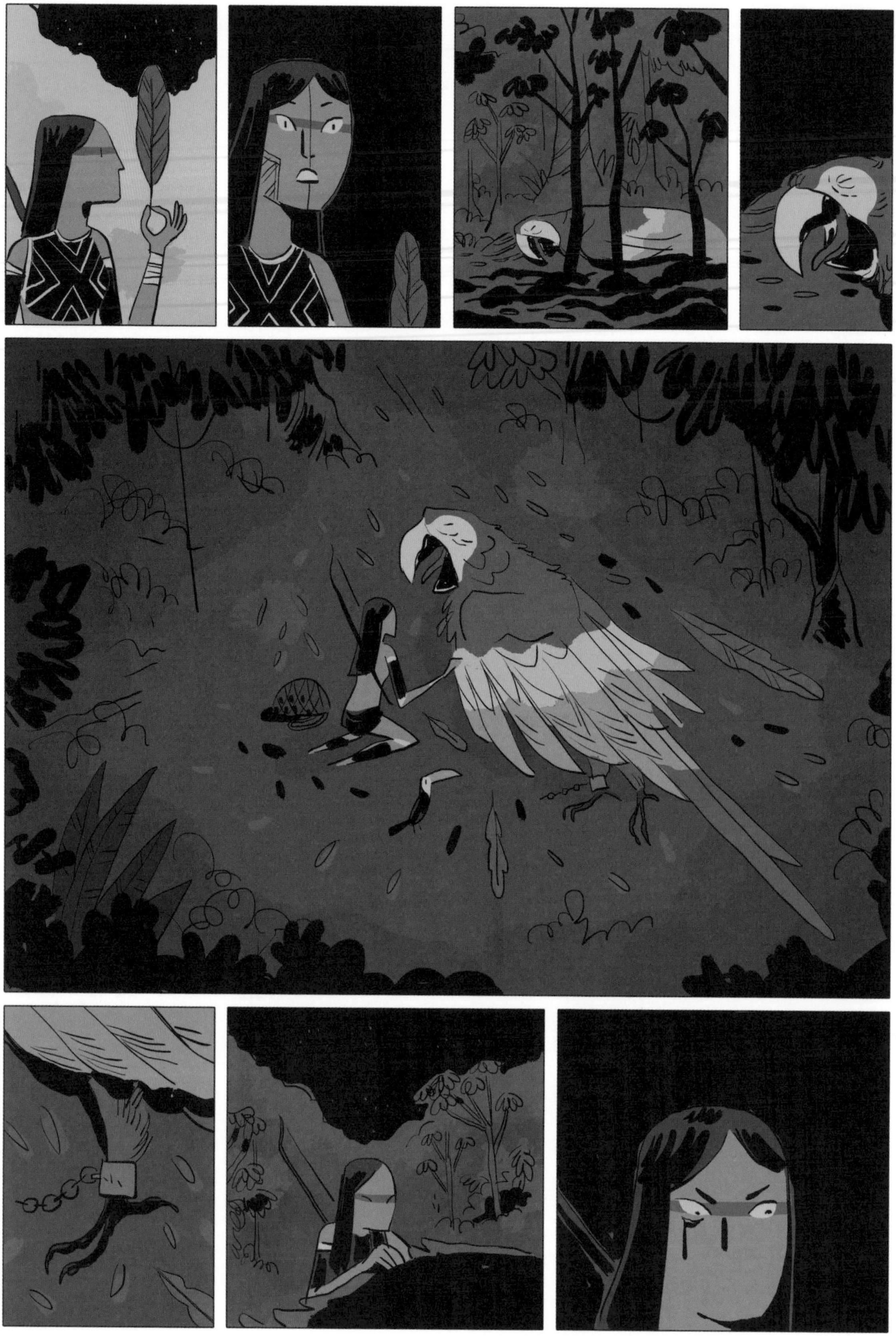

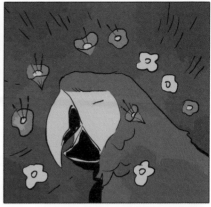
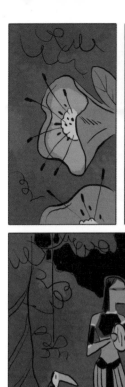

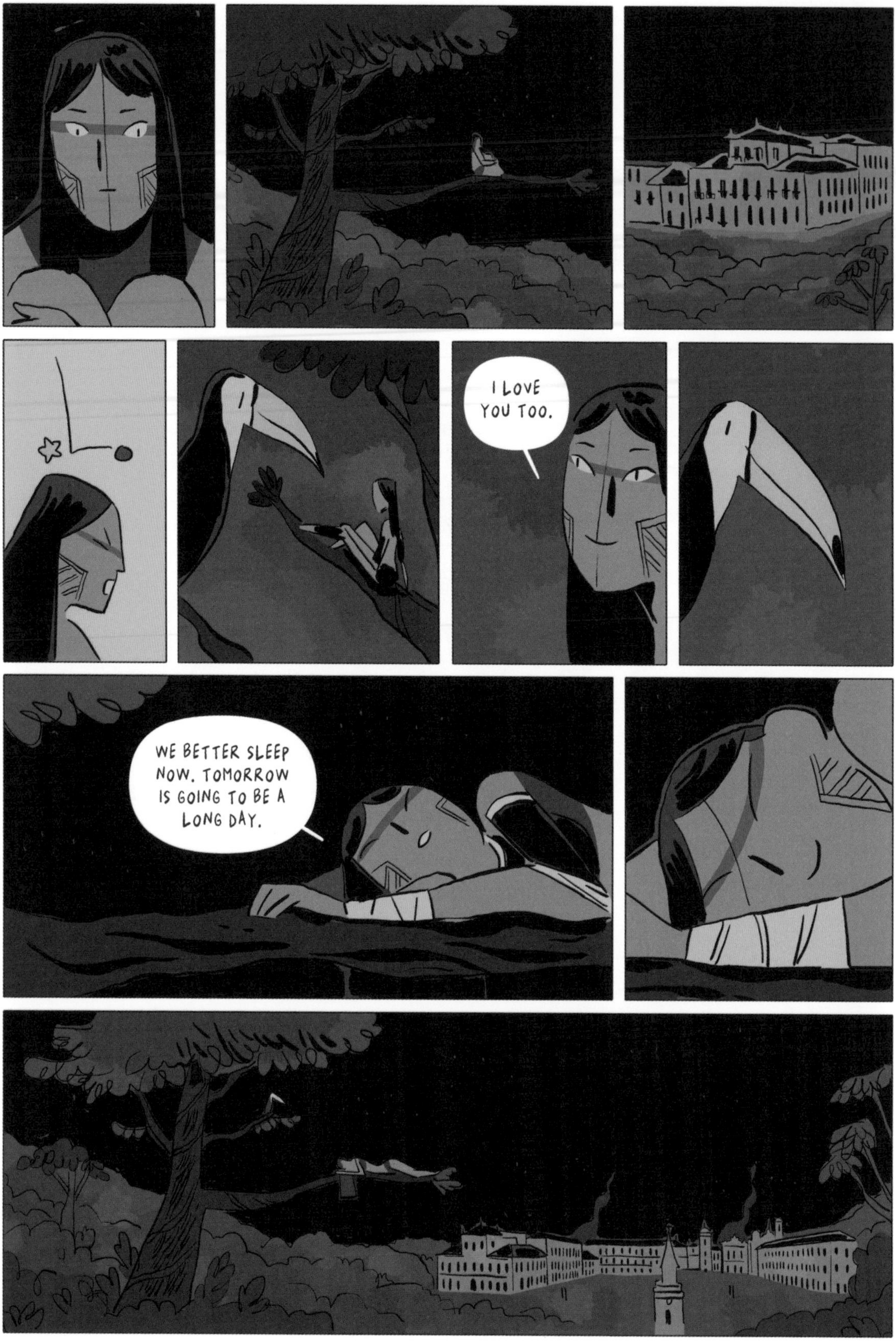
I LOVE YOU TOO.
WE BETTER SLEEP NOW. TOMORROW IS GOING TO BE A LONG DAY.

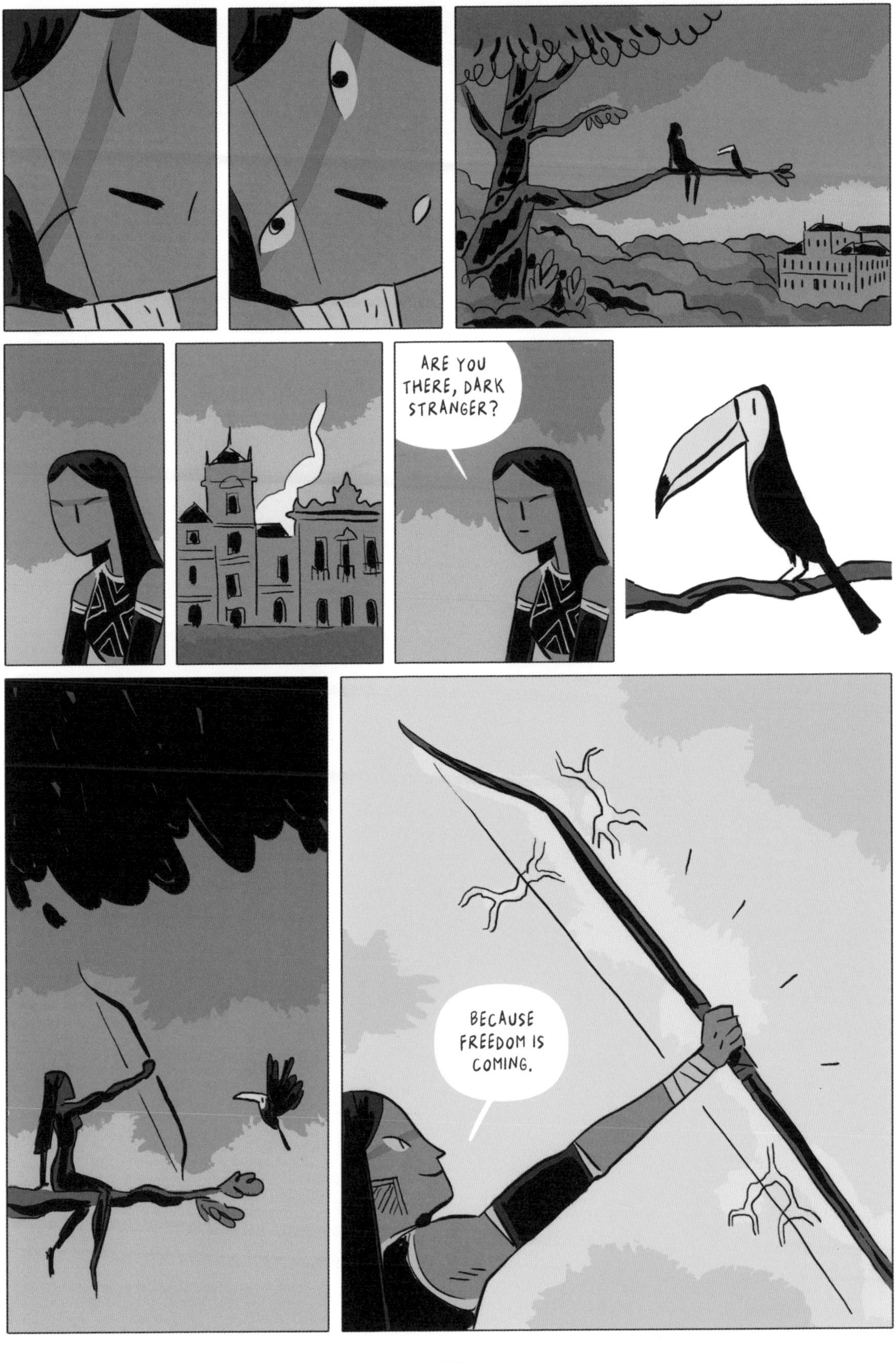
ARE YOU THERE, DARK STRANGER?
BECAUSE FREEDOM IS COMING.

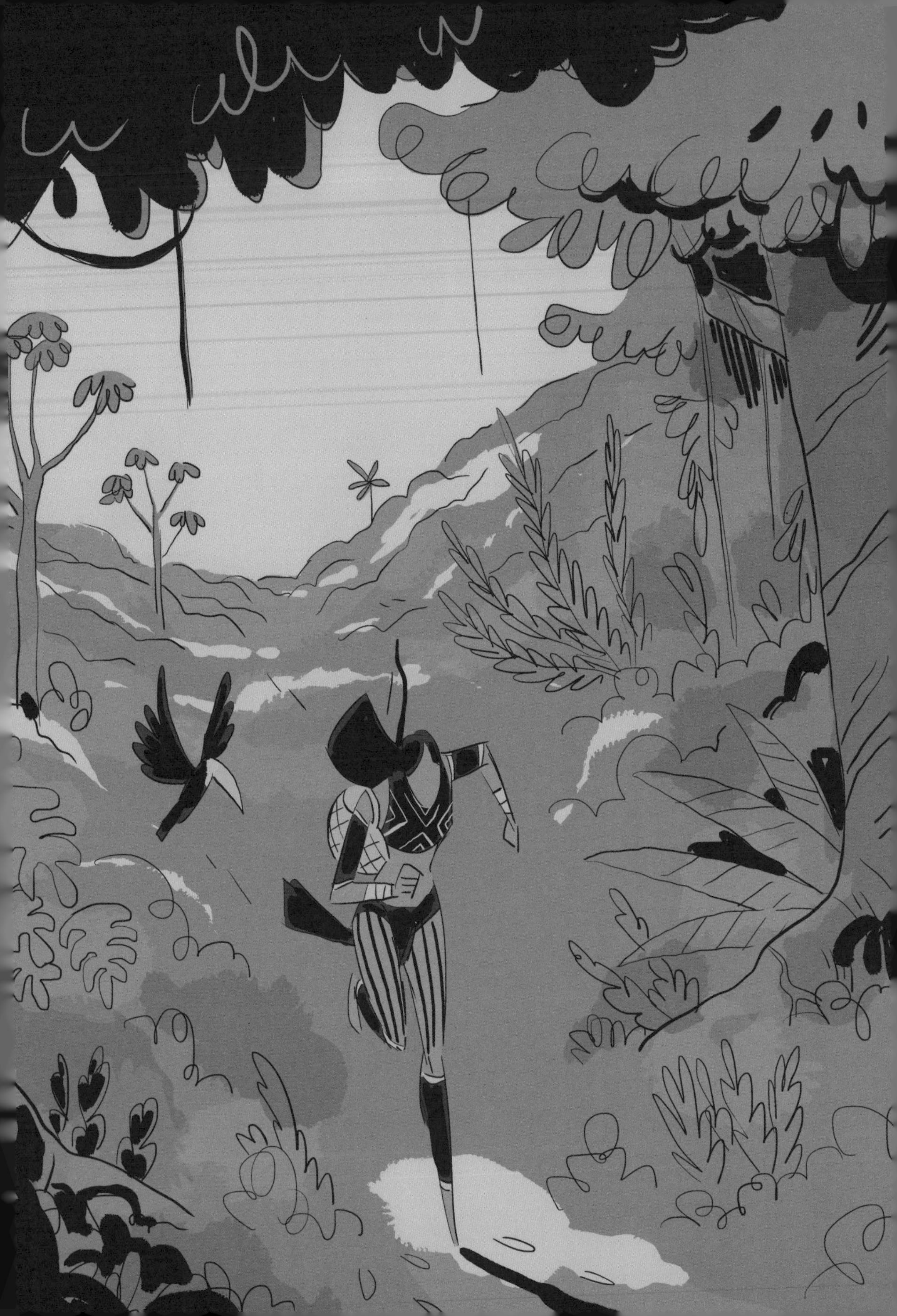

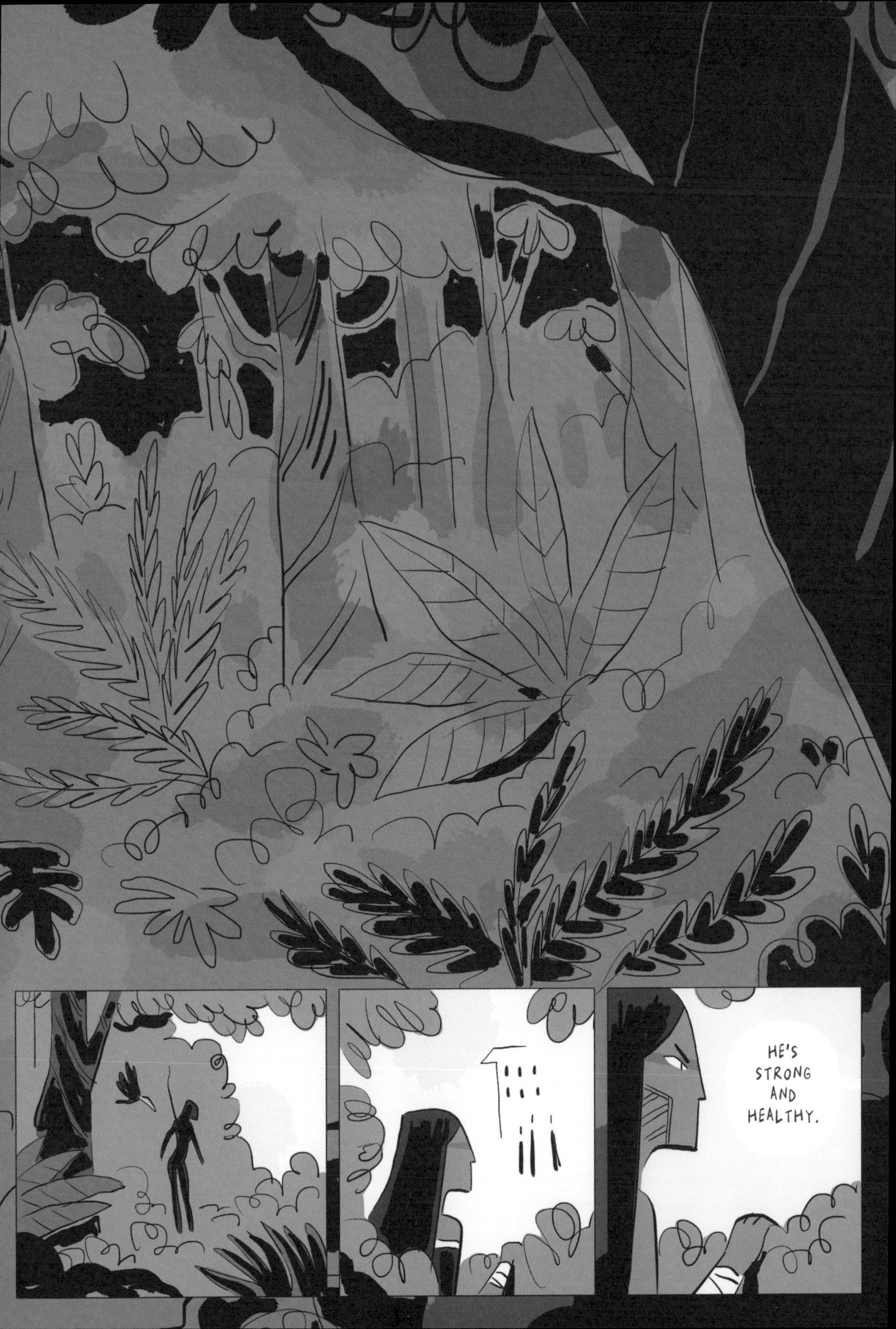
HE'S STRONG AND HEALTHY.

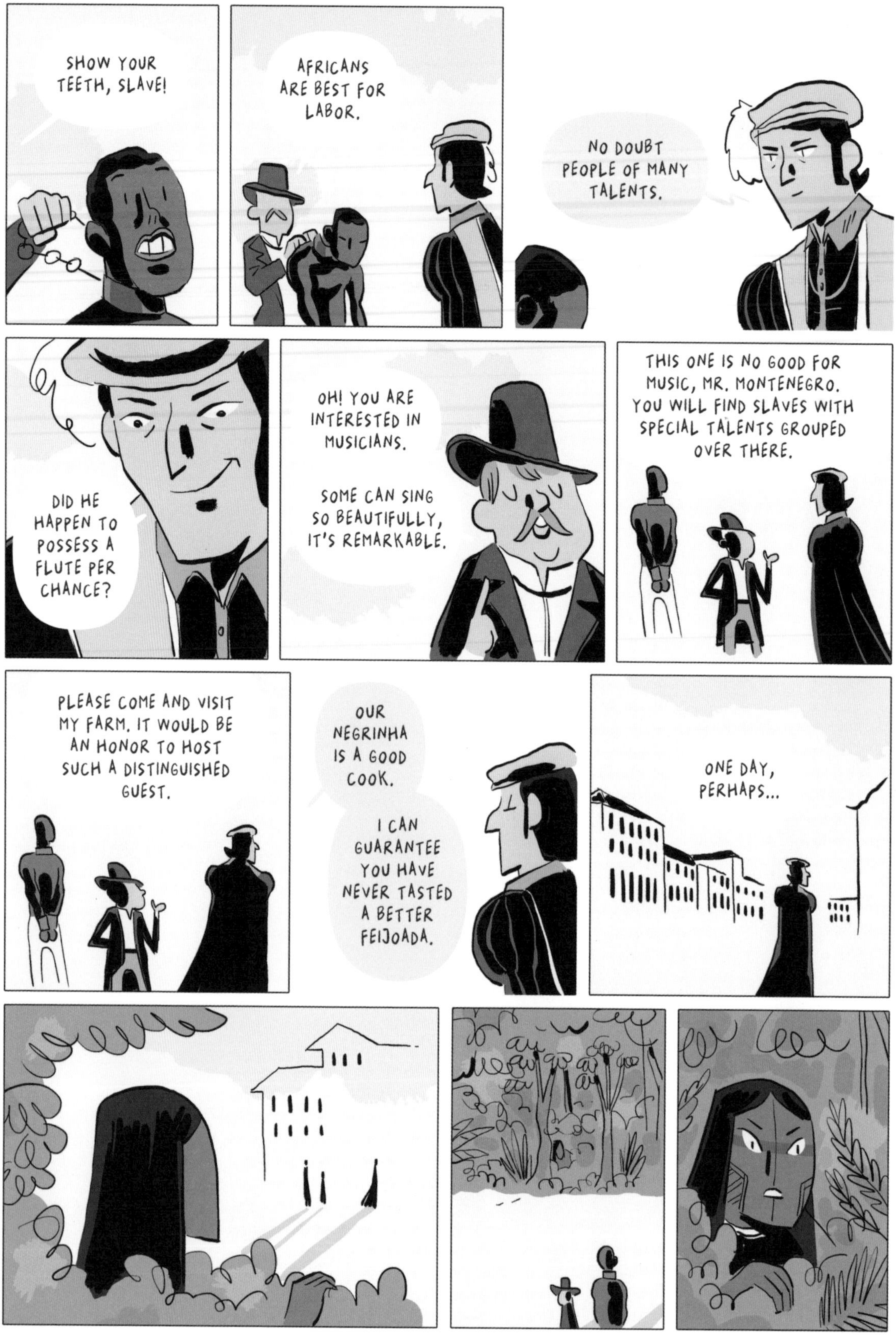
SHOW YOUR TEETH, SLAVE!
AFRICANS ARE BEST FOR LABOR.
NO DOUBT PEOPLE OF MANY TALENTS.
DID HE HAPPEN TO POSSESS A FLUTE PER CHANCE?
OH! YOU ARE INTERESTED IN MUSICIANS.
SOME CAN SING SO BEAUTIFULLY, IT'S REMARKABLE.
THIS ONE IS NO GOOD FOR MUSIC, MR. MONTENEGRO. YOU WILL FIND SLAVES WITH SPECIAL TALENTS GROUPED OVER THERE.
PLEASE COME AND VISIT MY FARM. IT WOULD BE AN HONOR TO HOST SUCH A DISTINGUISHED GUEST.
OUR NEGRINHA IS A GOOD COOK.
I CAN GUARANTEE YOU HAVE NEVER TASTED A BETTER FEIJOADA.
ONE DAY, PERHAPS...

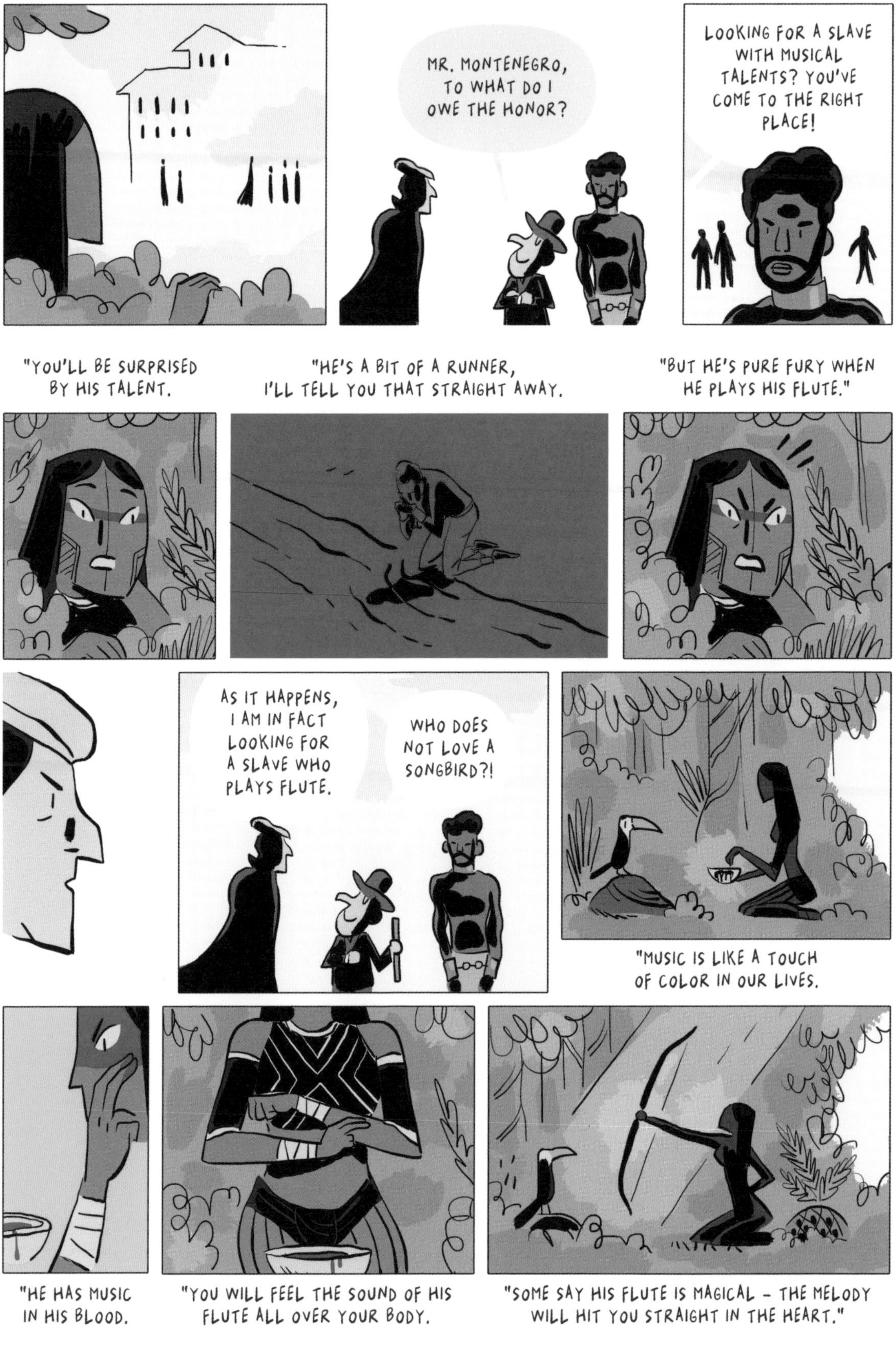
MR. MONTENEGRO, TO WHAT DO I OWE THE HONOR?
LOOKING FOR A SLAVE WITH MUSICAL TALENTS? YOU'VE COME TO THE RIGHT PLACE!
"YOU'LL BE SURPRISED BY HIS TALENT.
"HE'S A BIT OF A RUNNER, I'LL TELL YOU THAT STRAIGHT AWAY.
"BUT HE'S PURE FURY WHEN HE PLAYS HIS FLUTE."
AS IT HAPPENS, I AM IN FACT LOOKING FOR A SLAVE WHO PLAYS FLUTE.
WHO DOES NOT LOVE A SONGBIRD?!
"MUSIC IS LIKE A TOUCH OF COLOR IN OUR LIVES.
"HE HAS MUSIC IN HIS BLOOD.
"YOU WILL FEEL THE SOUND OF HIS FLUTE ALL OVER YOUR BODY.
"SOME SAY HIS FLUTE IS MAGICAL - THE MELODY WILL HIT YOU STRAIGHT IN THE HEART."

THAT'S QUITE HIGH PRAISE!

IT'S WELL DESERVED, BELIEVE ME.

THIS WILL MAKE YOU LAUGH...THESE FOLKS ARE SO SUPERSTITIOUS!

THEY SAY HIS FLUTE EVEN REVEALS MONSTERS! HA!

WHY DON'T WE REQUEST A DEMONSTRATION AND YOU CAN JUDGE FOR YOURSELF?

THAT WON'T BE NECESSARY. YOU CONVINCED ME.

I'LL TAKE THE FLUTE.

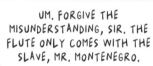

UM. FORGIVE THE MISUNDERSTANDING, SIR. THE FLUTE ONLY COMES WITH THE SLAVE, MR. MONTENEGRO.

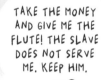

TAKE THE MONEY AND GIVE ME THE FLUTE! THE SLAVE DOES NOT SERVE ME. KEEP HIM.

SOLD!

IRACEMA?

58

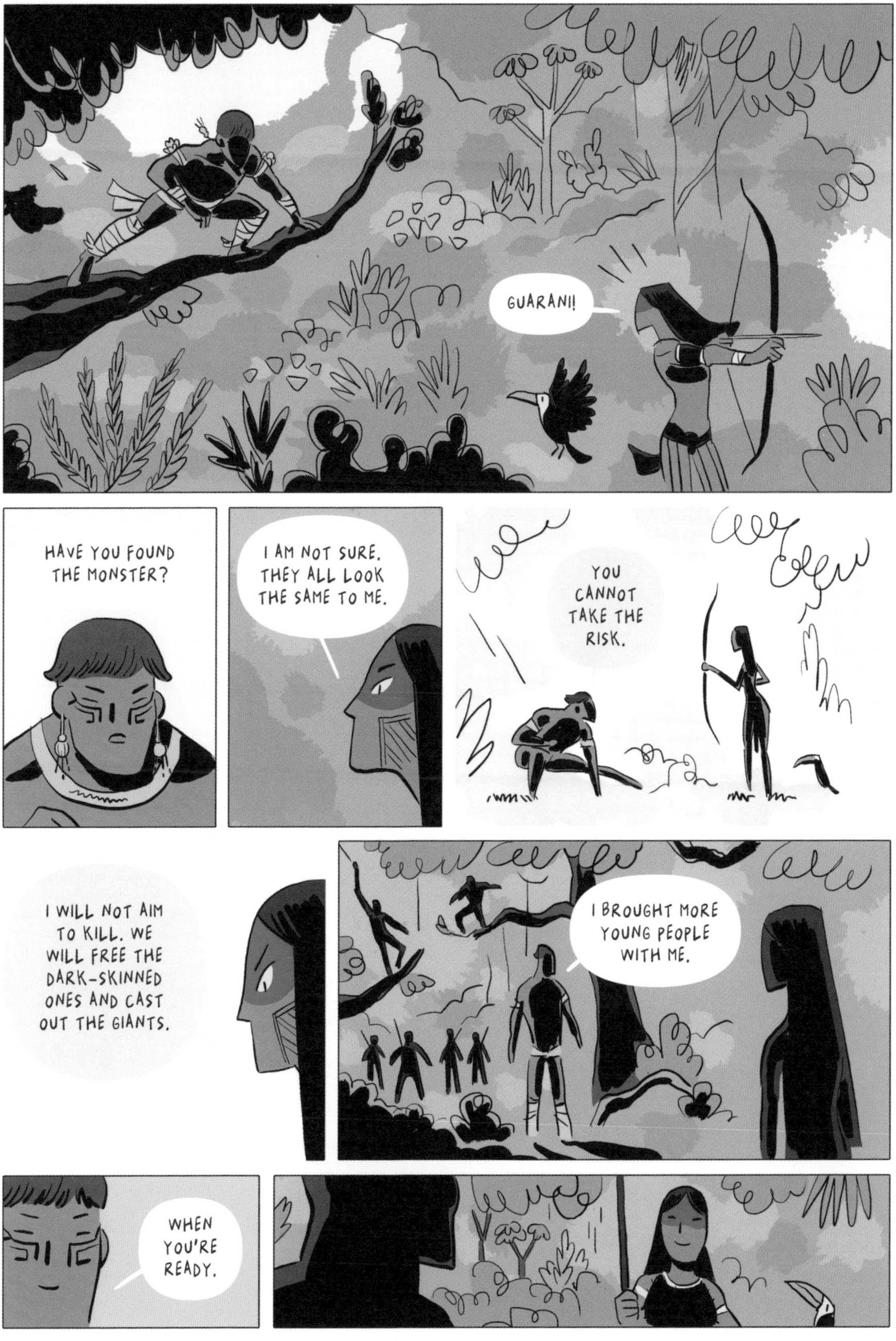
GUARANI!
HAVE YOU FOUND THE MONSTER?
I AM NOT SURE. THEY ALL LOOK THE SAME TO ME.
YOU CANNOT TAKE THE RISK.
I WILL NOT AIM TO KILL. WE WILL FREE THE DARK-SKINNED ONES AND CAST OUT THE GIANTS.
I BROUGHT MORE YOUNG PEOPLE WITH ME.
WHEN YOU'RE READY.

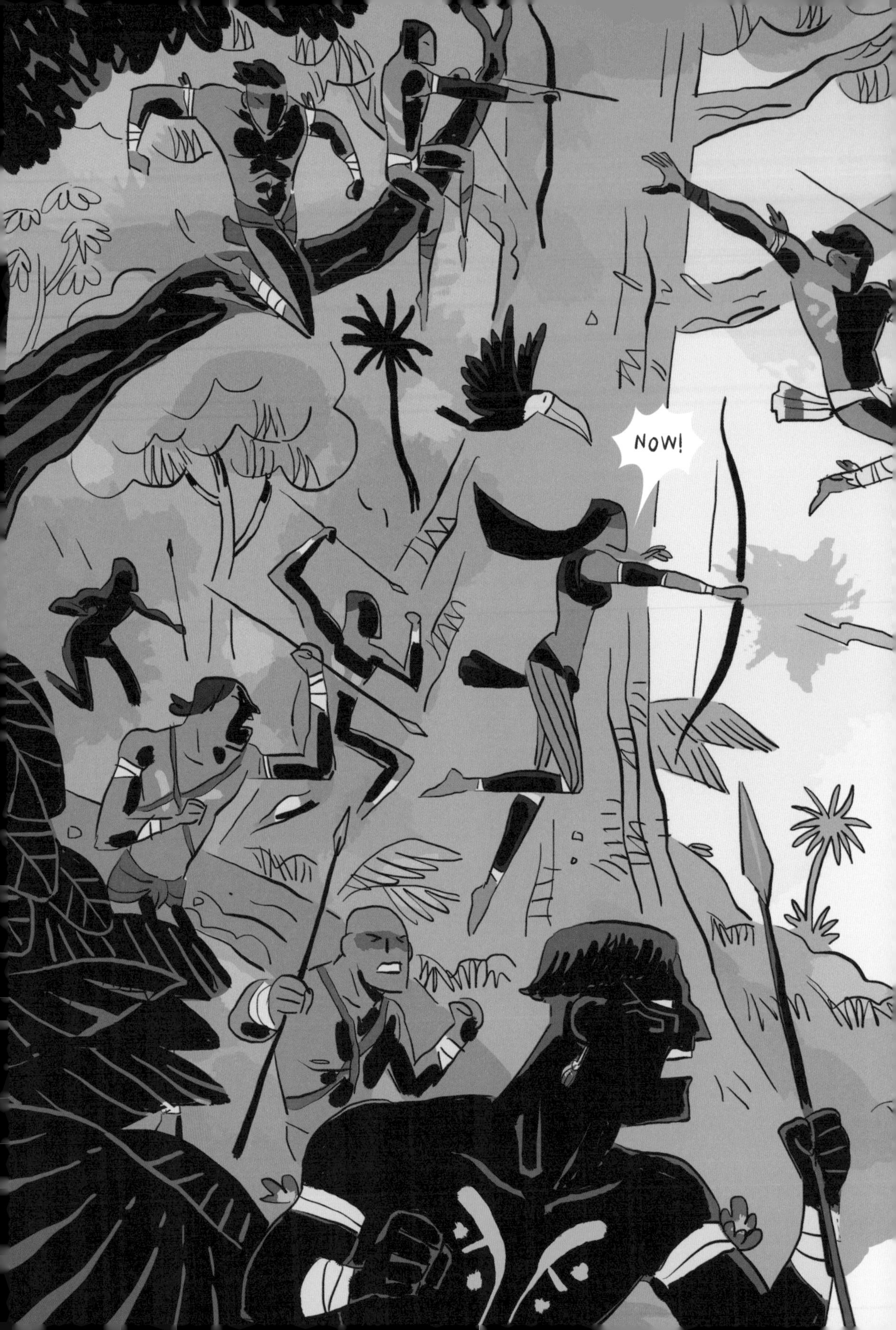
NOW!

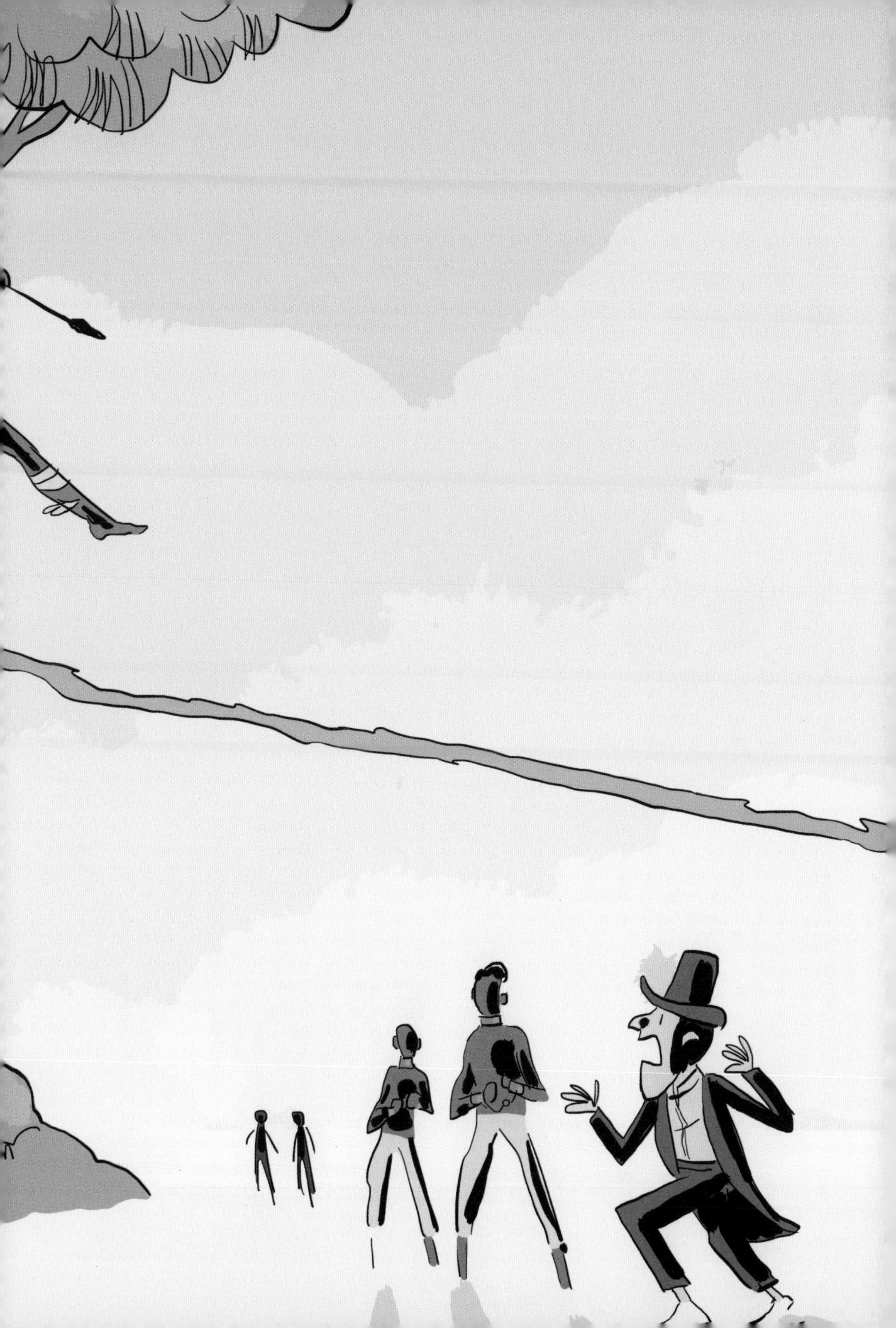

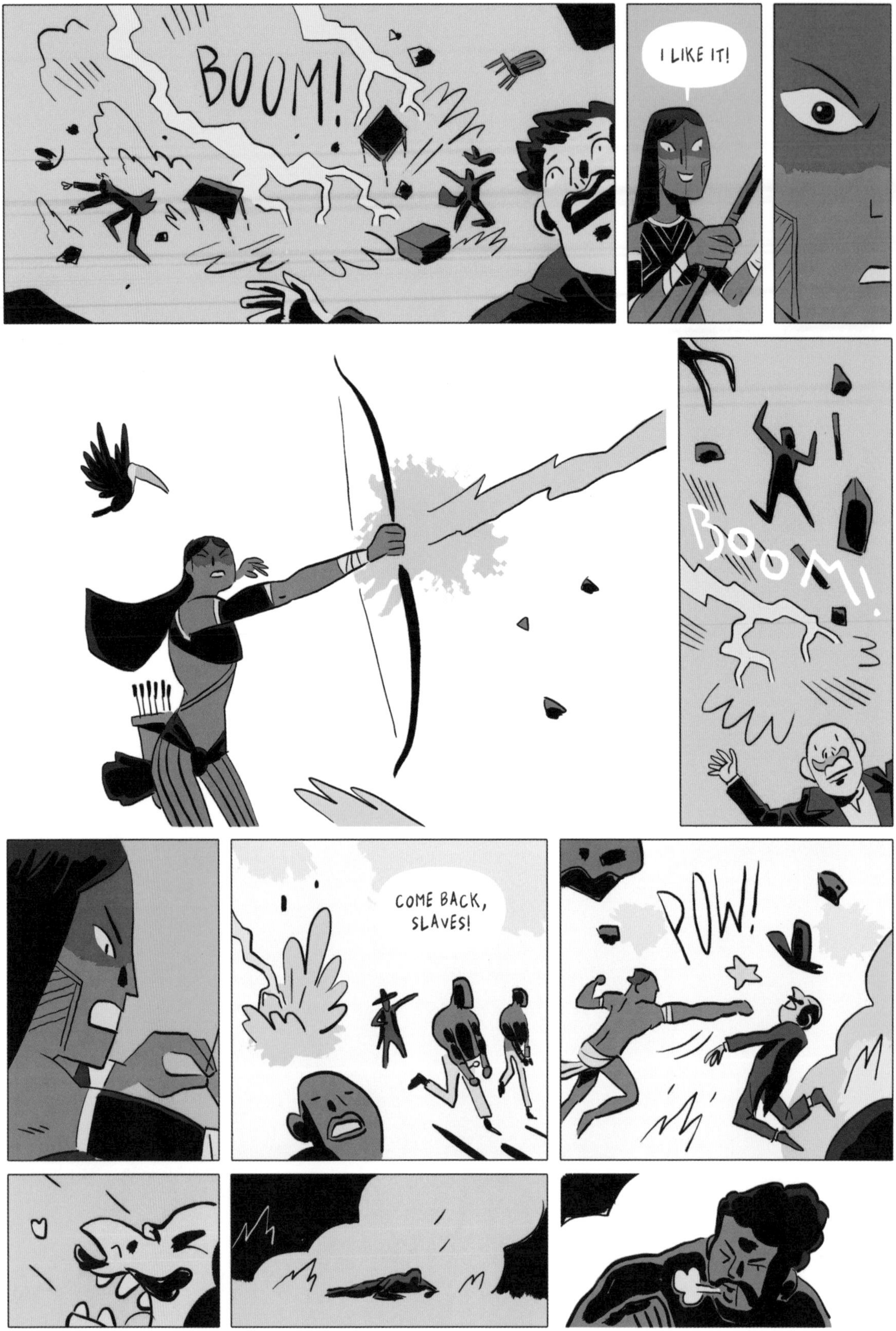
BOOM!
I LIKE IT!
BOOM!
COME BACK, SLAVES!
POW!

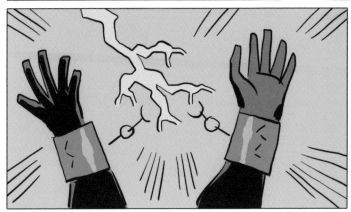

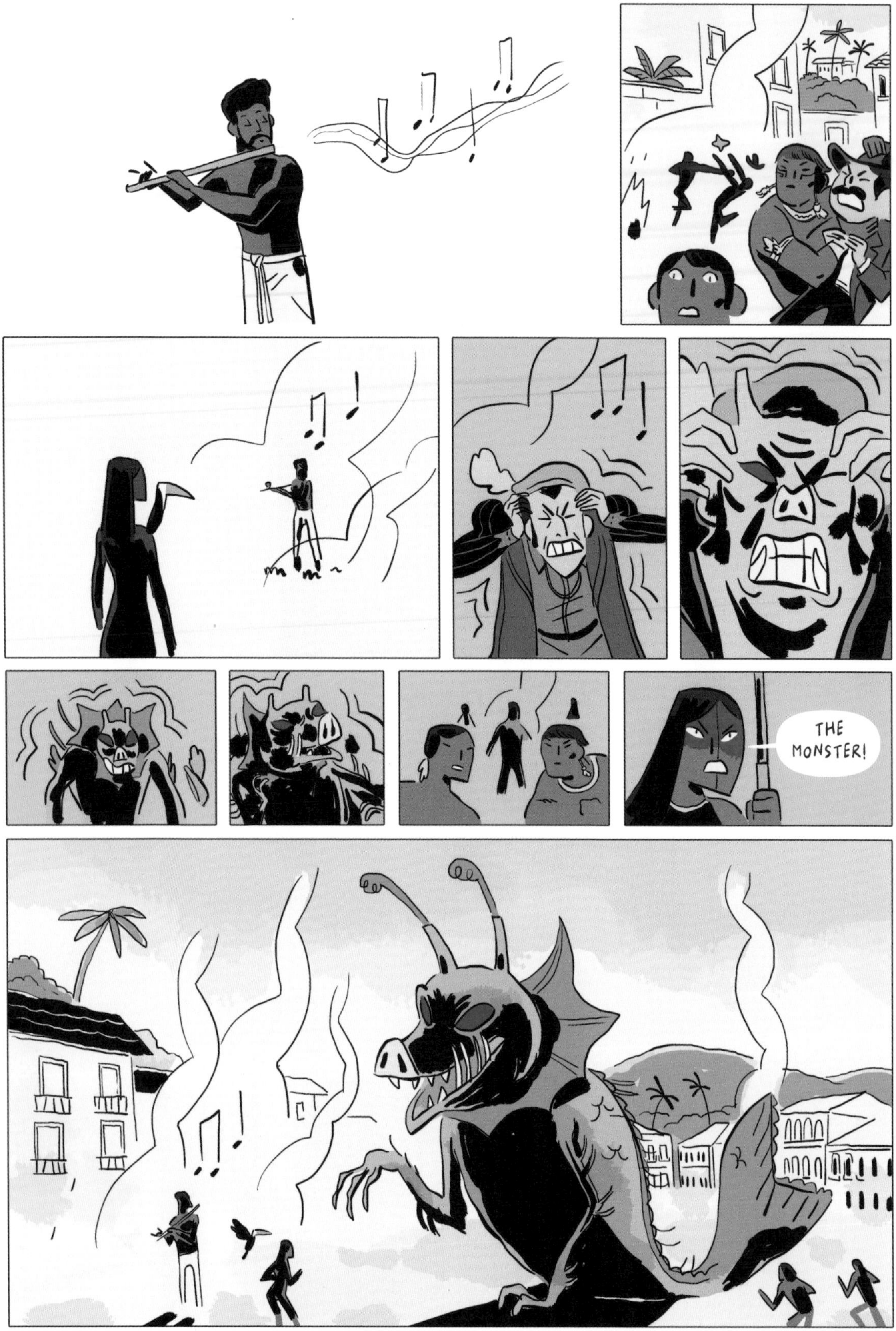
THE MONSTER!

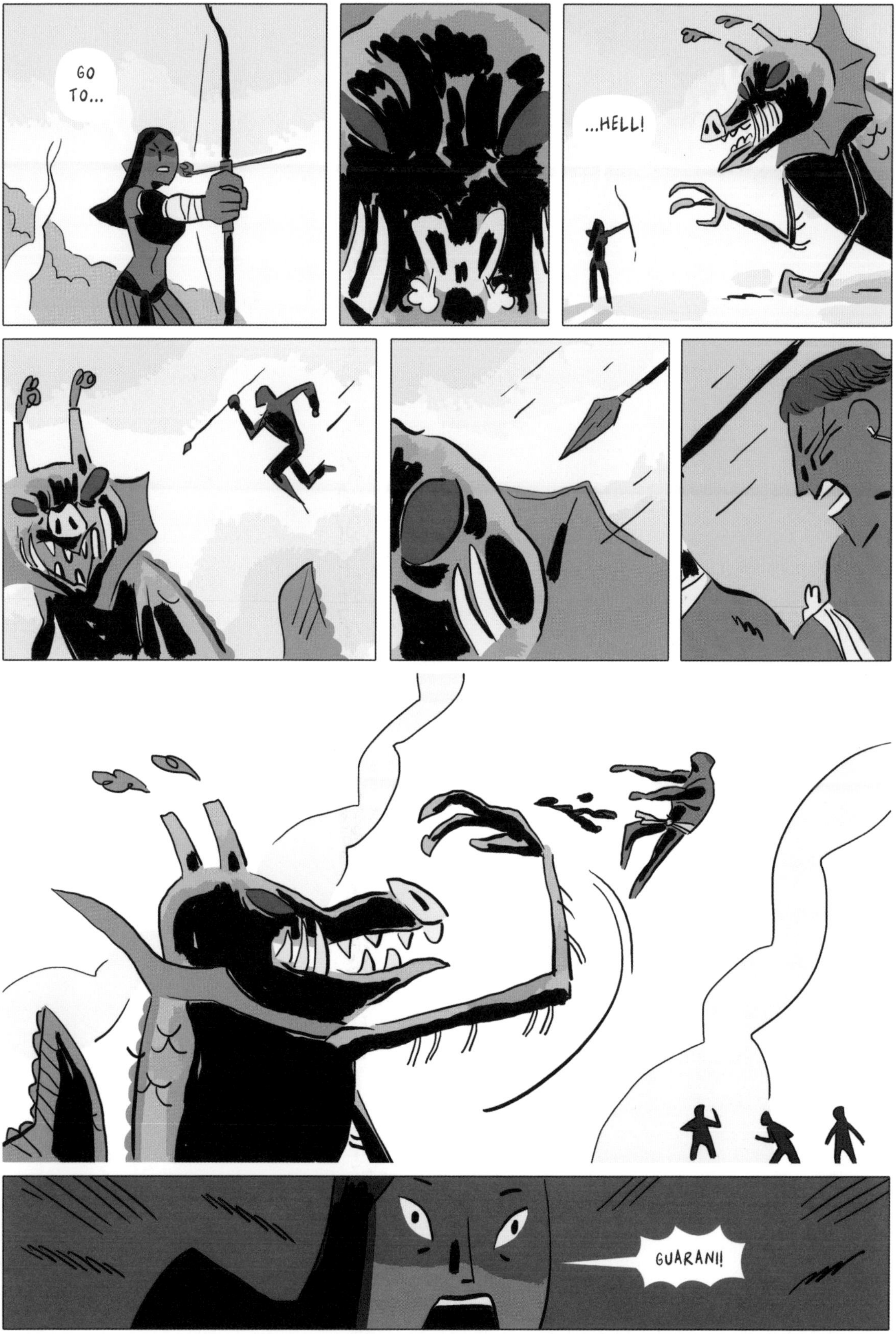
GO TO...
...HELL!
GUARANI!

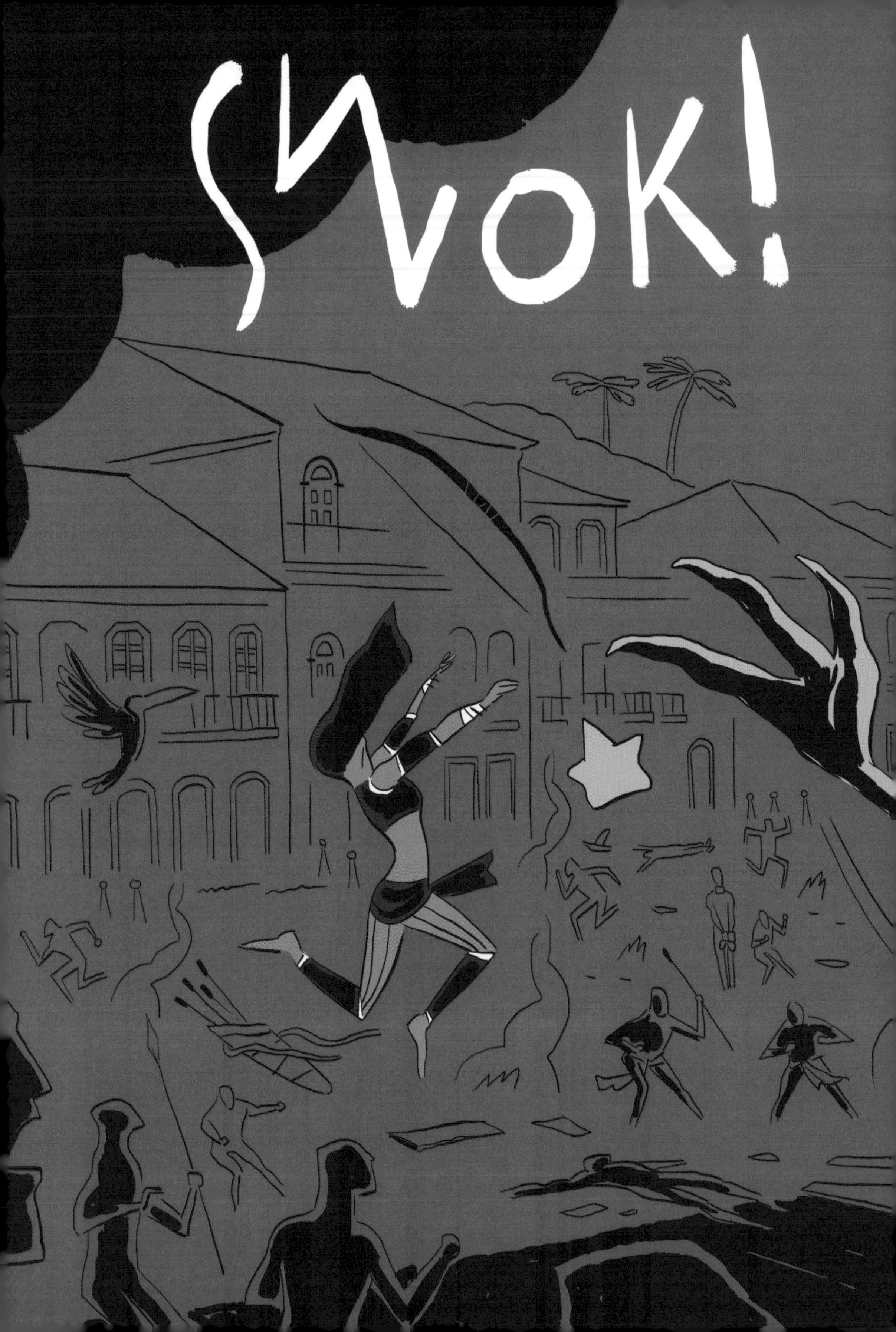
SNOK!

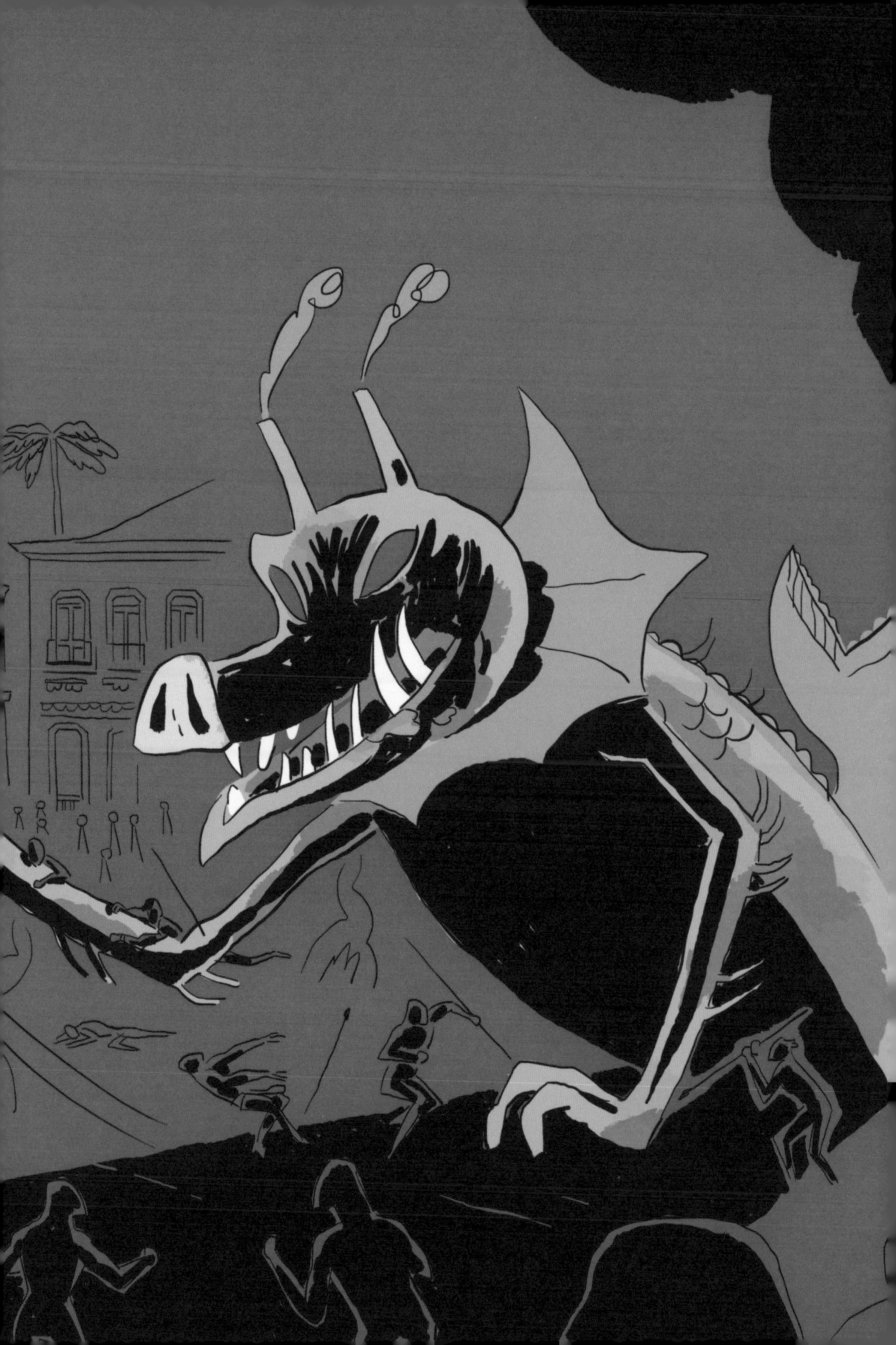

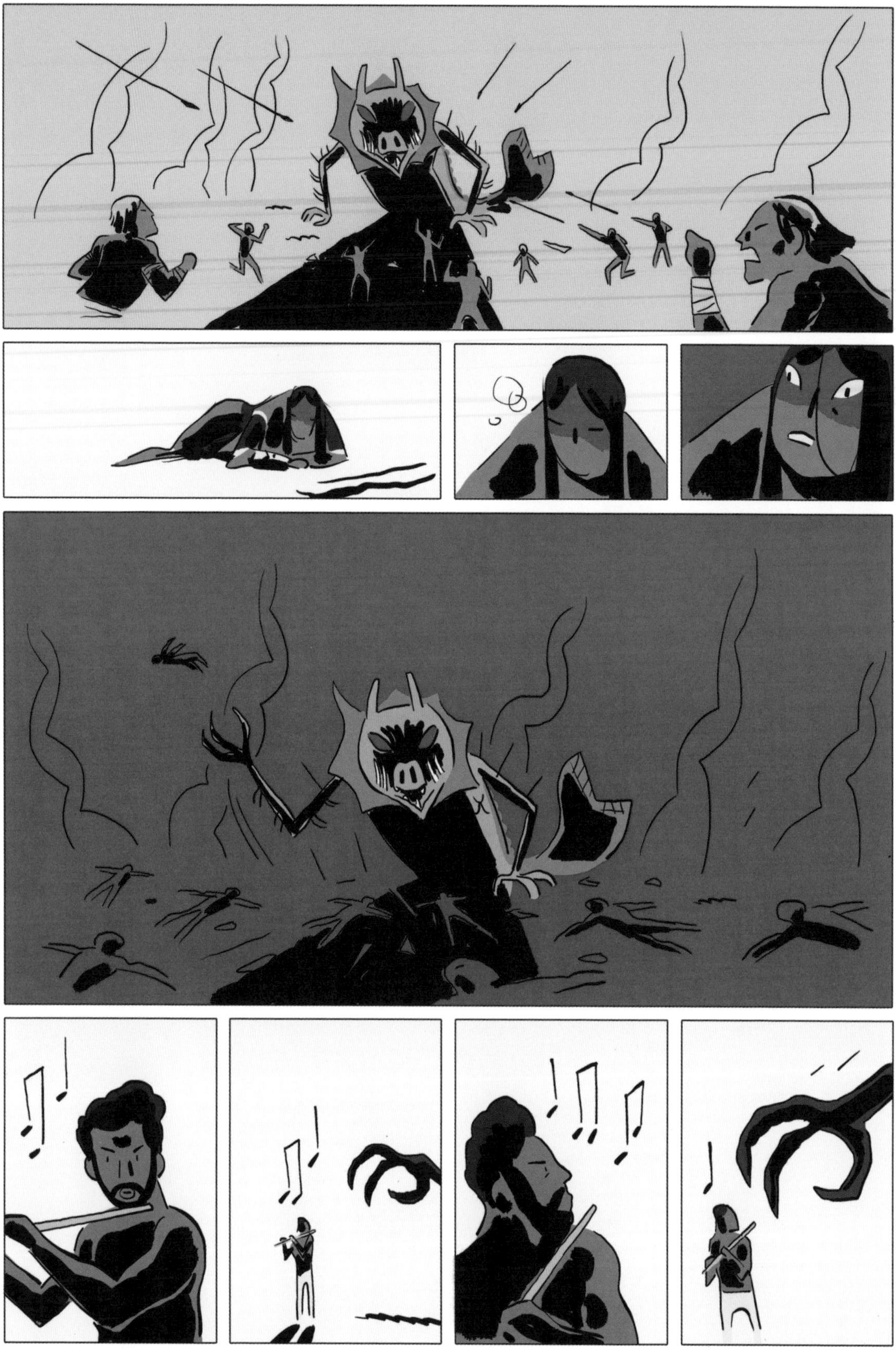

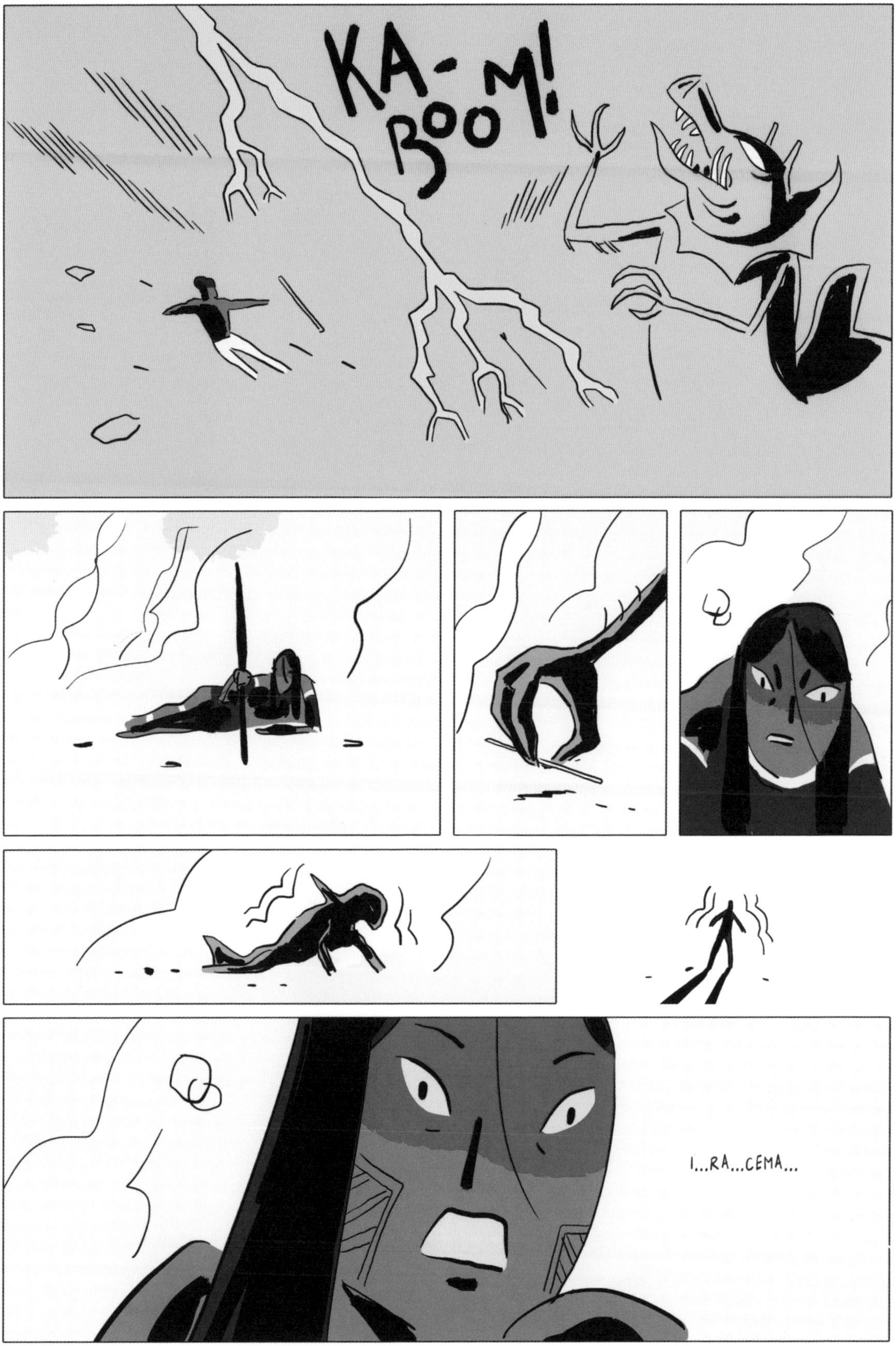
KA-BOOM!
I...RA...CEMA...

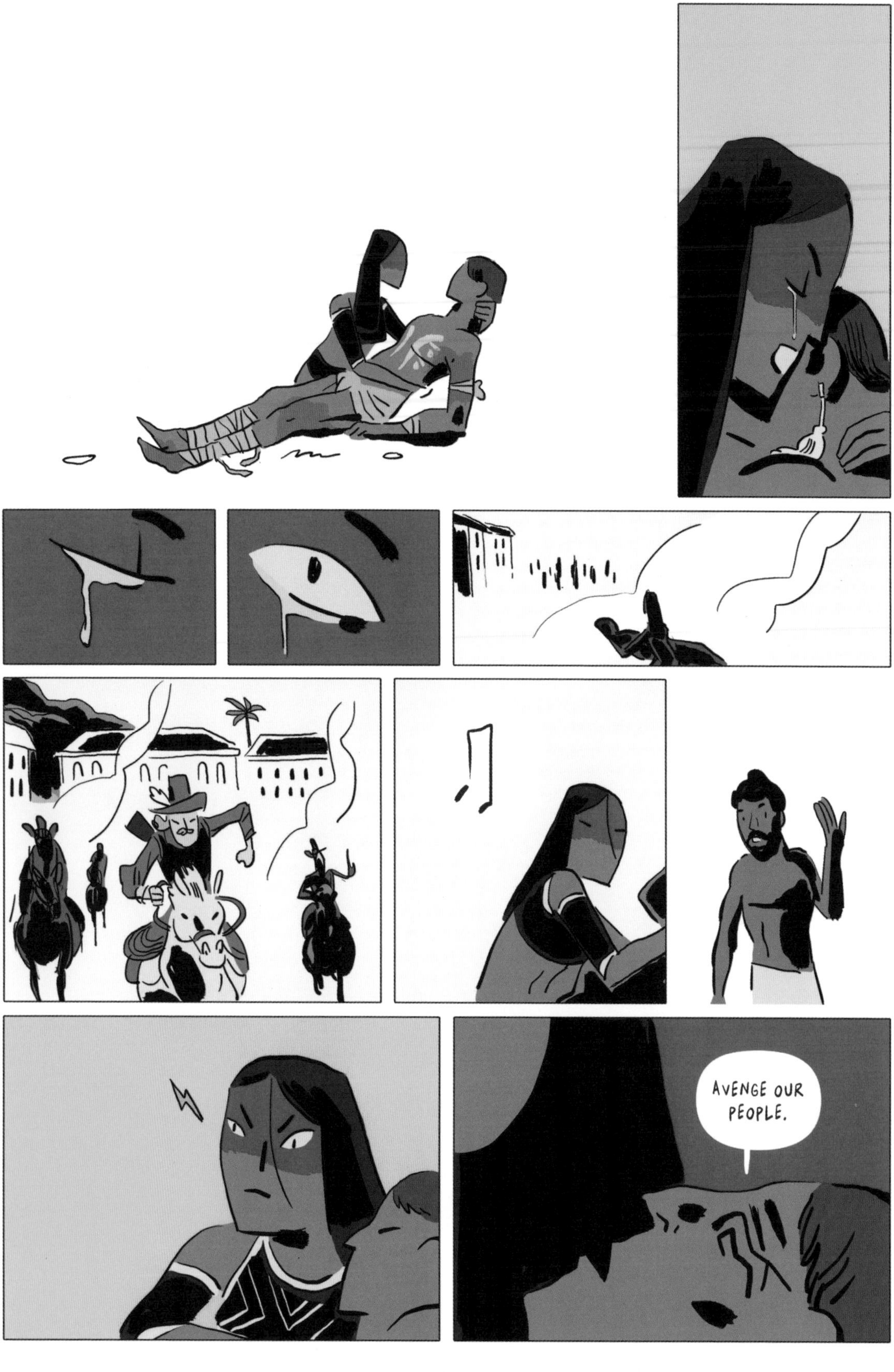
AVENGE OUR PEOPLE.

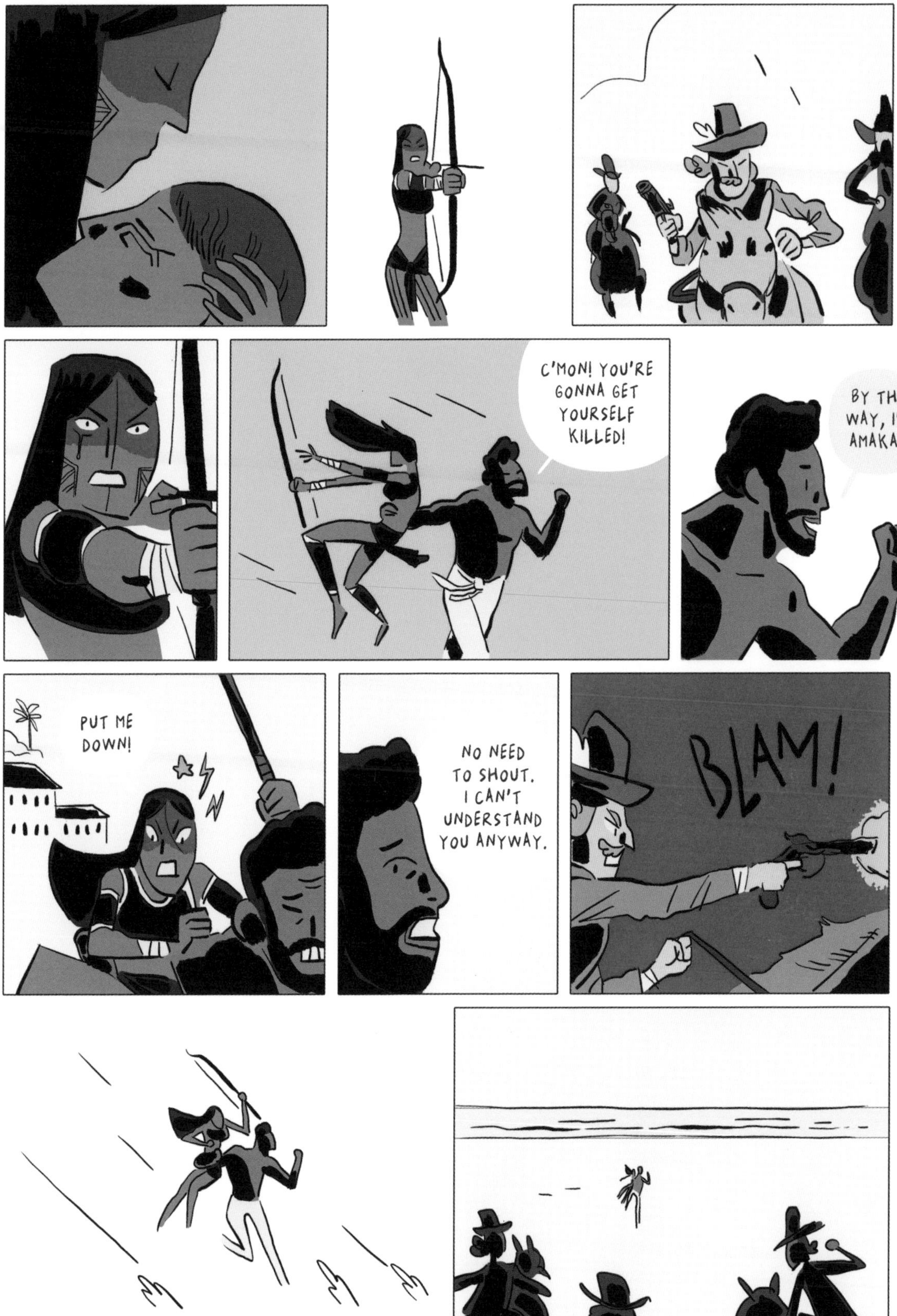
C'MON! YOU'RE GONNA GET YOURSELF KILLED!
BY THE WAY, I'M AMAKAI.
PUT ME DOWN!
NO NEED TO SHOUT. I CAN'T UNDERSTAND YOU ANYWAY.
BLAM!

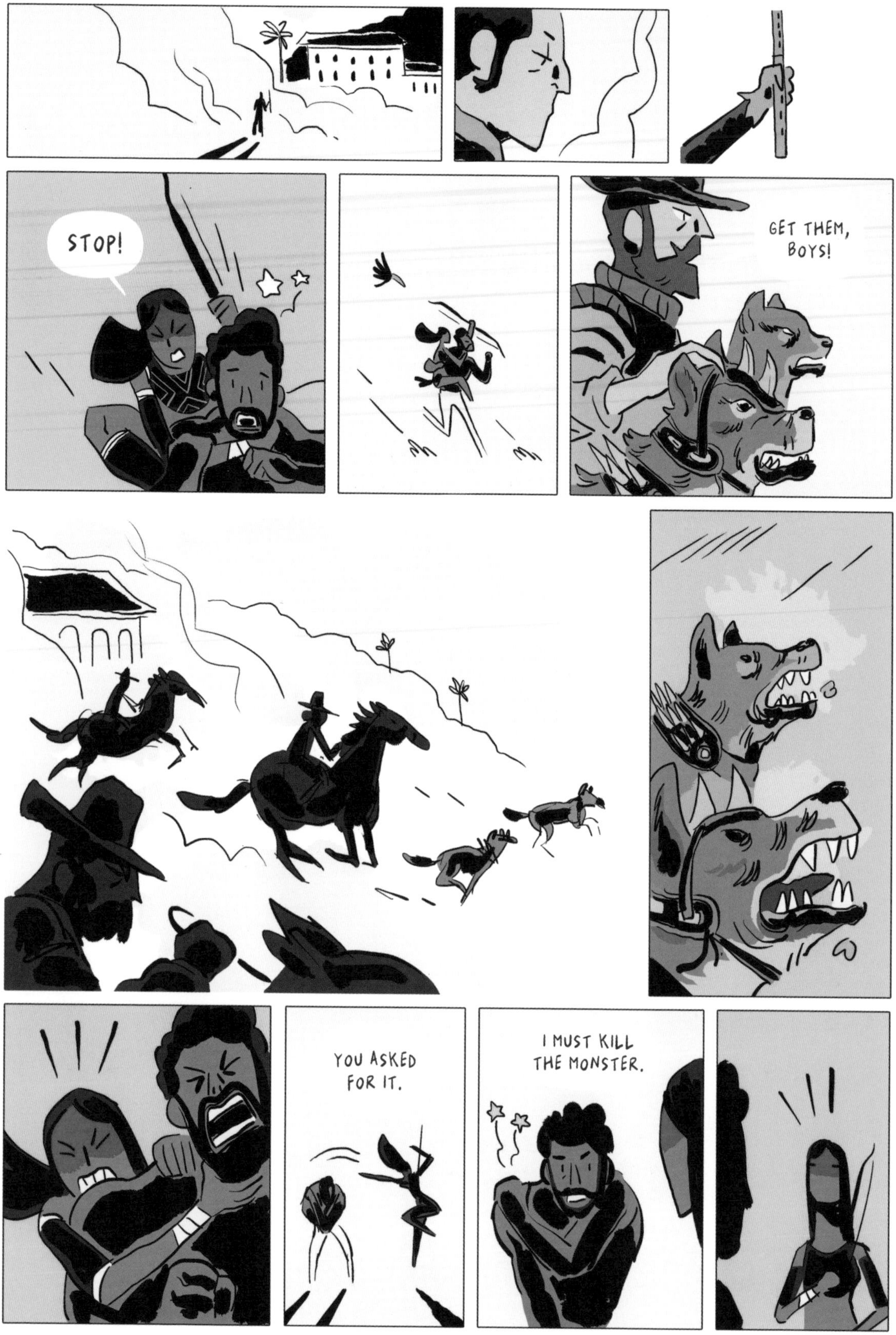
STOP!
GET THEM, BOYS!
YOU ASKED FOR IT.
I MUST KILL THE MONSTER.

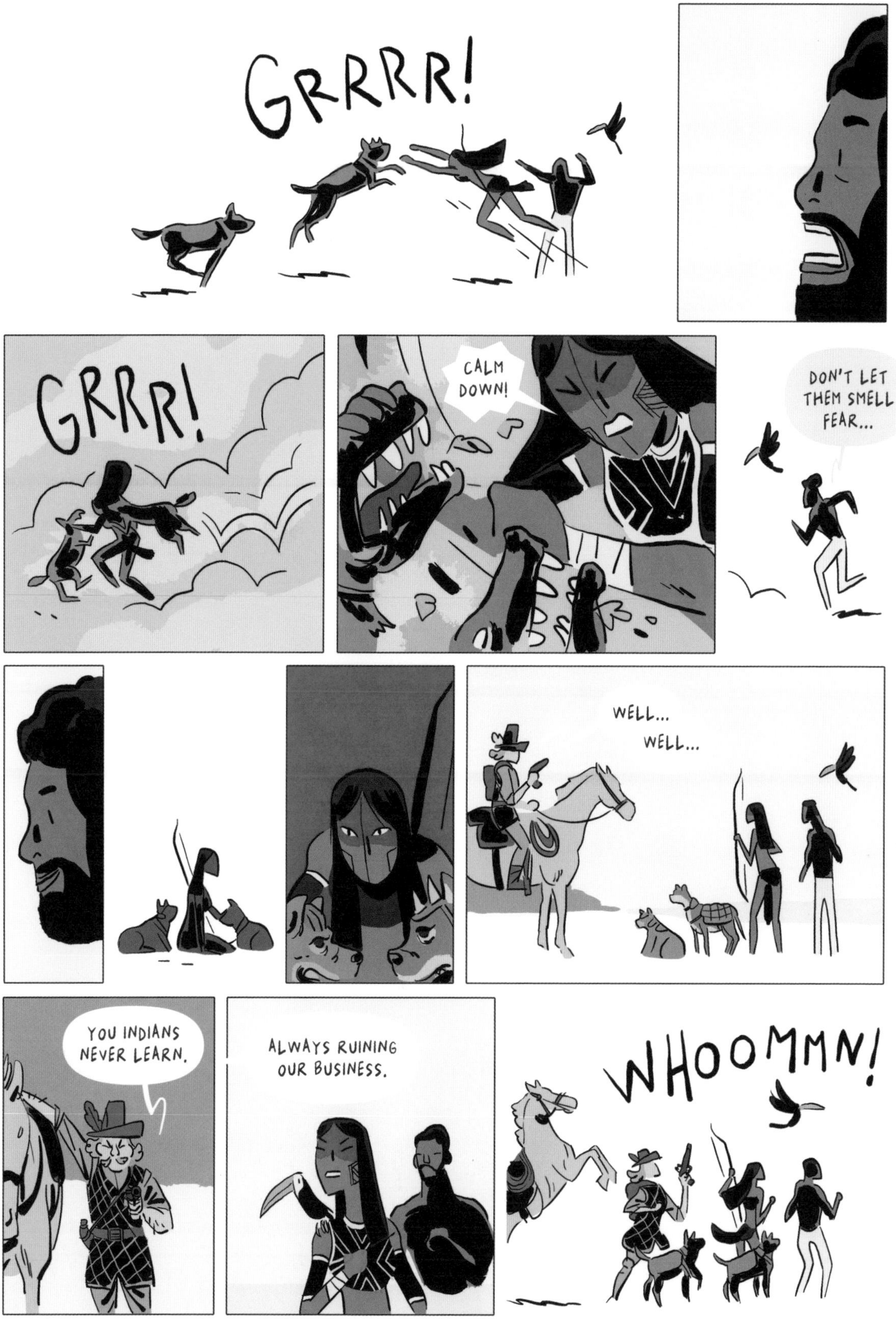
GRRRR!
GRRR!
CALM DOWN!
DON'T LET THEM SMELL FEAR...
WELL...
WELL...
YOU INDIANS NEVER LEARN.
ALWAYS RUINING OUR BUSINESS.
WHOOMMN!

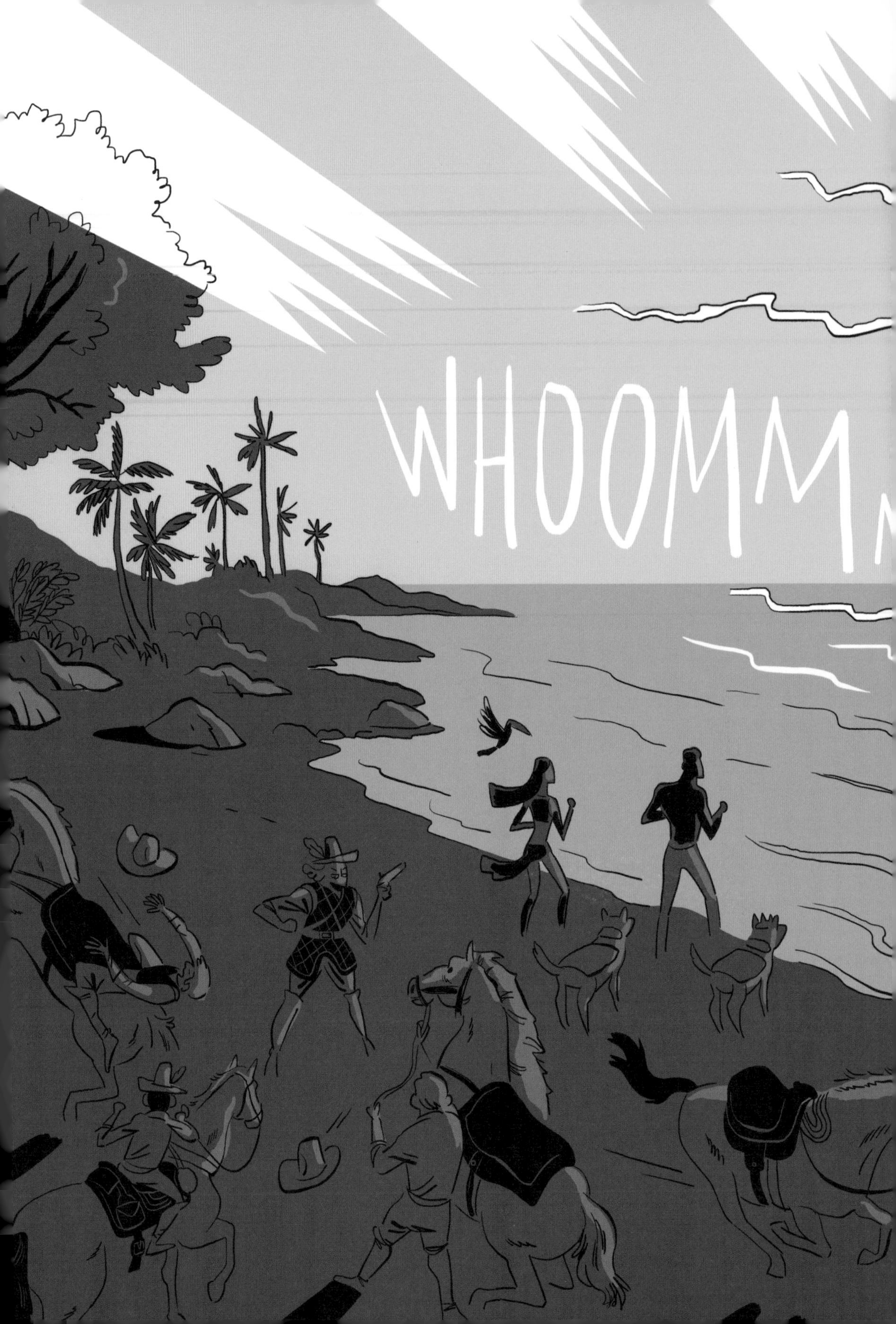
WHOOMM

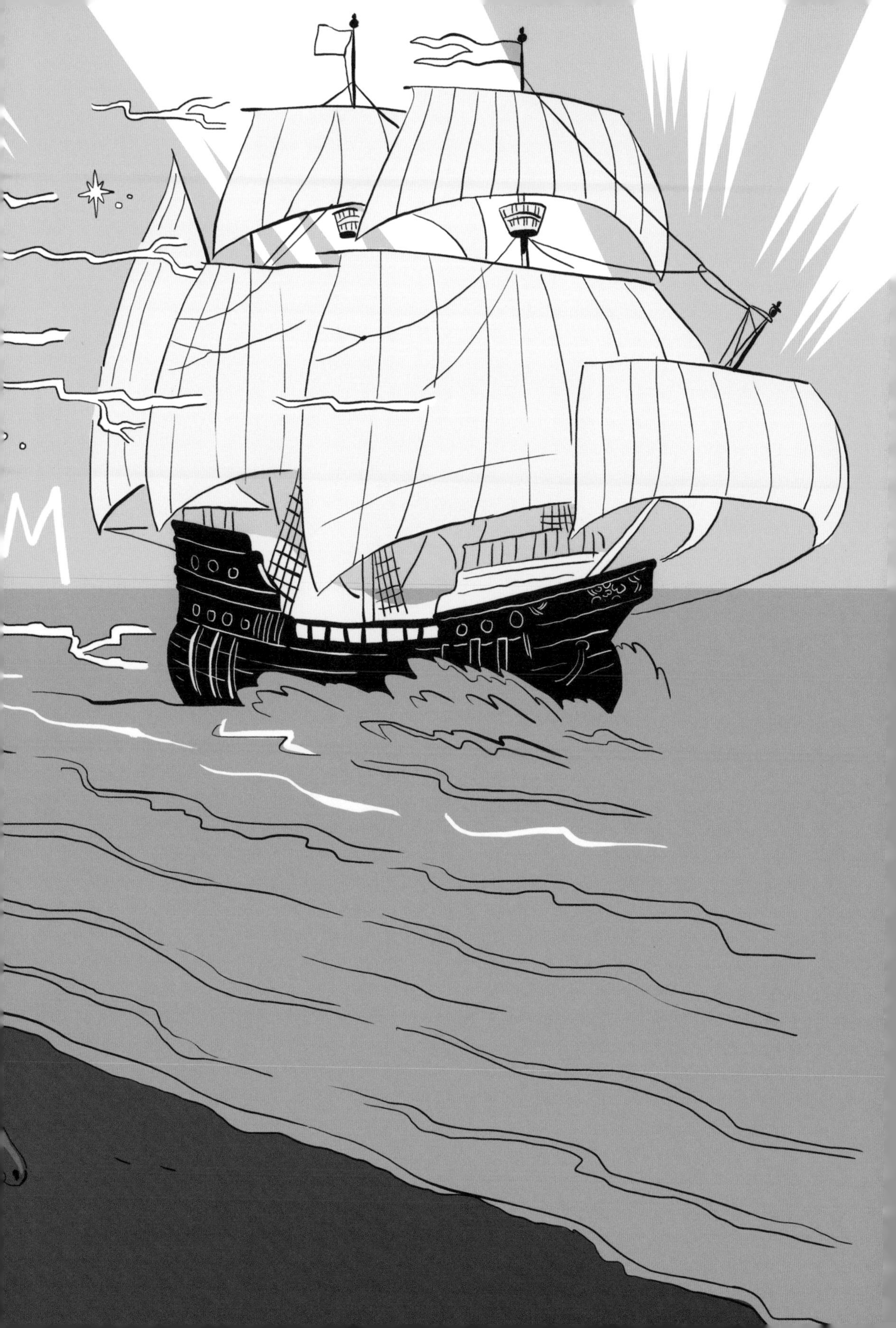
M

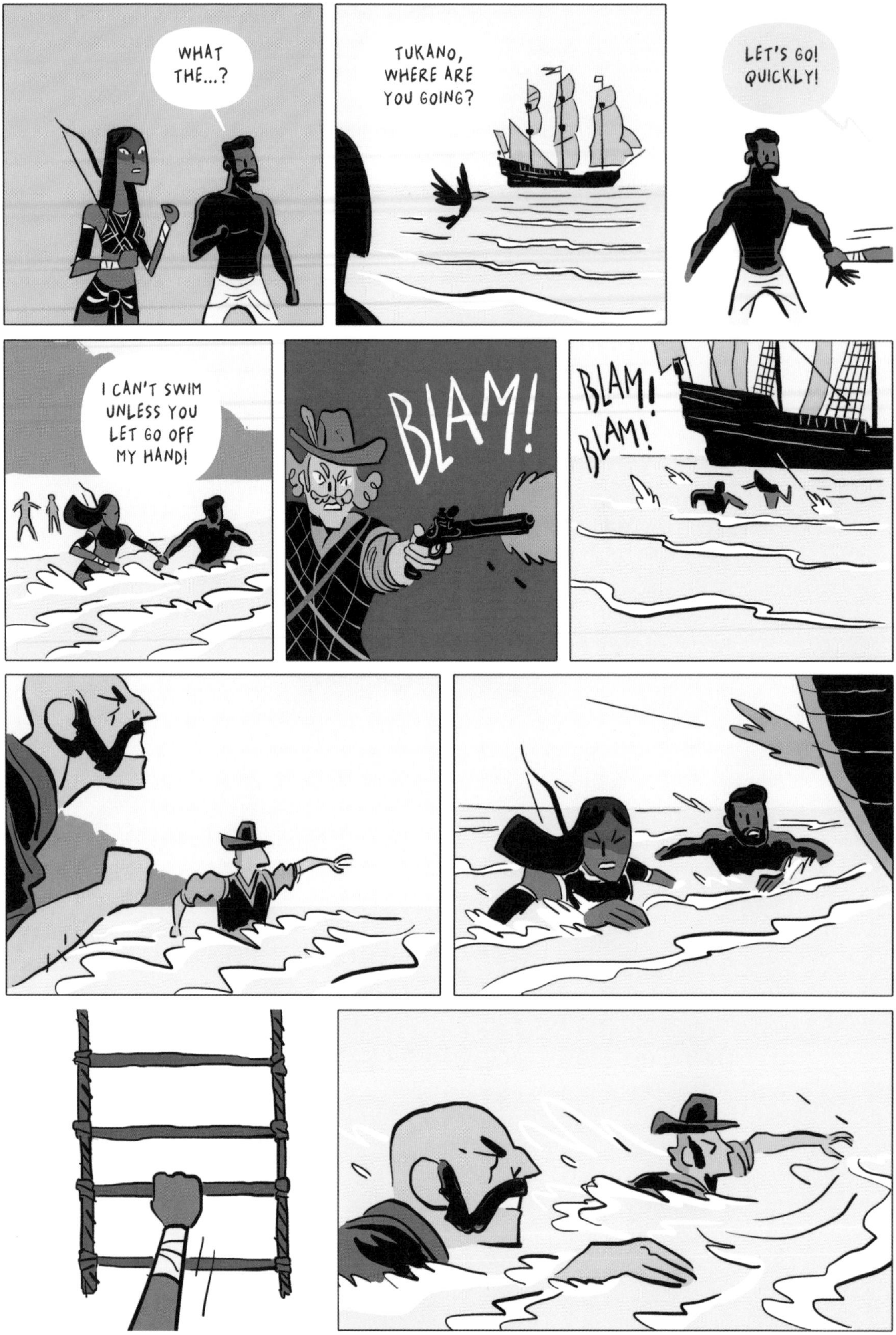

WHAT THE...?
TUKANO, WHERE ARE YOU GOING?
LET'S GO! QUICKLY!
I CAN'T SWIM UNLESS YOU LET GO OFF MY HAND!
BLAM!
BLAM! BLAM!

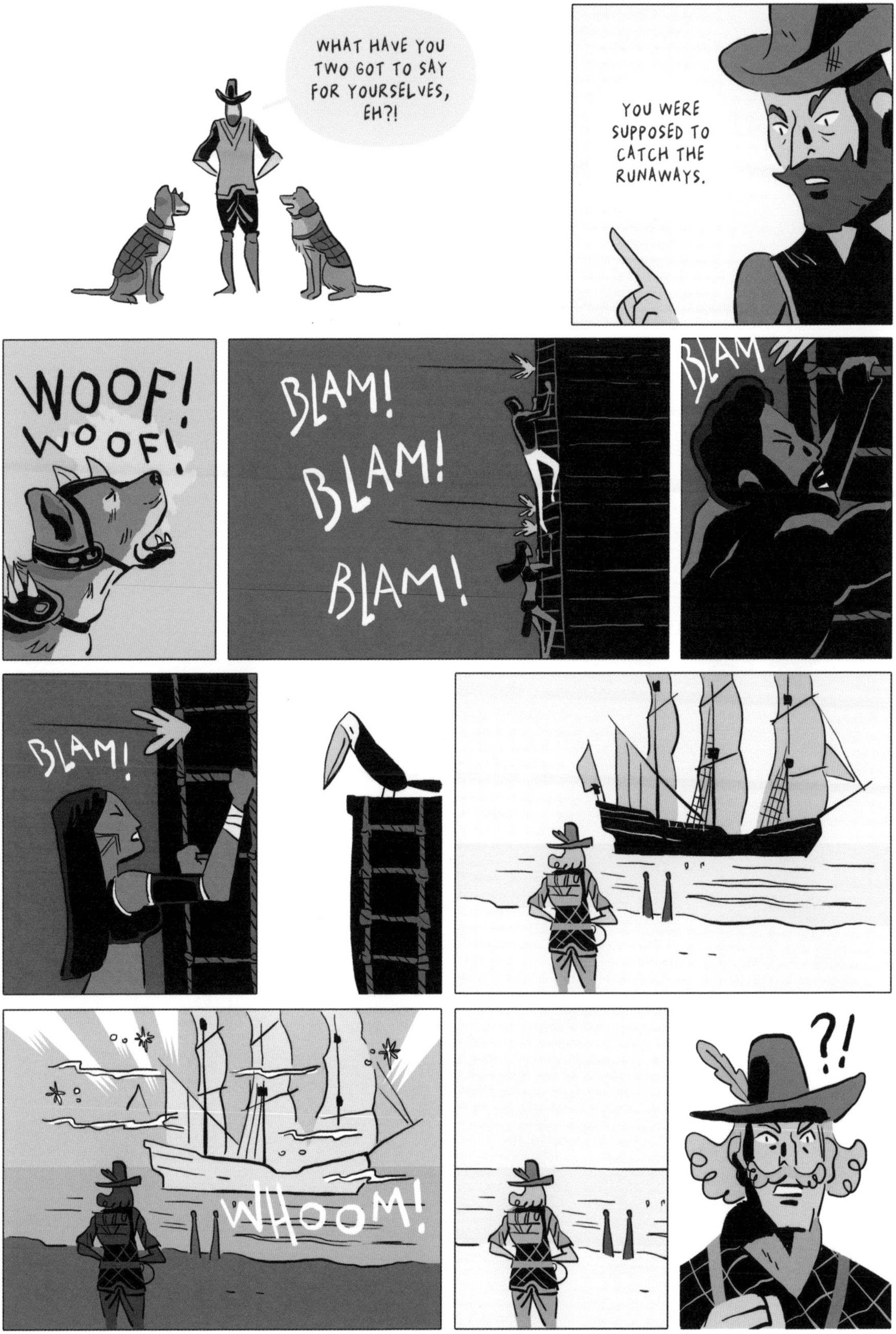
WHAT HAVE YOU TWO GOT TO SAY FOR YOURSELVES, EH?!
YOU WERE SUPPOSED TO CATCH THE RUNAWAYS.
WOOF! WOOF!
BLAM! BLAM! BLAM!
BLAM
BLAM!
WHOOM!
?!

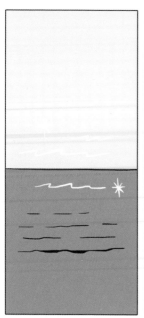

WHOOMNN

TUKANO?

MAN, WE ARE GETTING INTO SOME DEEP TROUBLE.

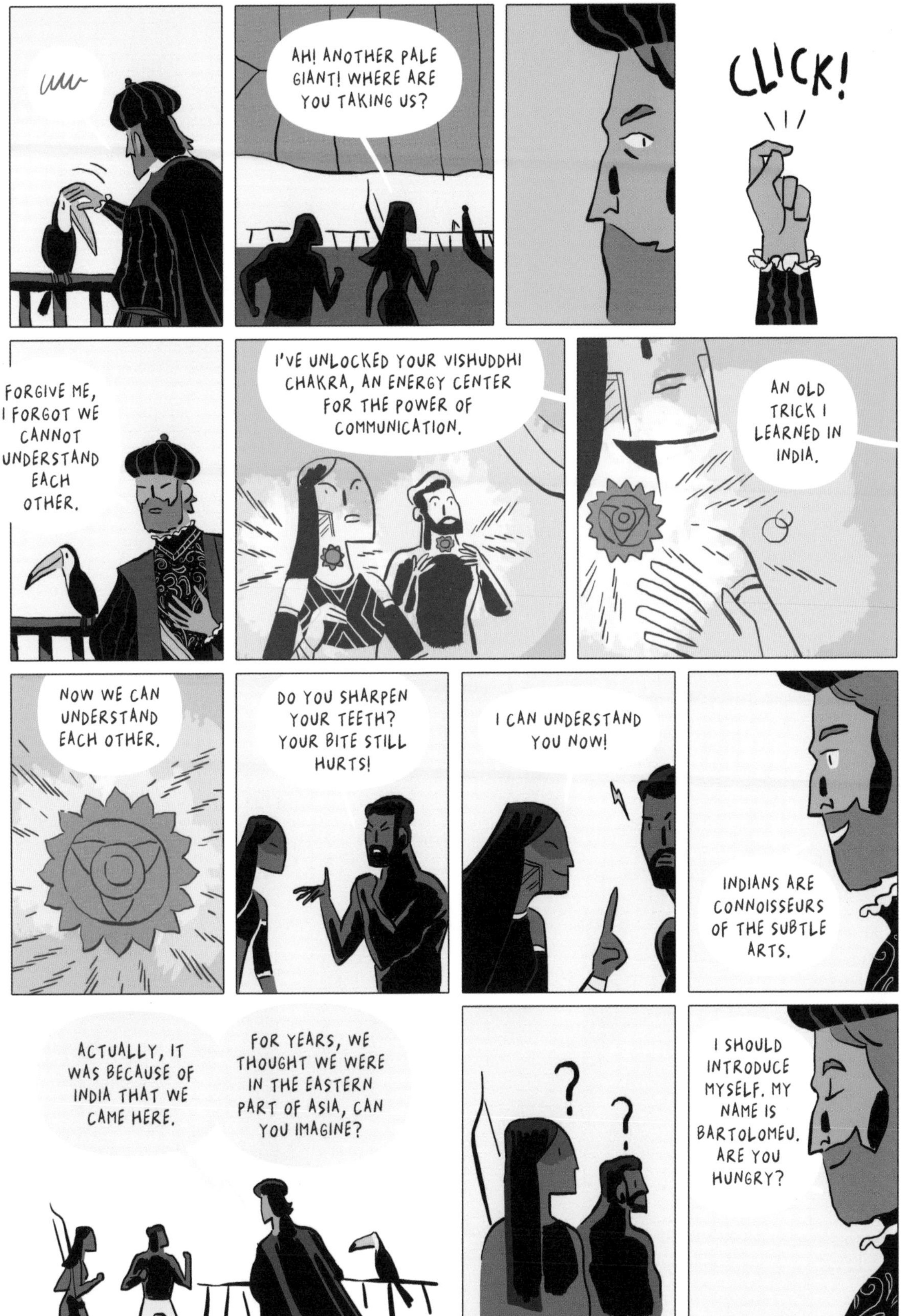
uuw
AH! ANOTHER PALE GIANT! WHERE ARE YOU TAKING US?
CLICK!
FORGIVE ME, I FORGOT WE CANNOT UNDERSTAND EACH OTHER.
I'VE UNLOCKED YOUR VISHUDDHI CHAKRA, AN ENERGY CENTER FOR THE POWER OF COMMUNICATION.
AN OLD TRICK I LEARNED IN INDIA.
NOW WE CAN UNDERSTAND EACH OTHER.
DO YOU SHARPEN YOUR TEETH? YOUR BITE STILL HURTS!
I CAN UNDERSTAND YOU NOW!
INDIANS ARE CONNOISSEURS OF THE SUBTLE ARTS.
ACTUALLY, IT WAS BECAUSE OF INDIA THAT WE CAME HERE.
FOR YEARS, WE THOUGHT WE WERE IN THE EASTERN PART OF ASIA, CAN YOU IMAGINE?
? ?
I SHOULD INTRODUCE MYSELF. MY NAME IS BARTOLOMEU. ARE YOU HUNGRY?

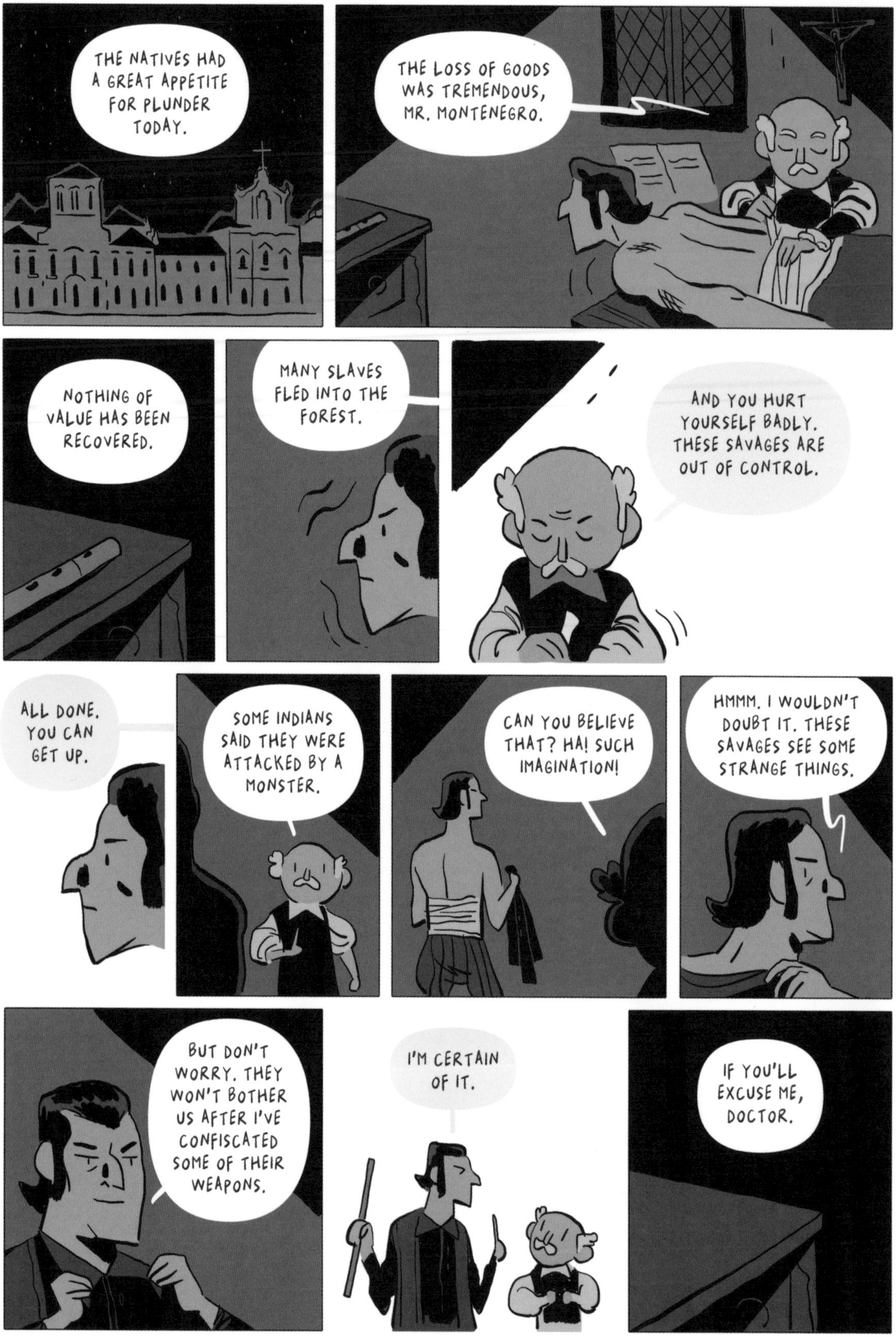
THE NATIVES HAD A GREAT APPETITE FOR PLUNDER TODAY.
THE LOSS OF GOODS WAS TREMENDOUS, MR. MONTENEGRO.
NOTHING OF VALUE HAS BEEN RECOVERED.
MANY SLAVES FLED INTO THE FOREST.
AND YOU HURT YOURSELF BADLY. THESE SAVAGES ARE OUT OF CONTROL.
ALL DONE. YOU CAN GET UP.
SOME INDIANS SAID THEY WERE ATTACKED BY A MONSTER.
CAN YOU BELIEVE THAT? HA! SUCH IMAGINATION!
HMMM. I WOULDN'T DOUBT IT. THESE SAVAGES SEE SOME STRANGE THINGS.
BUT DON'T WORRY. THEY WON'T BOTHER US AFTER I'VE CONFISCATED SOME OF THEIR WEAPONS.
I'M CERTAIN OF IT.
IF YOU'LL EXCUSE ME, DOCTOR.

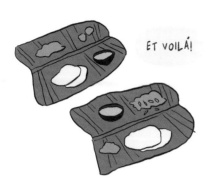

ET VOILÁ!

I HOPE IT'S NOT TOO SPICY.

TURMERIC, CINNAMON, NUTMEG — THESE SPICES ARE MORE VALUABLE THAN GOLD.

NOT BAD!

COLUMBUS WOULD NEVER HAVE COME HERE IF IT HADN'T BEEN FOR THEM.

YOU COOKED THIS?

WELL, NOT EXACTLY.

HE HELPS ME WITH THE SHIP.

BUT PLEASE, DON'T TALK TO HIM.

HE IS NOT FROM THIS WORLD.

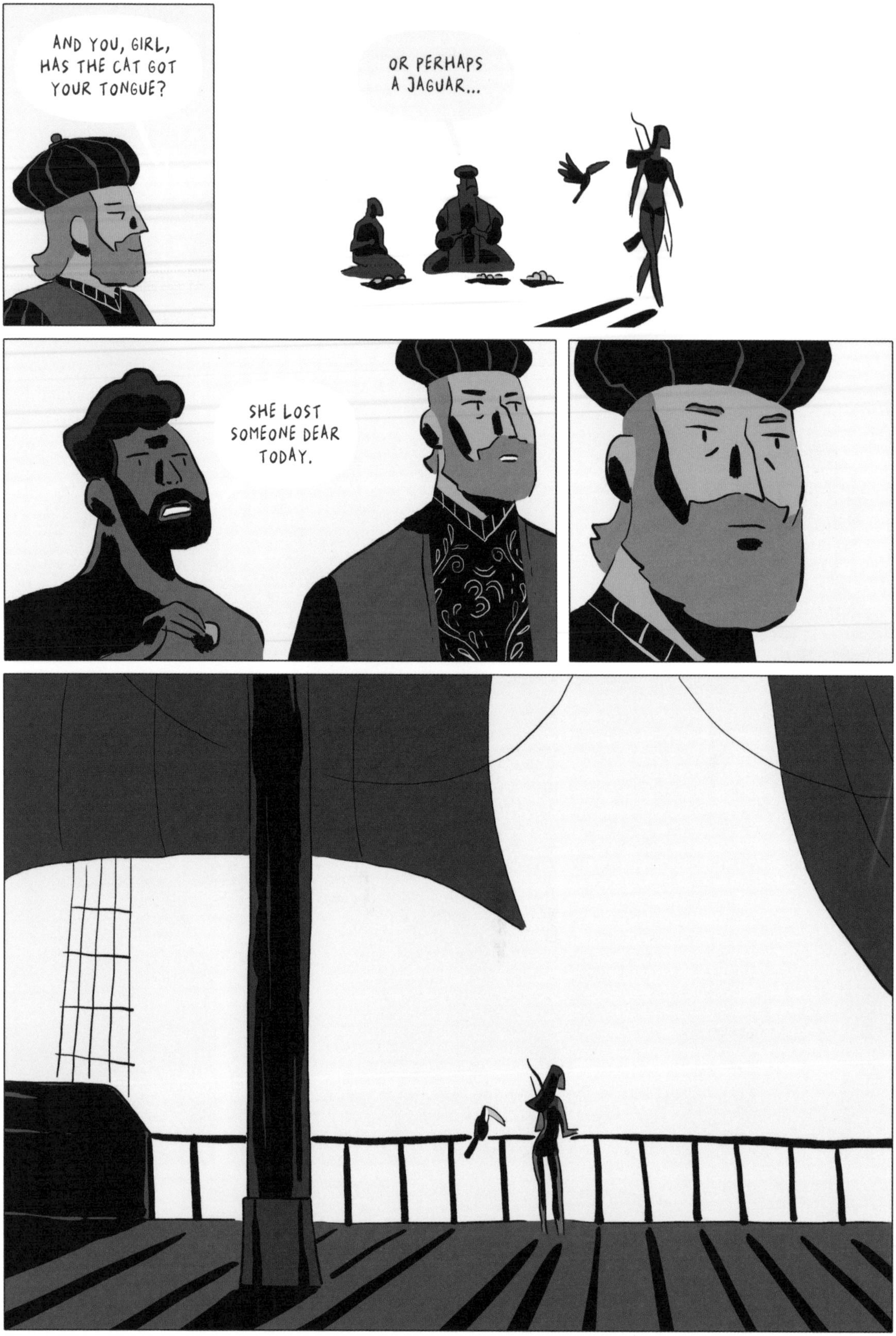
AND YOU, GIRL, HAS THE CAT GOT YOUR TONGUE?
OR PERHAPS A JAGUAR...
SHE LOST SOMEONE DEAR TODAY.

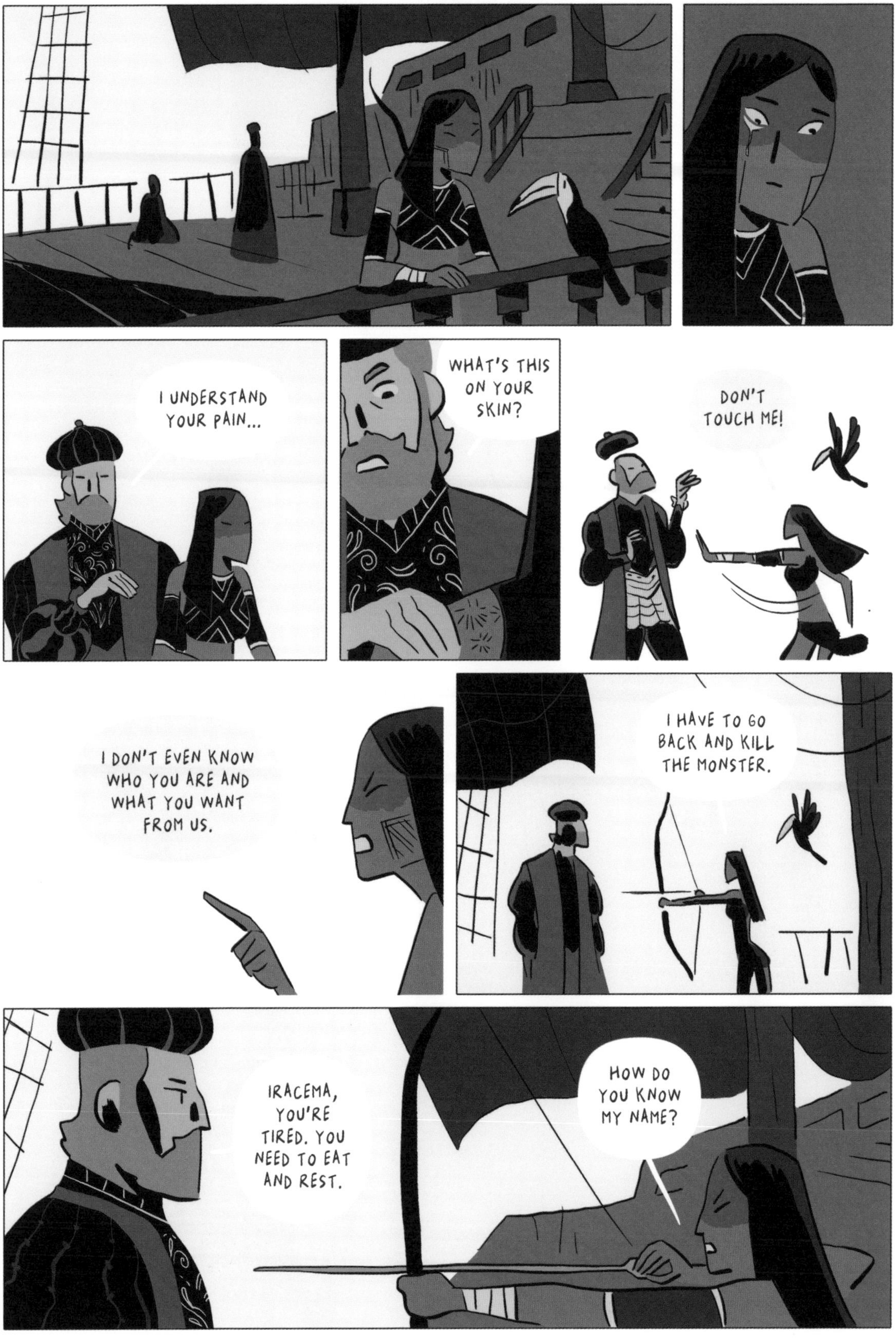
I UNDERSTAND YOUR PAIN...
WHAT'S THIS ON YOUR SKIN?
DON'T TOUCH ME!
I DON'T EVEN KNOW WHO YOU ARE AND WHAT YOU WANT FROM US.
I HAVE TO GO BACK AND KILL THE MONSTER.
IRACEMA, YOU'RE TIRED. YOU NEED TO EAT AND REST.
HOW DO YOU KNOW MY NAME?

THE INDIAN SAGES WHO SENT ME TO YOU, KNOW MORE THAN JUST YOUR NAME.

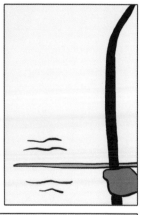

PLEASE...

ACCEPT AT LEAST THIS FRUIT.

"HERE WE COME."

THIS IS THE PERFECT PLACE TO SPEND THE NIGHT.

AN UNINHABITED ISLAND.

I UNDERSTAND THE WORRY OF SPENDING THE NIGHT ON A STRANGER'S SHIP.

ESPECIALLY WITH A BIG EAGLE HEADED MAN ROAMING AROUND.

I'LL EXPLAIN EVERYTHING TOMORROW.

"AMAKAI, TELL ME, DO YOU TRUST HIM?"

DO YOU TRUST BARTOLOMEU?

HE OFFERED ME THE FIRST DECENT MEAL I HAD IN MONTHS.

THAT WOULD MAKE HIM THE CLOSEST WHITE MAN TO MY CONFIDENCE. NOT THAT HE HAS A LOT OF COMPETITION.

PLUS, I NOTICED YOUR BIRD LIKES THE GUY.

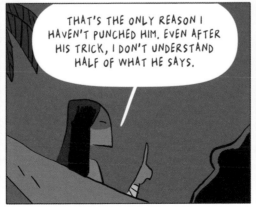

THAT'S THE ONLY REASON I HAVEN'T PUNCHED HIM. EVEN AFTER HIS TRICK, I DON'T UNDERSTAND HALF OF WHAT HE SAYS.

I DON'T THINK I TRUST HIM. AND YOU SHOULDN'T EITHER.

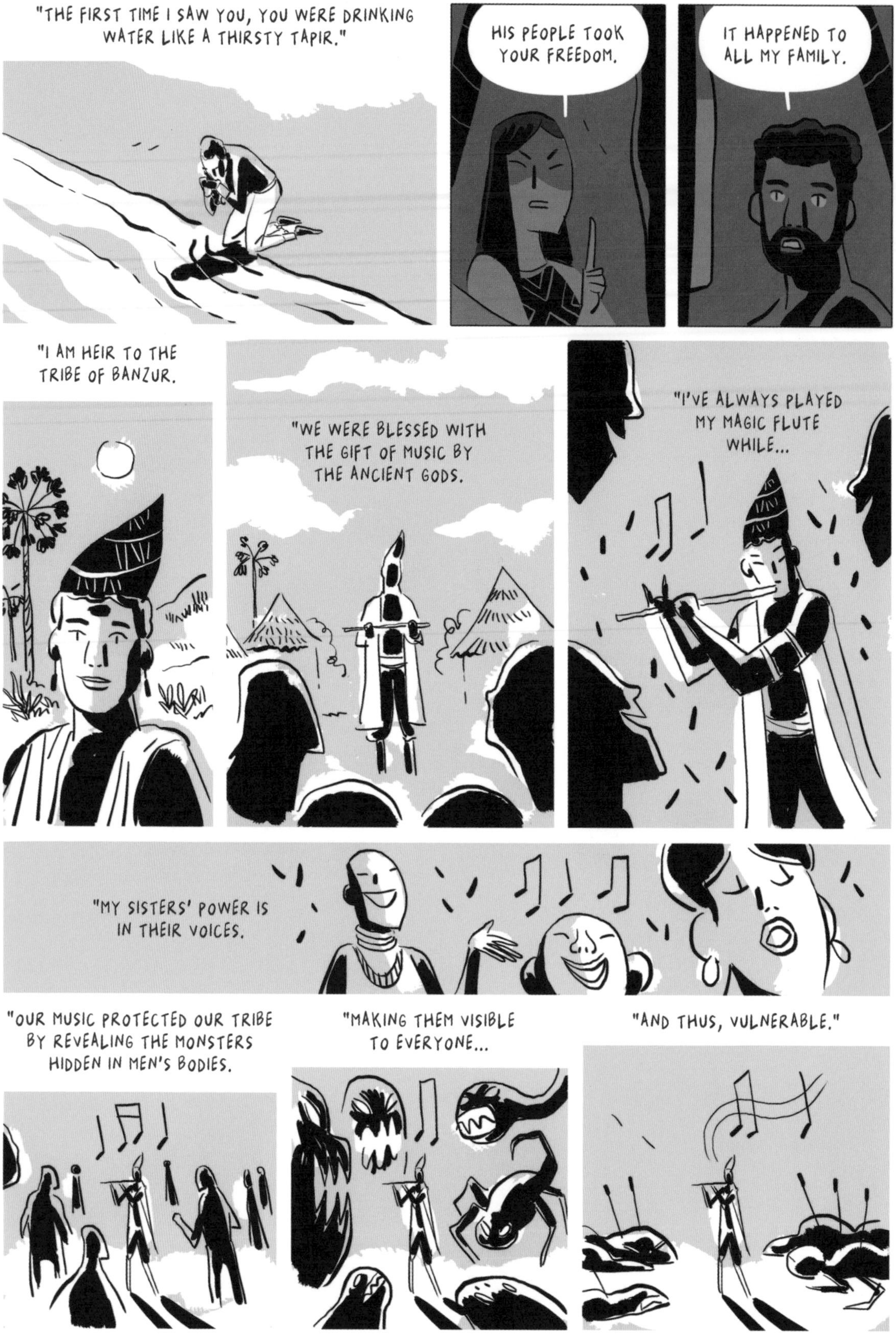
"THE FIRST TIME I SAW YOU, YOU WERE DRINKING WATER LIKE A THIRSTY TAPIR."
HIS PEOPLE TOOK YOUR FREEDOM.
IT HAPPENED TO ALL MY FAMILY.
"I AM HEIR TO THE TRIBE OF BANZUR.
"WE WERE BLESSED WITH THE GIFT OF MUSIC BY THE ANCIENT GODS.
"I'VE ALWAYS PLAYED MY MAGIC FLUTE WHILE...
"MY SISTERS' POWER IS IN THEIR VOICES.
"OUR MUSIC PROTECTED OUR TRIBE BY REVEALING THE MONSTERS HIDDEN IN MEN'S BODIES.
"MAKING THEM VISIBLE TO EVERYONE...
"AND THUS, VULNERABLE."

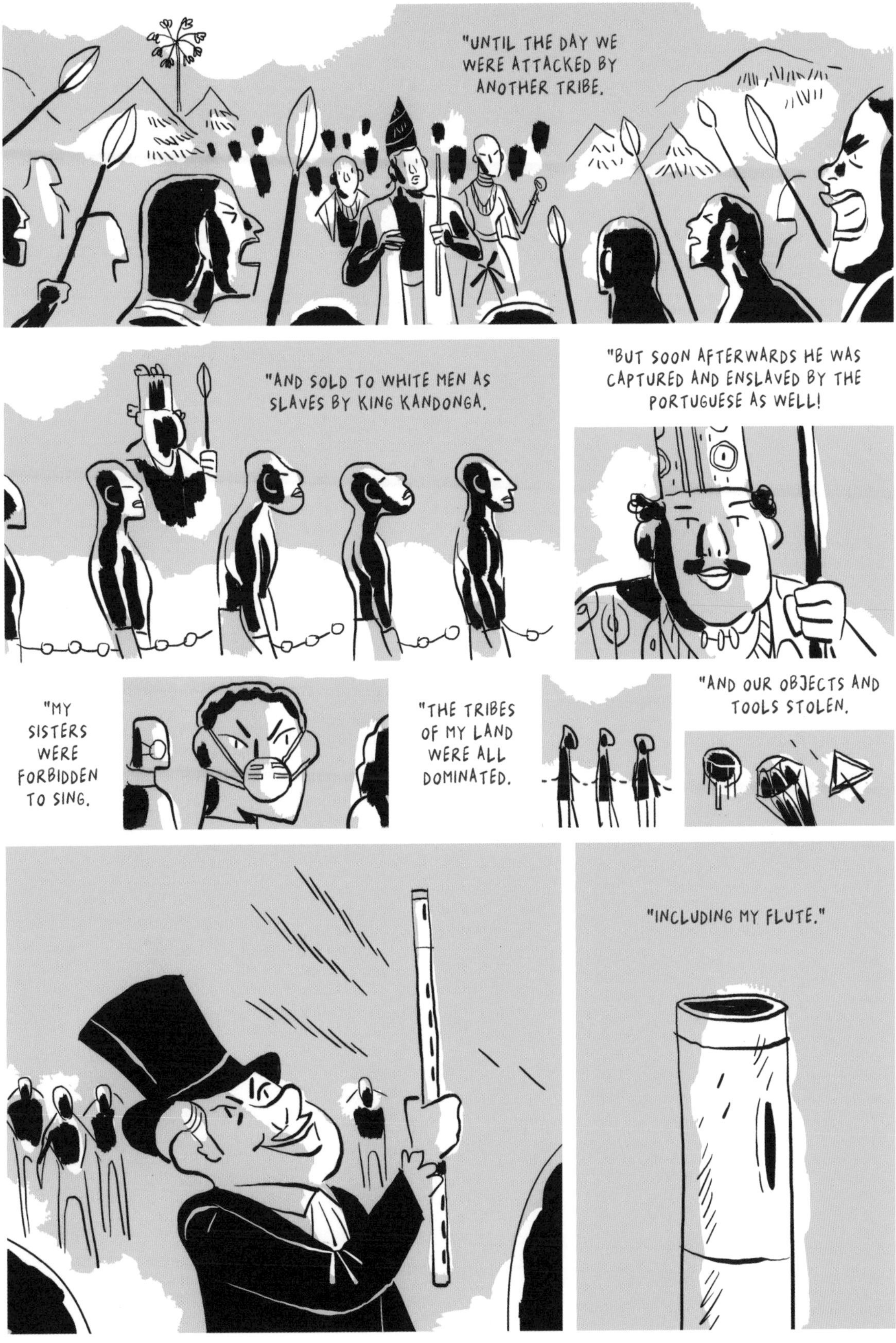
"UNTIL THE DAY WE WERE ATTACKED BY ANOTHER TRIBE.
"AND SOLD TO WHITE MEN AS SLAVES BY KING KANDONGA.
"BUT SOON AFTERWARDS HE WAS CAPTURED AND ENSLAVED BY THE PORTUGUESE AS WELL!
"MY SISTERS WERE FORBIDDEN TO SING.
"THE TRIBES OF MY LAND WERE ALL DOMINATED.
"AND OUR OBJECTS AND TOOLS STOLEN.
"INCLUDING MY FLUTE."

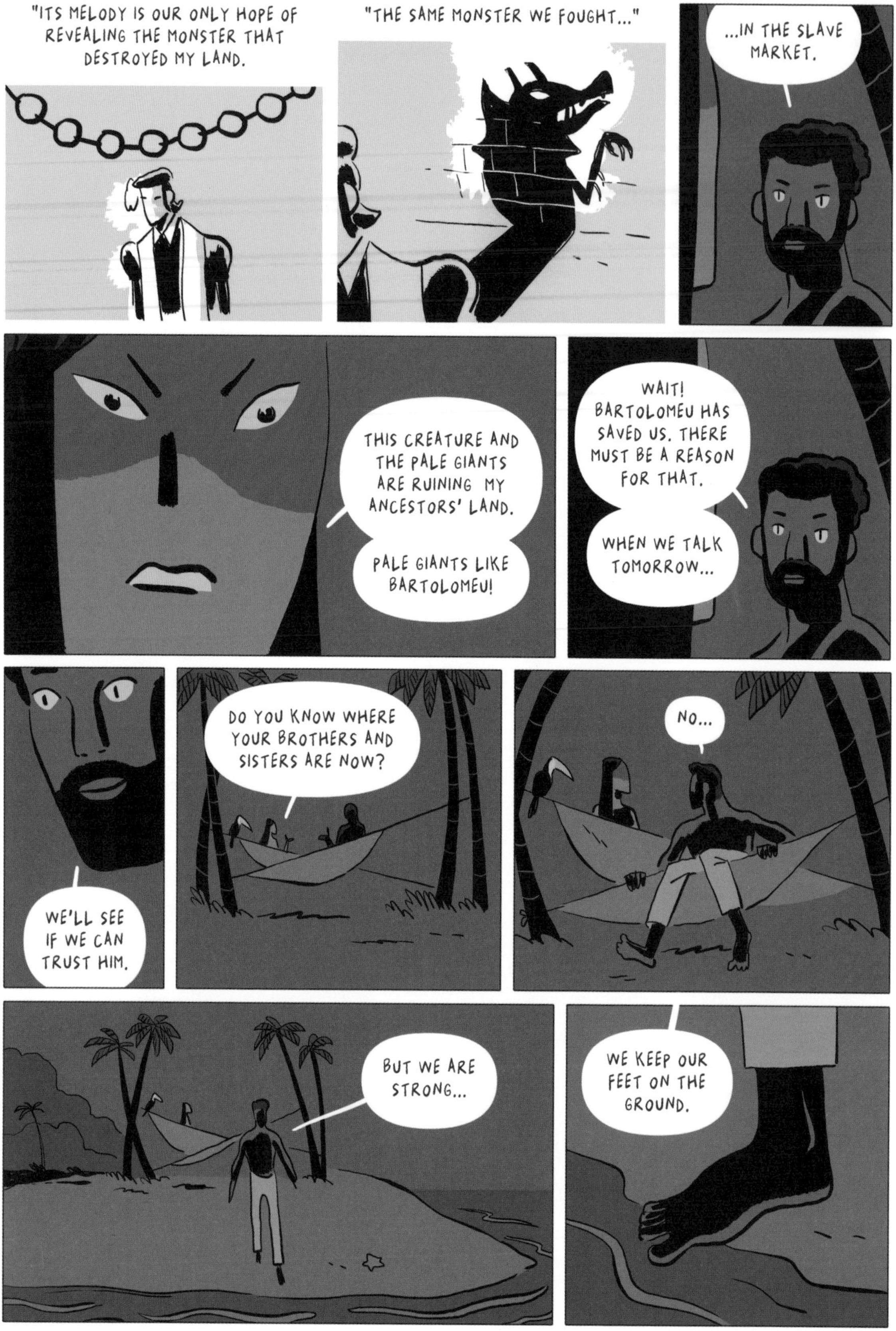
"ITS MELODY IS OUR ONLY HOPE OF REVEALING THE MONSTER THAT DESTROYED MY LAND.
"THE SAME MONSTER WE FOUGHT..."
...IN THE SLAVE MARKET.
THIS CREATURE AND THE PALE GIANTS ARE RUINING MY ANCESTORS' LAND.
PALE GIANTS LIKE BARTOLOMEU!
WAIT! BARTOLOMEU HAS SAVED US. THERE MUST BE A REASON FOR THAT.
WHEN WE TALK TOMORROW...
WE'LL SEE IF WE CAN TRUST HIM.
DO YOU KNOW WHERE YOUR BROTHERS AND SISTERS ARE NOW?
NO...
BUT WE ARE STRONG...
WE KEEP OUR FEET ON THE GROUND.

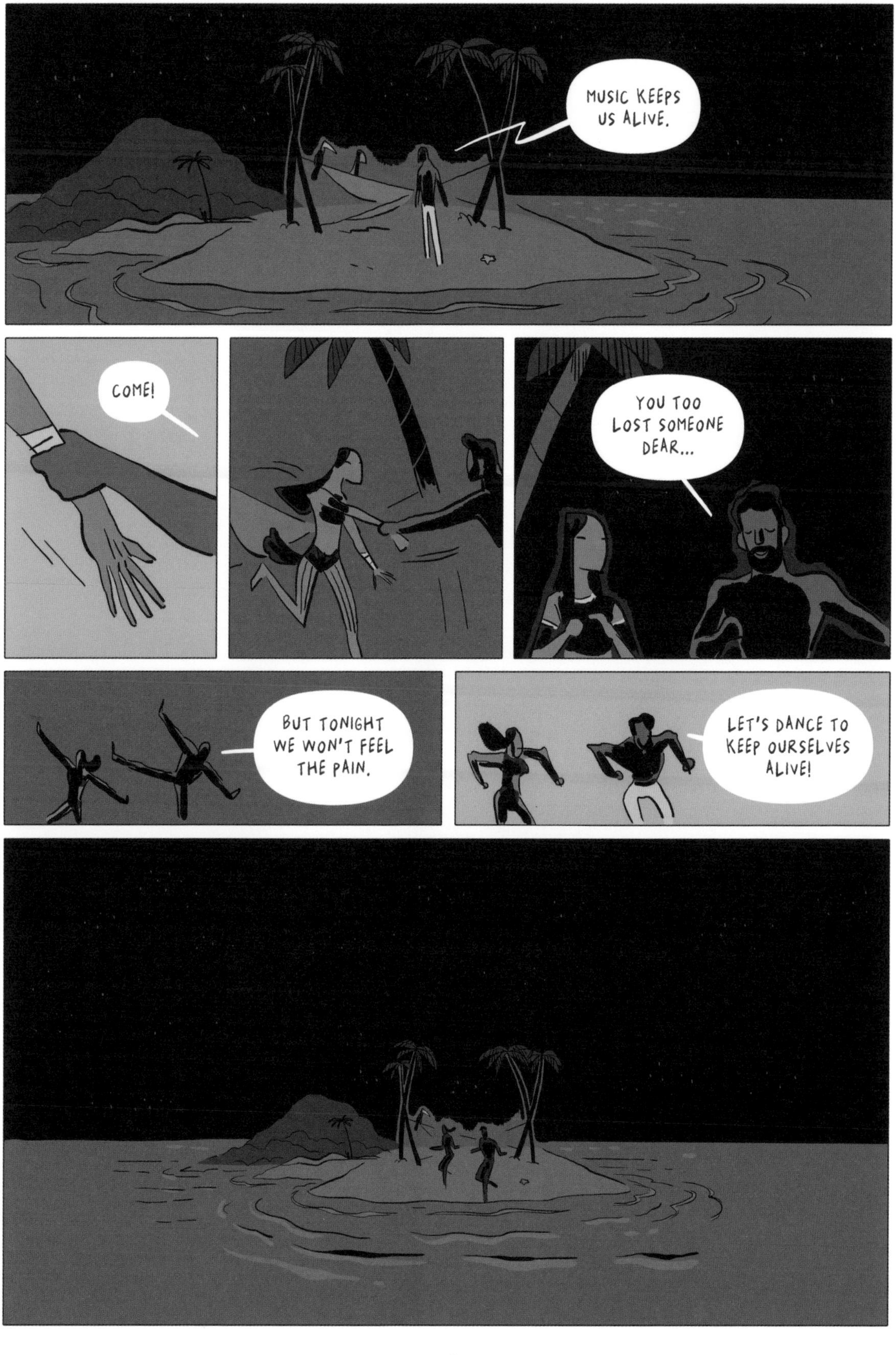
MUSIC KEEPS US ALIVE.
COME!
YOU TOO LOST SOMEONE DEAR...
BUT TONIGHT WE WON'T FEEL THE PAIN.
LET'S DANCE TO KEEP OURSELVES ALIVE!

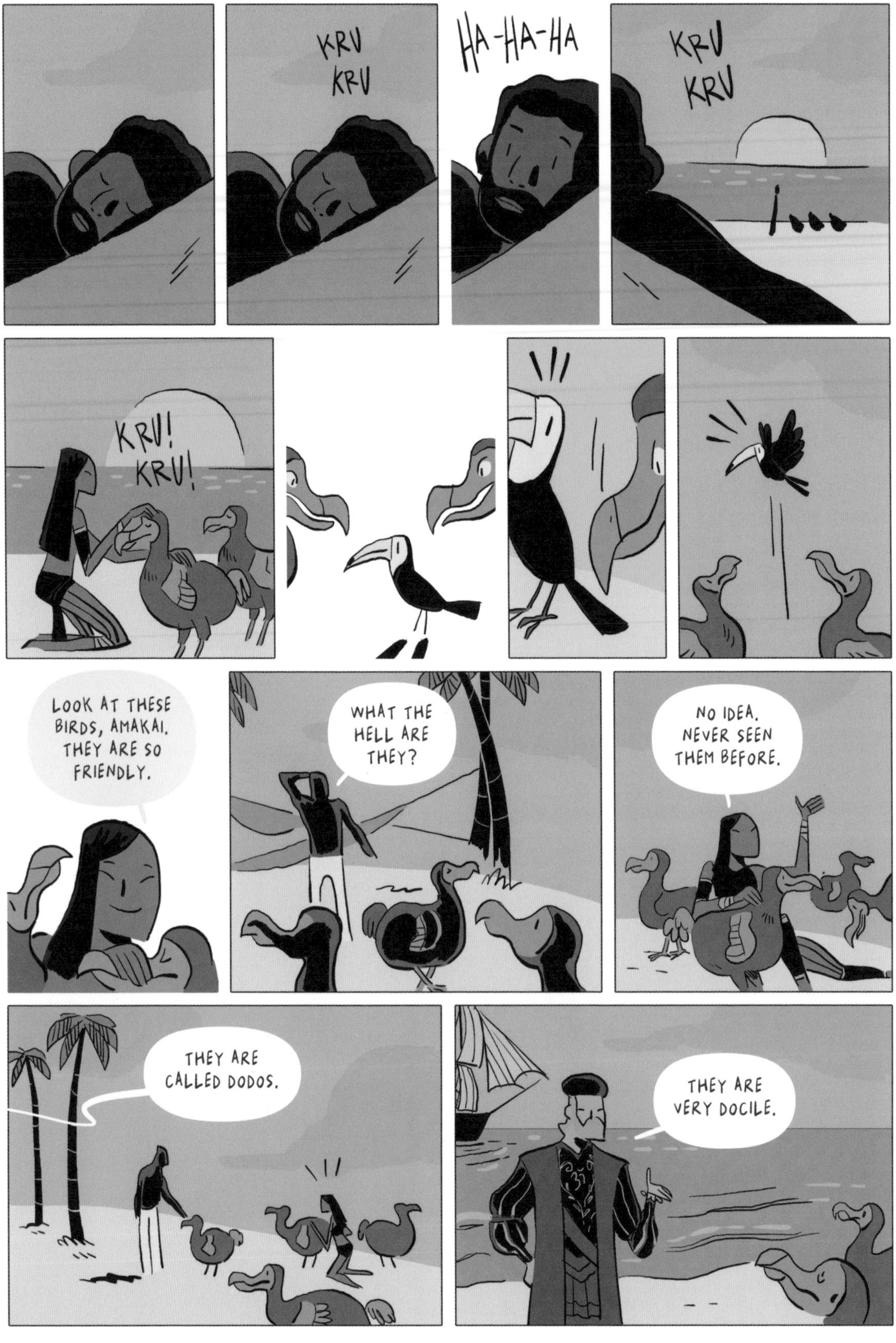
KRU
KRU
HA-HA-HA
KRU
KRU
KRU!
KRU!
LOOK AT THESE BIRDS, AMAKAI. THEY ARE SO FRIENDLY.
WHAT THE HELL ARE THEY?
NO IDEA. NEVER SEEN THEM BEFORE.
THEY ARE CALLED DODOS.
THEY ARE VERY DOCILE.

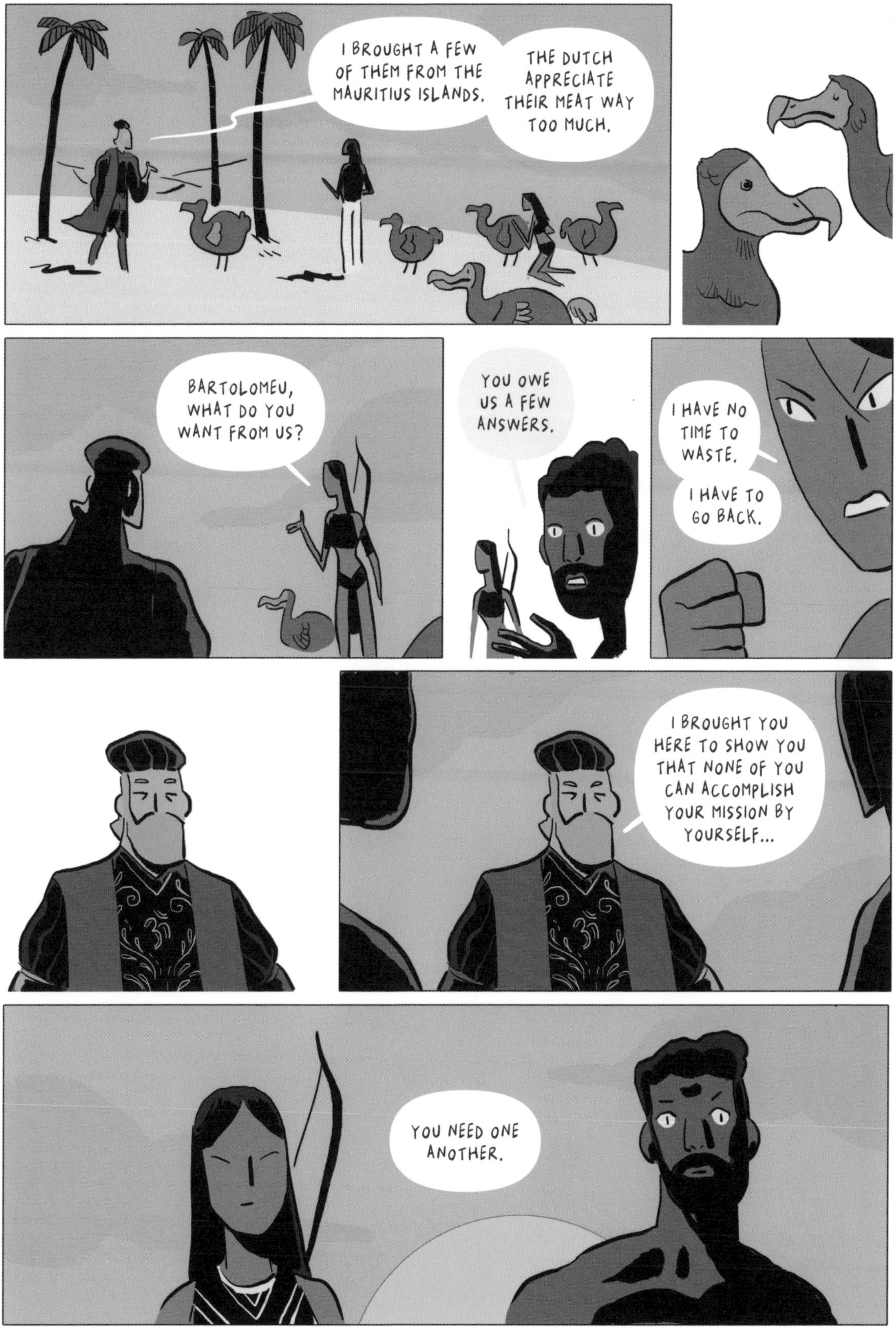
I BROUGHT A FEW OF THEM FROM THE MAURITIUS ISLANDS.
THE DUTCH APPRECIATE THEIR MEAT WAY TOO MUCH.
BARTOLOMEU, WHAT DO YOU WANT FROM US?
YOU OWE US A FEW ANSWERS.
I HAVE NO TIME TO WASTE.
I HAVE TO GO BACK.
I BROUGHT YOU HERE TO SHOW YOU THAT NONE OF YOU CAN ACCOMPLISH YOUR MISSION BY YOURSELF...
YOU NEED ONE ANOTHER.

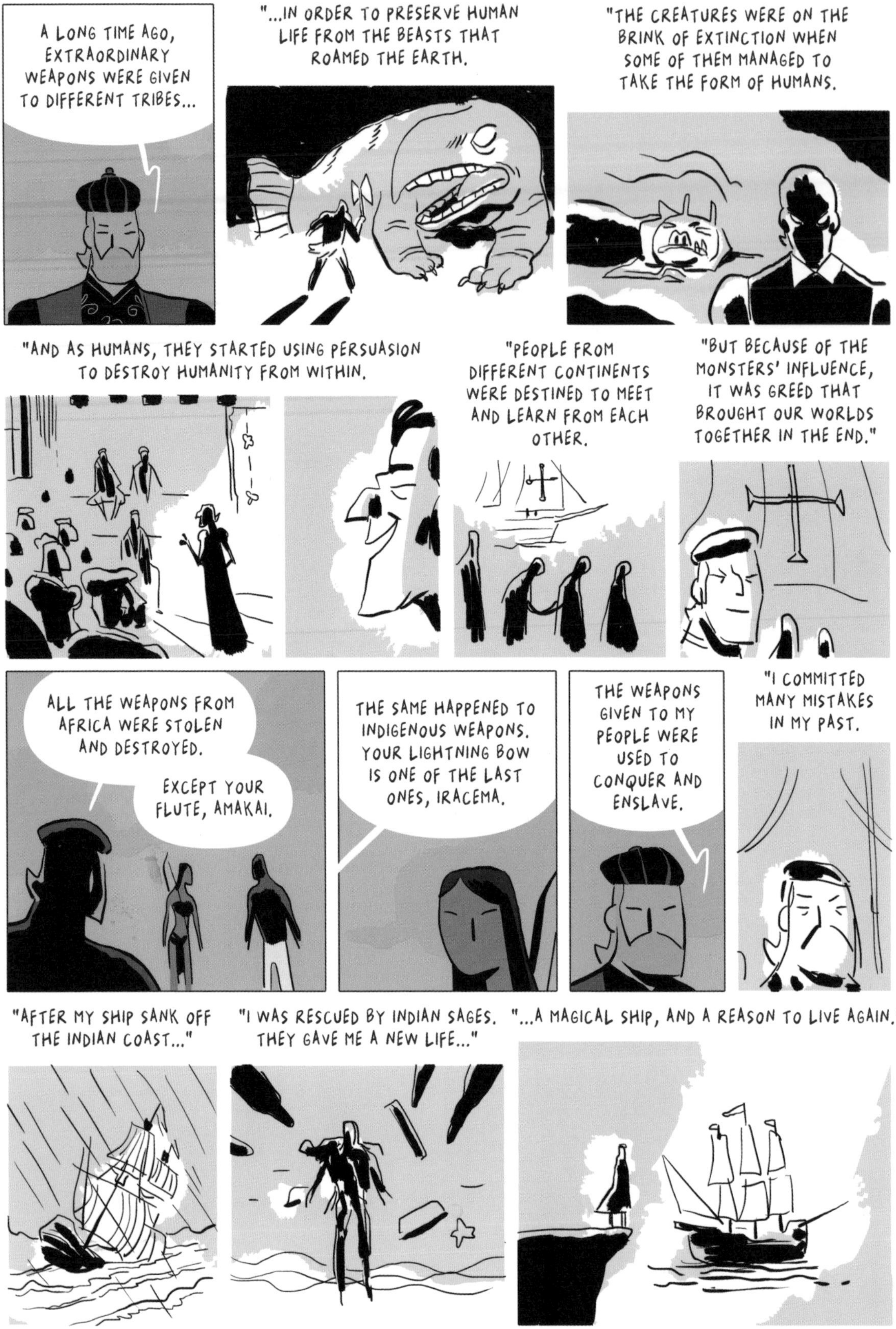
A LONG TIME AGO, EXTRAORDINARY WEAPONS WERE GIVEN TO DIFFERENT TRIBES...
"...IN ORDER TO PRESERVE HUMAN LIFE FROM THE BEASTS THAT ROAMED THE EARTH.
"THE CREATURES WERE ON THE BRINK OF EXTINCTION WHEN SOME OF THEM MANAGED TO TAKE THE FORM OF HUMANS.
"AND AS HUMANS, THEY STARTED USING PERSUASION TO DESTROY HUMANITY FROM WITHIN.
"PEOPLE FROM DIFFERENT CONTINENTS WERE DESTINED TO MEET AND LEARN FROM EACH OTHER.
"BUT BECAUSE OF THE MONSTERS' INFLUENCE, IT WAS GREED THAT BROUGHT OUR WORLDS TOGETHER IN THE END."
ALL THE WEAPONS FROM AFRICA WERE STOLEN AND DESTROYED.
EXCEPT YOUR FLUTE, AMAKAI.
THE SAME HAPPENED TO INDIGENOUS WEAPONS. YOUR LIGHTNING BOW IS ONE OF THE LAST ONES, IRACEMA.
THE WEAPONS GIVEN TO MY PEOPLE WERE USED TO CONQUER AND ENSLAVE.
"I COMMITTED MANY MISTAKES IN MY PAST.
"AFTER MY SHIP SANK OFF THE INDIAN COAST..."
"I WAS RESCUED BY INDIAN SAGES. THEY GAVE ME A NEW LIFE..."
"...A MAGICAL SHIP, AND A REASON TO LIVE AGAIN."

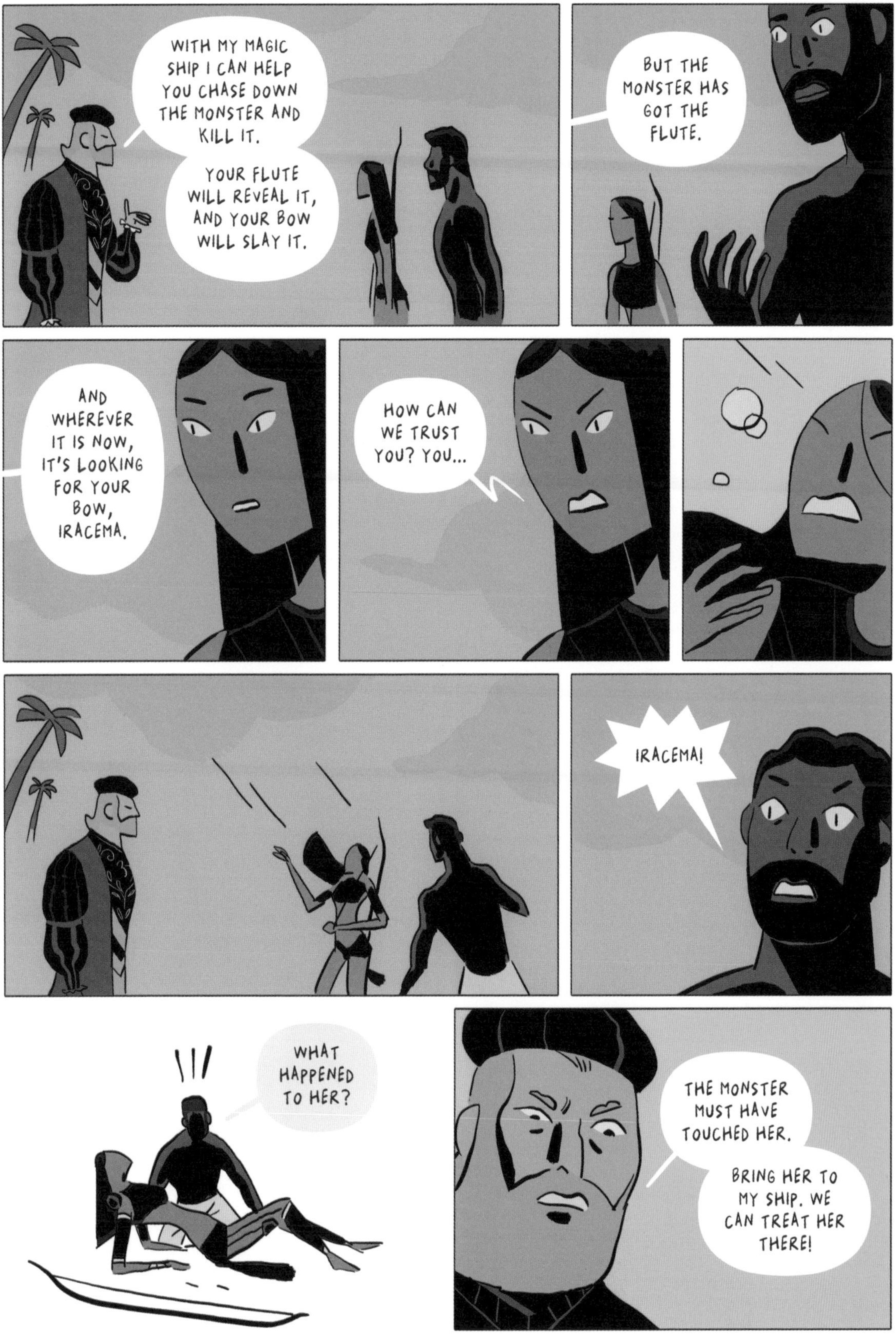
WITH MY MAGIC SHIP I CAN HELP YOU CHASE DOWN THE MONSTER AND KILL IT.
YOUR FLUTE WILL REVEAL IT, AND YOUR BOW WILL SLAY IT.
BUT THE MONSTER HAS GOT THE FLUTE.
AND WHEREVER IT IS NOW, IT'S LOOKING FOR YOUR BOW, IRACEMA.
HOW CAN WE TRUST YOU? YOU...
IRACEMA!
WHAT HAPPENED TO HER?
THE MONSTER MUST HAVE TOUCHED HER.
BRING HER TO MY SHIP. WE CAN TREAT HER THERE!

C'MON, IRACEMA. YOU ARE TOUGH!

THE VIRUS IS SPREADING THROUGH HER BODY.

LET HER REST.

MY ASSISTANT WILL TAKE GOOD CARE OF HER.

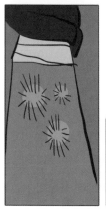

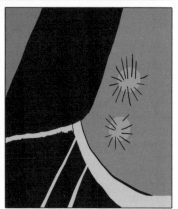

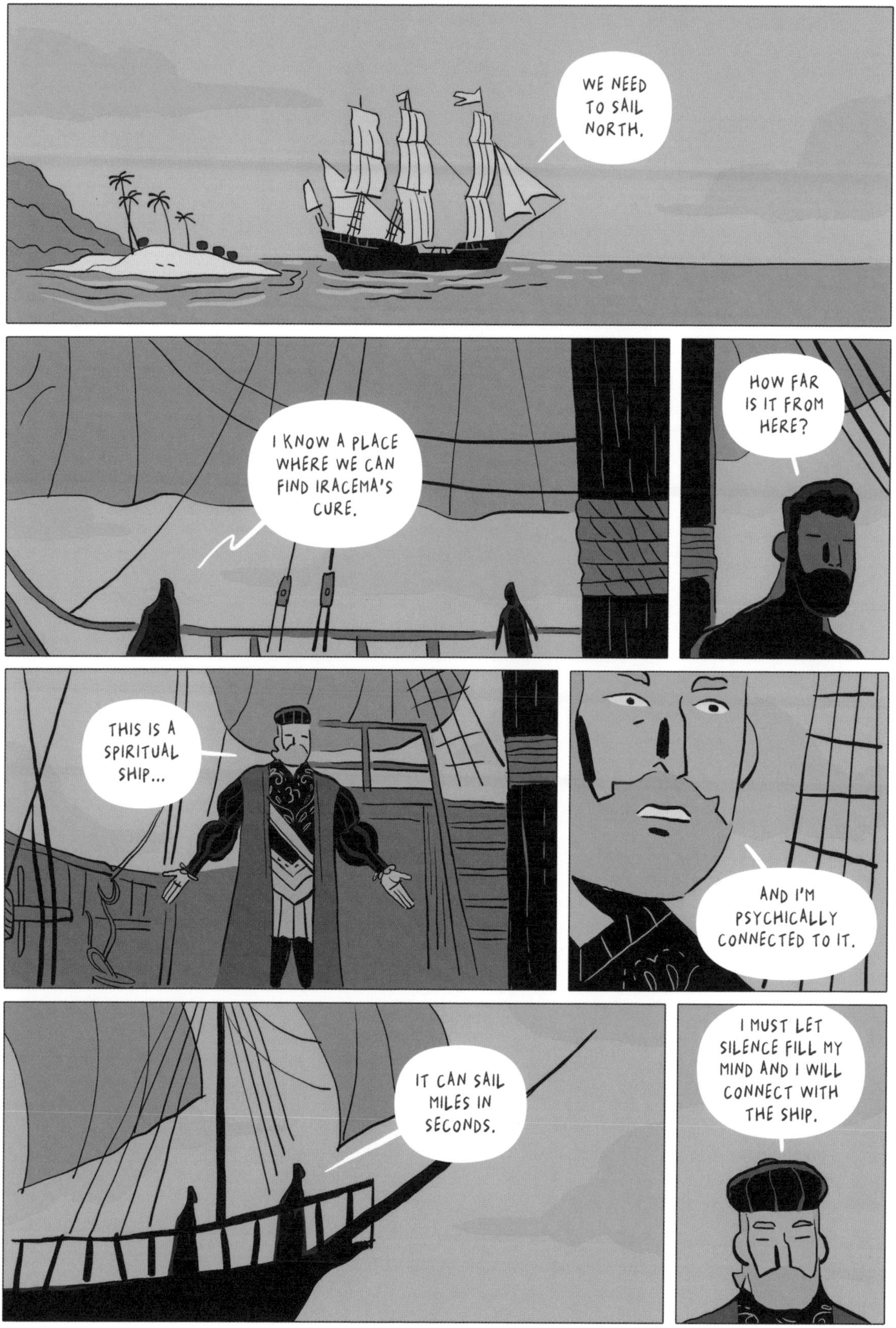
WE NEED TO SAIL NORTH.
I KNOW A PLACE WHERE WE CAN FIND IRACEMA'S CURE.
HOW FAR IS IT FROM HERE?
THIS IS A SPIRITUAL SHIP...
AND I'M PSYCHICALLY CONNECTED TO IT.
IT CAN SAIL MILES IN SECONDS.
I MUST LET SILENCE FILL MY MIND AND I WILL CONNECT WITH THE SHIP.

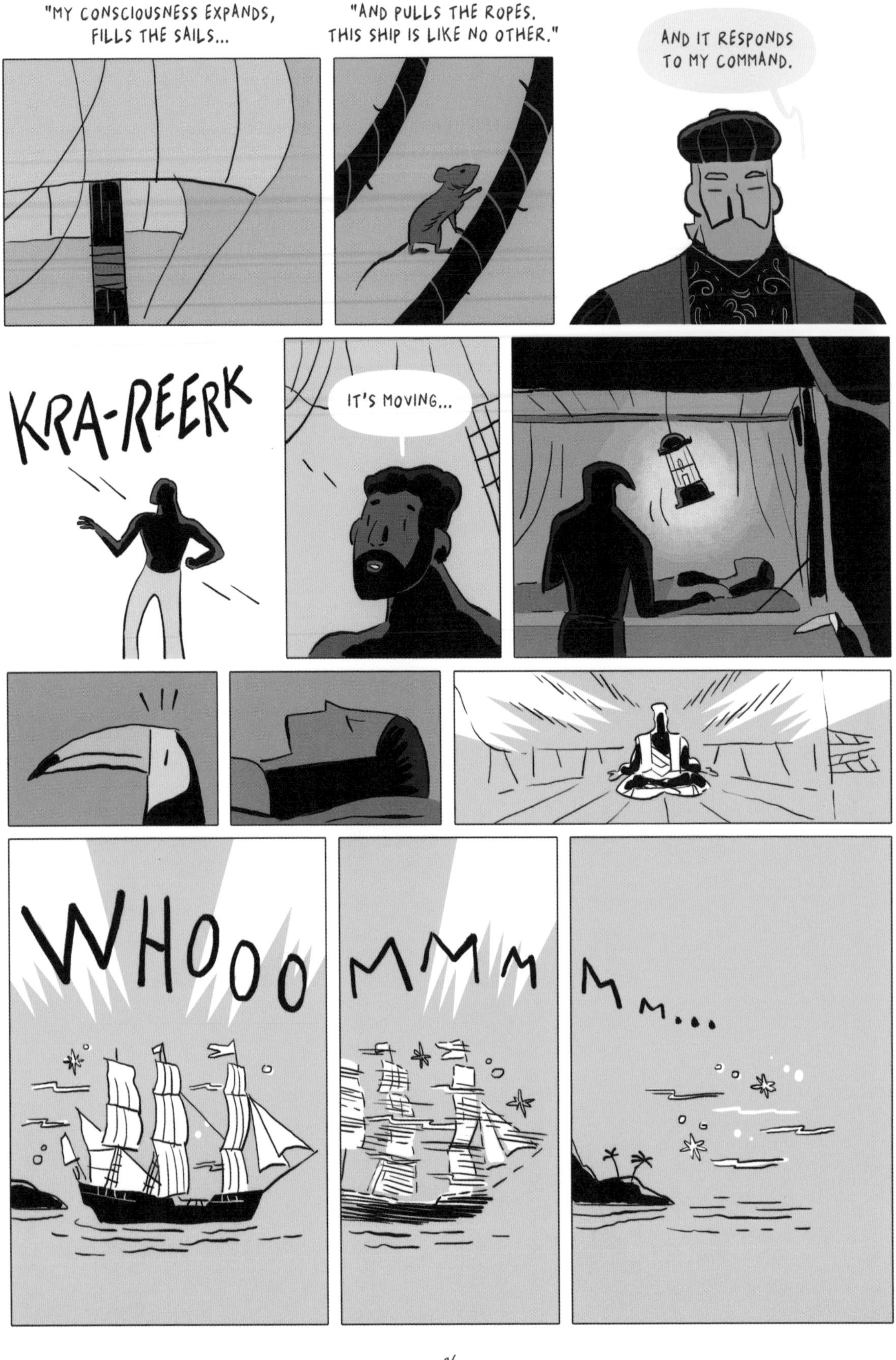
"MY CONSCIOUSNESS EXPANDS, FILLS THE SAILS...
"AND PULLS THE ROPES. THIS SHIP IS LIKE NO OTHER."
AND IT RESPONDS TO MY COMMAND.
KRA-REERK
IT'S MOVING...
WHOOOMMMMm...

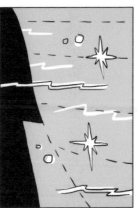

IT'S HERE!

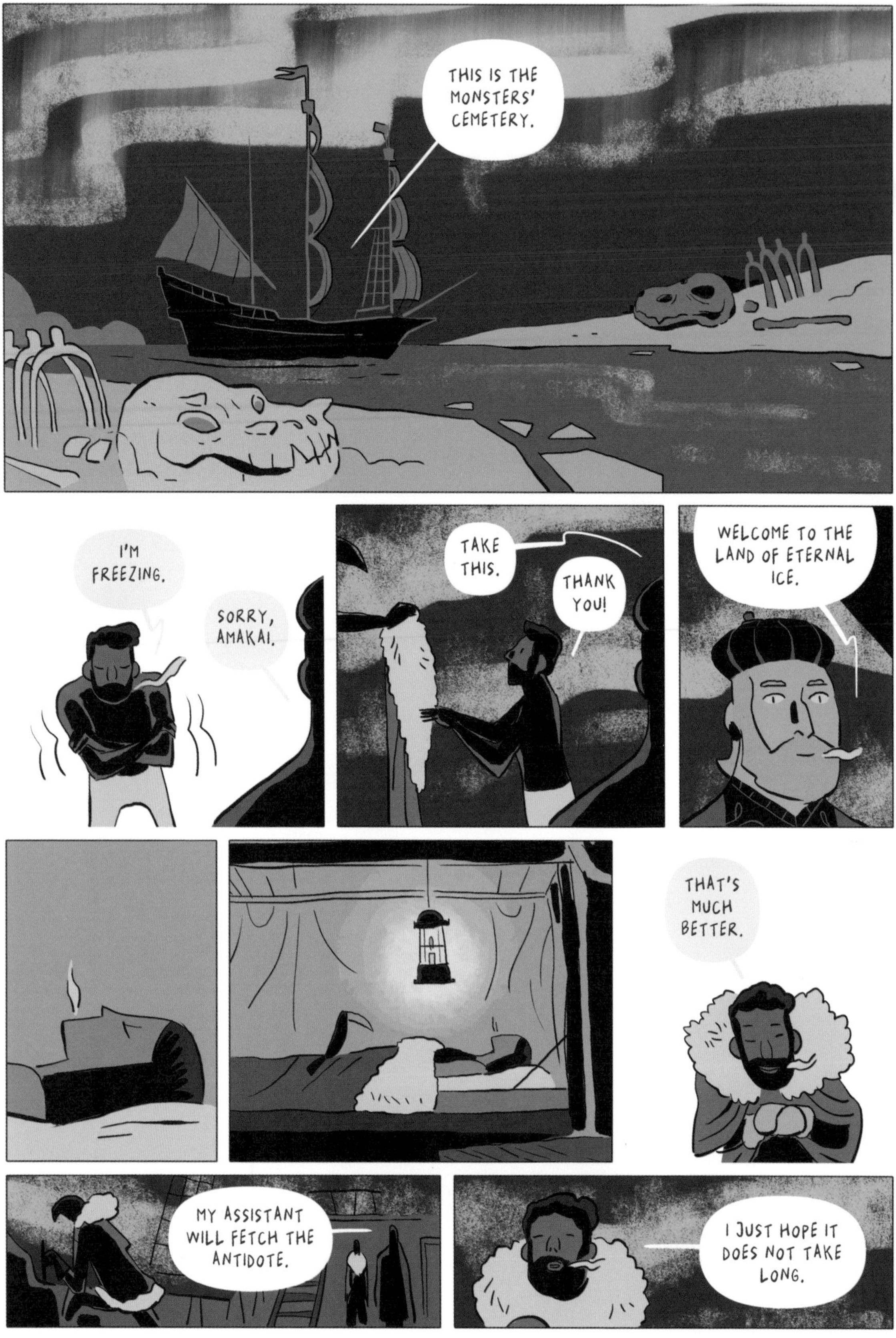
THIS IS THE MONSTERS' CEMETERY.
I'M FREEZING.
SORRY, AMAKAI.
TAKE THIS.
THANK YOU!
WELCOME TO THE LAND OF ETERNAL ICE.
THAT'S MUCH BETTER.
MY ASSISTANT WILL FETCH THE ANTIDOTE.
I JUST HOPE IT DOES NOT TAKE LONG.

THUD!

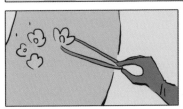

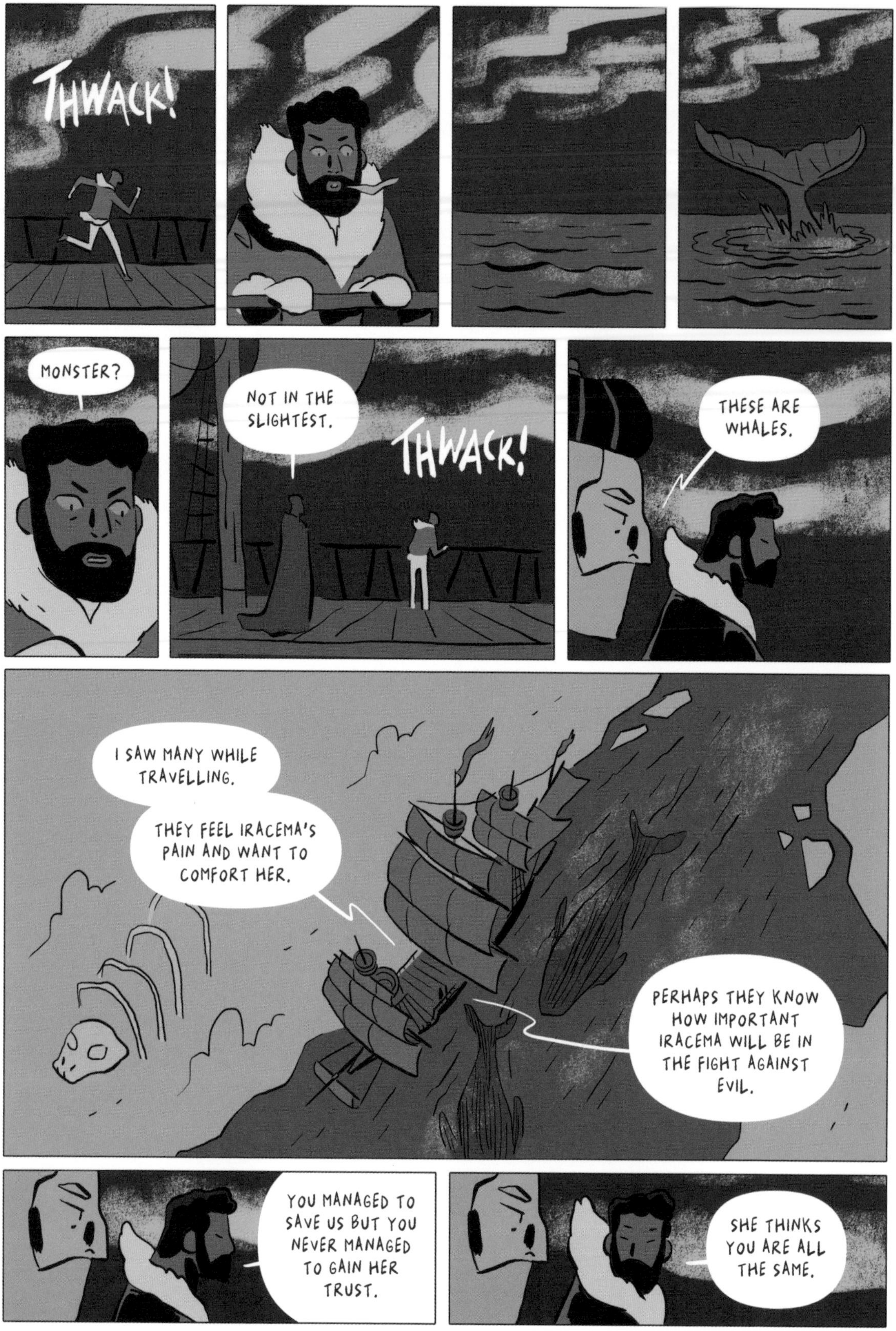
THWACK!
MONSTER?
NOT IN THE SLIGHTEST.
THWACK!
THESE ARE WHALES.
I SAW MANY WHILE TRAVELLING.
THEY FEEL IRACEMA'S PAIN AND WANT TO COMFORT HER.
PERHAPS THEY KNOW HOW IMPORTANT IRACEMA WILL BE IN THE FIGHT AGAINST EVIL.
YOU MANAGED TO SAVE US BUT YOU NEVER MANAGED TO GAIN HER TRUST.
SHE THINKS YOU ARE ALL THE SAME.

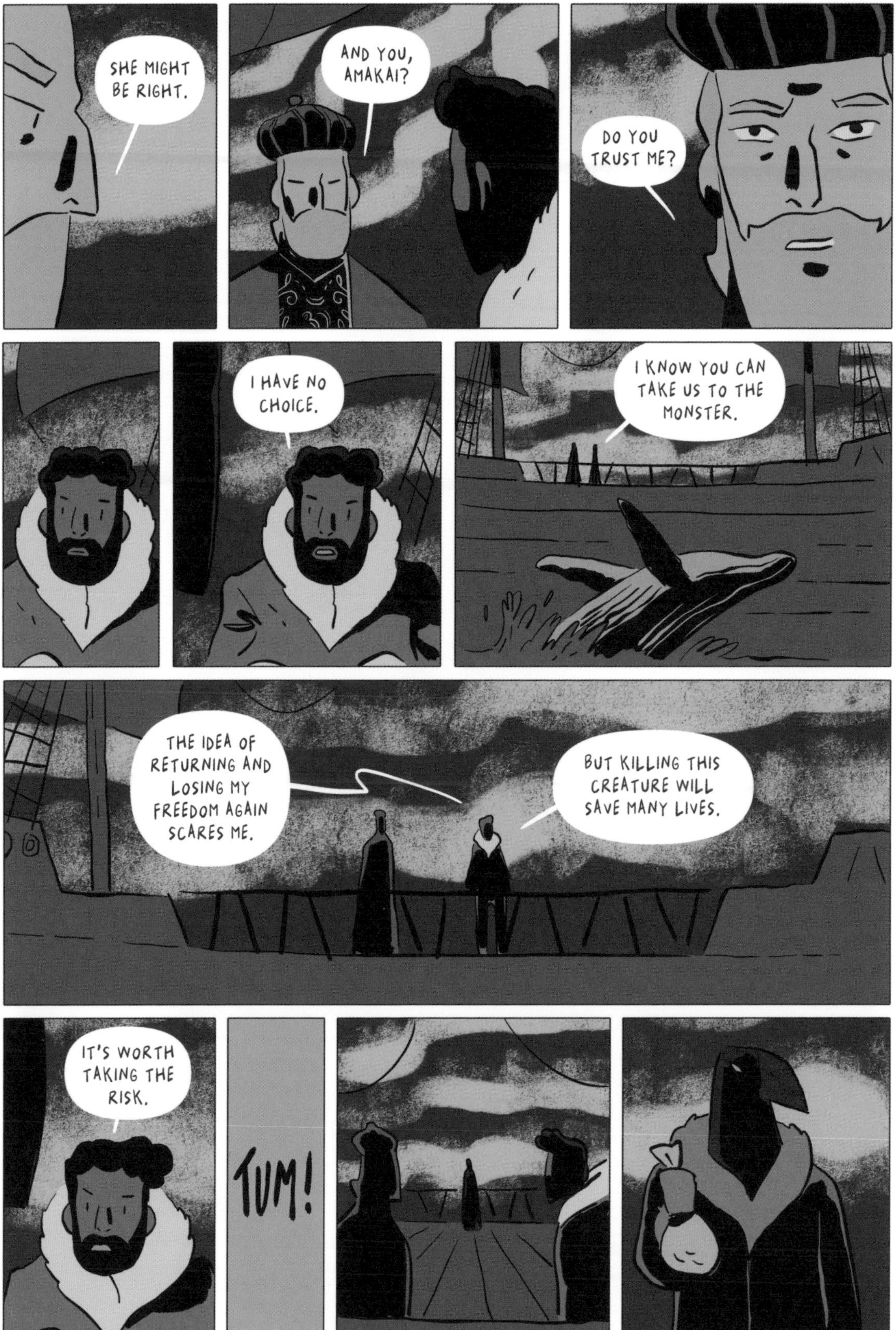
SHE MIGHT BE RIGHT.
AND YOU, AMAKAI?
DO YOU TRUST ME?
I HAVE NO CHOICE.
I KNOW YOU CAN TAKE US TO THE MONSTER.
THE IDEA OF RETURNING AND LOSING MY FREEDOM AGAIN SCARES ME.
BUT KILLING THIS CREATURE WILL SAVE MANY LIVES.
IT'S WORTH TAKING THE RISK.
TUM!

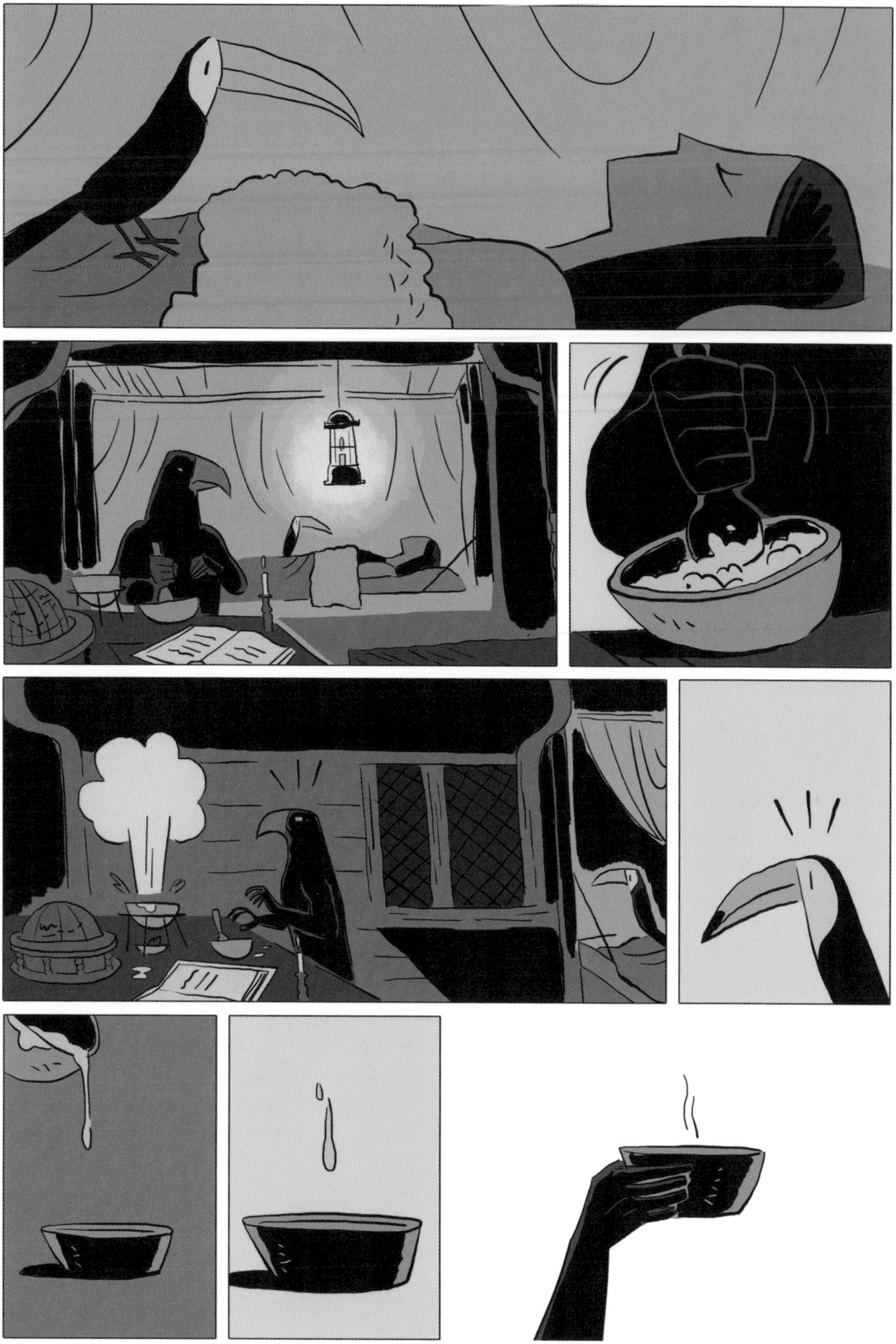

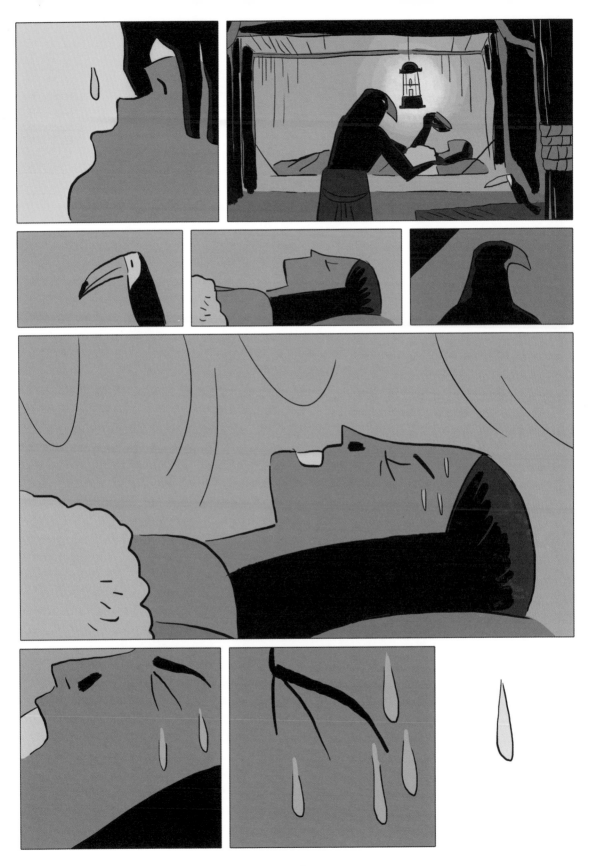

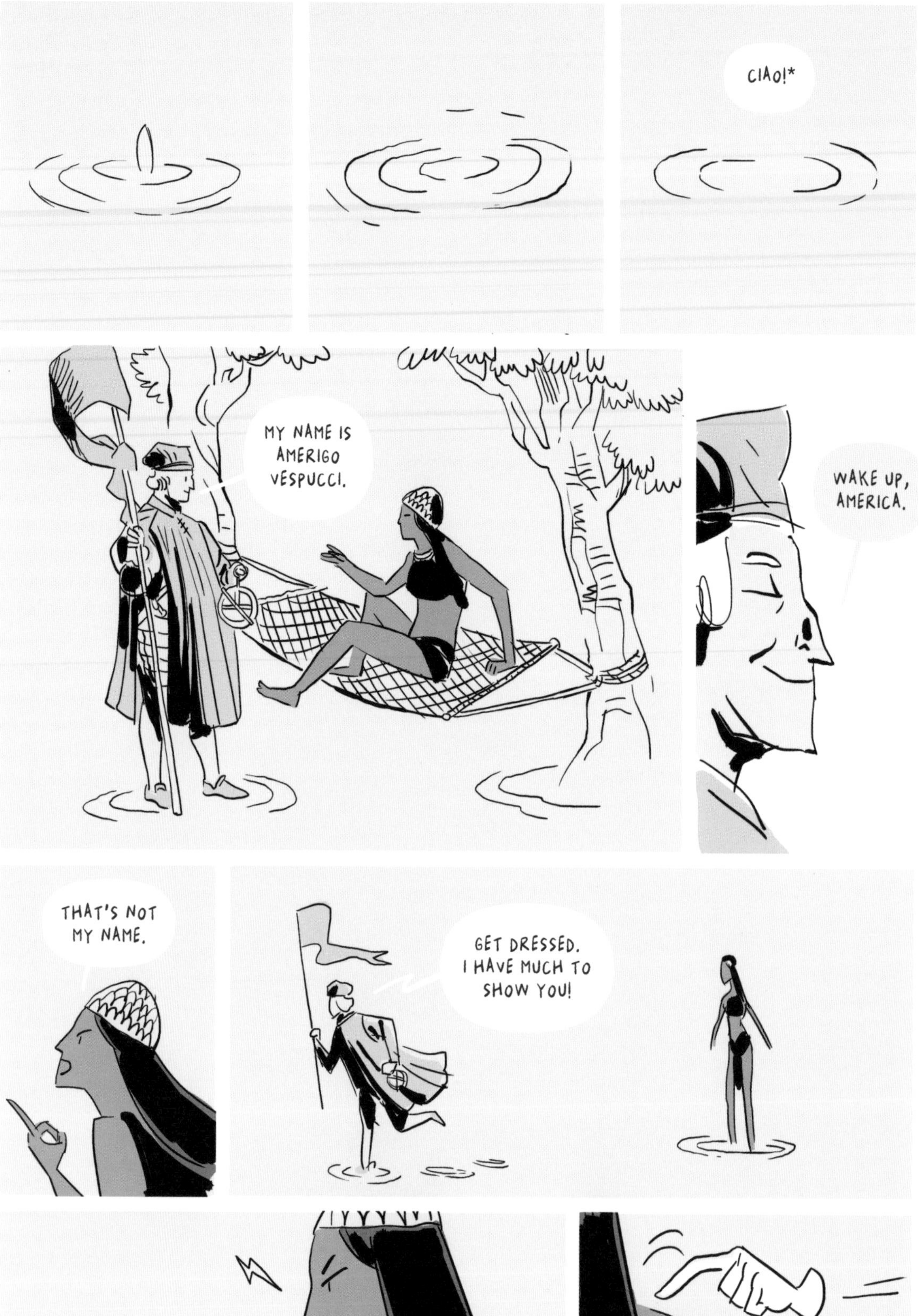
CIAO!*
MY NAME IS AMERIGO VESPUCCI.
WAKE UP, AMERICA.
THAT'S NOT MY NAME.
GET DRESSED. I HAVE MUCH TO SHOW YOU!

*HELLO!

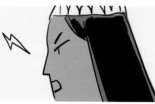

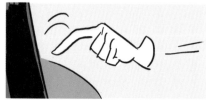

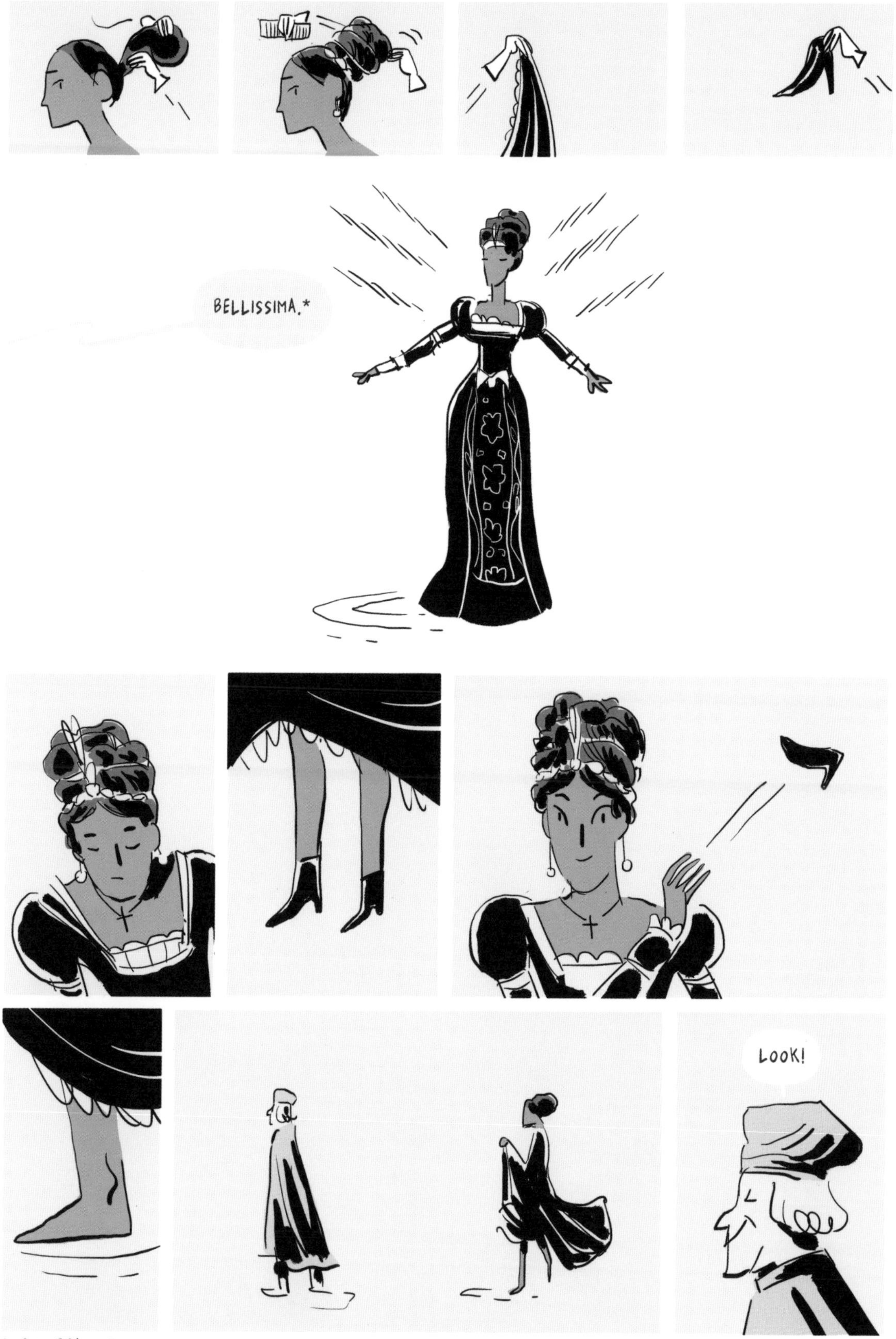
BELLISSIMA.*
LOOK!

*VERY BEAUTIFUL

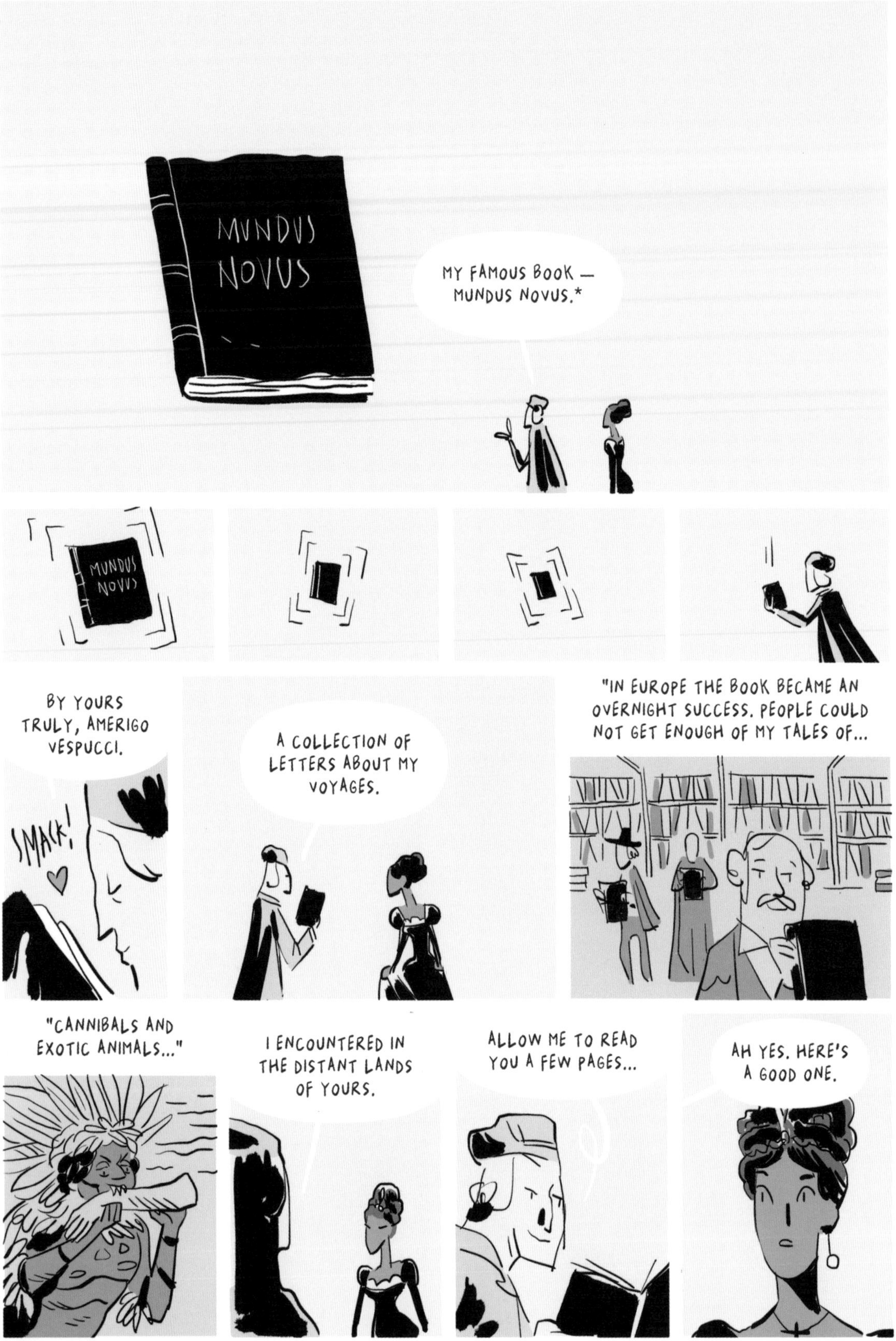
MUNDUS NOVUS
MY FAMOUS BOOK — MUNDUS NOVUS.*
MUNDUS NOVUS
BY YOURS TRULY, AMERIGO VESPUCCI.
SMACK!
A COLLECTION OF LETTERS ABOUT MY VOYAGES.
"IN EUROPE THE BOOK BECAME AN OVERNIGHT SUCCESS. PEOPLE COULD NOT GET ENOUGH OF MY TALES OF...
"CANNIBALS AND EXOTIC ANIMALS..."
I ENCOUNTERED IN THE DISTANT LANDS OF YOURS.
ALLOW ME TO READ YOU A FEW PAGES...
AH YES. HERE'S A GOOD ONE.

*NEW WORLD

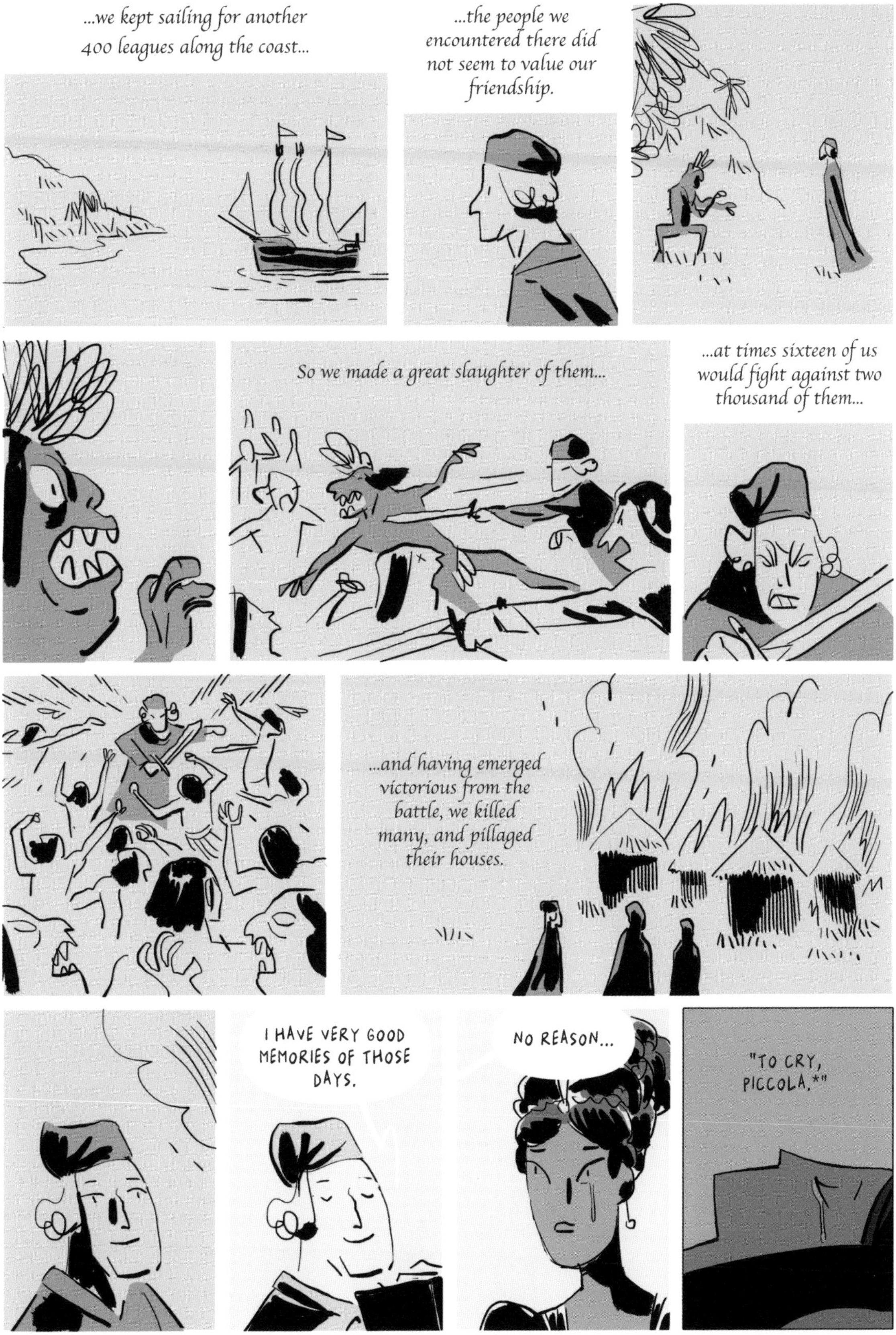

...we kept sailing for another 400 leagues along the coast...
...the people we encountered there did not seem to value our friendship.
So we made a great slaughter of them...
...at times sixteen of us would fight against two thousand of them...
...and having emerged victorious from the battle, we killed many, and pillaged their houses.
I HAVE VERY GOOD MEMORIES OF THOSE DAYS.
NO REASON...
"TO CRY, PICCOLA.*"

*LITTLE GIRL

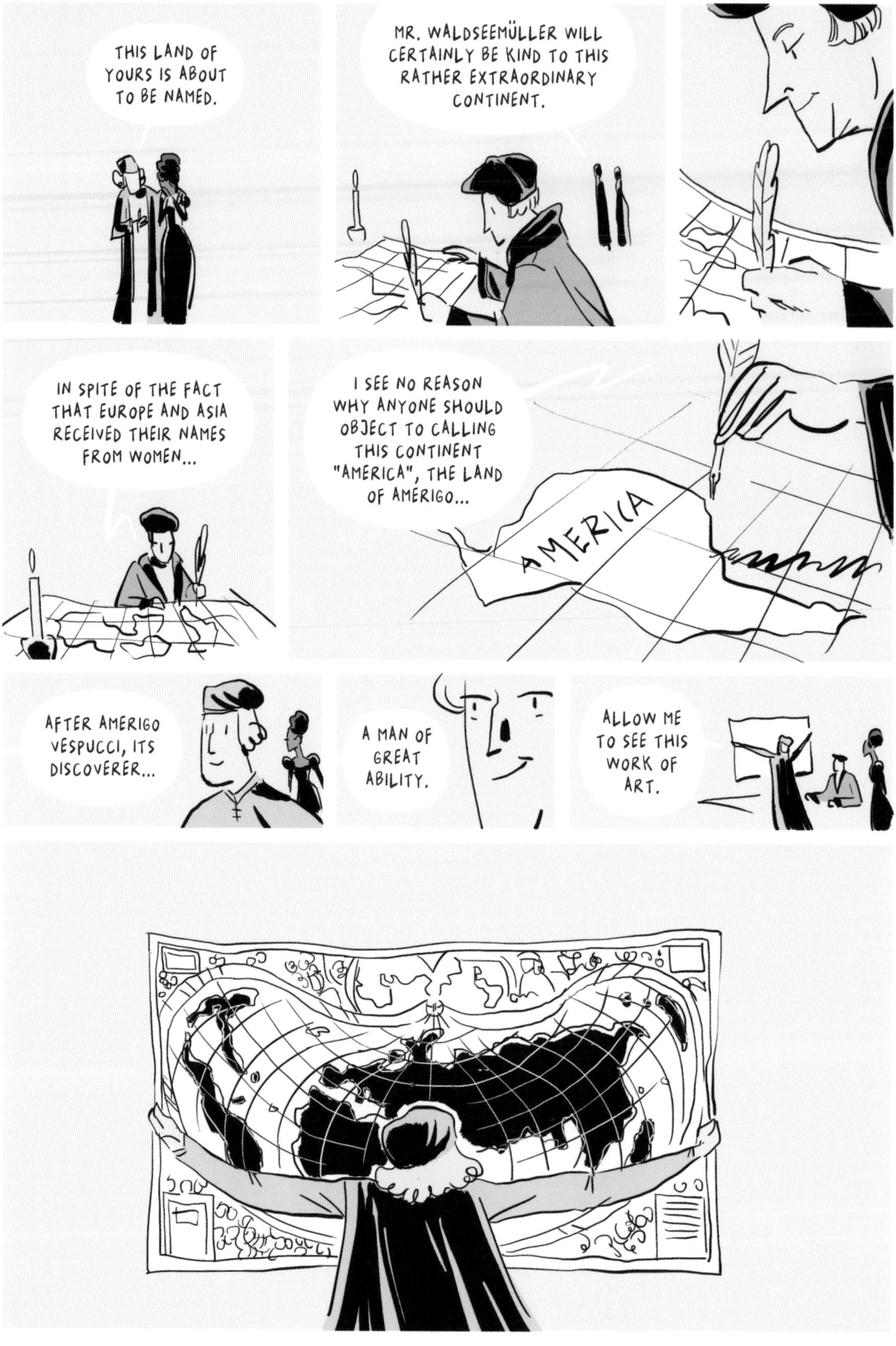
THIS LAND OF YOURS IS ABOUT TO BE NAMED.
MR. WALDSEEMÜLLER WILL CERTAINLY BE KIND TO THIS RATHER EXTRAORDINARY CONTINENT.
IN SPITE OF THE FACT THAT EUROPE AND ASIA RECEIVED THEIR NAMES FROM WOMEN...
I SEE NO REASON WHY ANYONE SHOULD OBJECT TO CALLING THIS CONTINENT "AMERICA", THE LAND OF AMERIGO...
AMERICA
AFTER AMERIGO VESPUCCI, ITS DISCOVERER...
A MAN OF GREAT ABILITY.
ALLOW ME TO SEE THIS WORK OF ART.

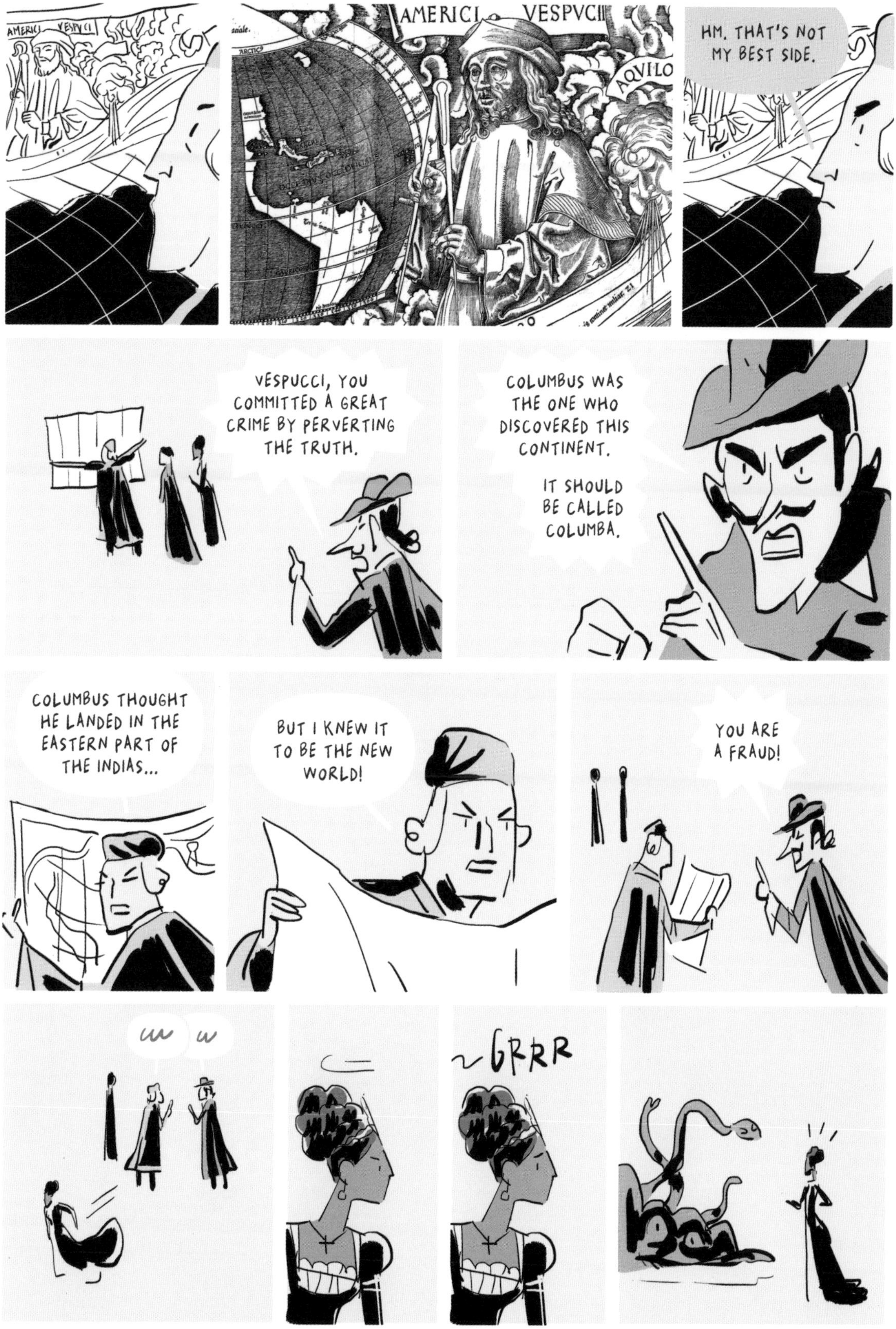
AMERICI VESPVCII
AQVILO
HM. THAT'S NOT MY BEST SIDE.
VESPUCCI, YOU COMMITTED A GREAT CRIME BY PERVERTING THE TRUTH.
COLUMBUS WAS THE ONE WHO DISCOVERED THIS CONTINENT.
IT SHOULD BE CALLED COLUMBA.
COLUMBUS THOUGHT HE LANDED IN THE EASTERN PART OF THE INDIAS...
BUT I KNEW IT TO BE THE NEW WORLD!
YOU ARE A FRAUD!
GRRR

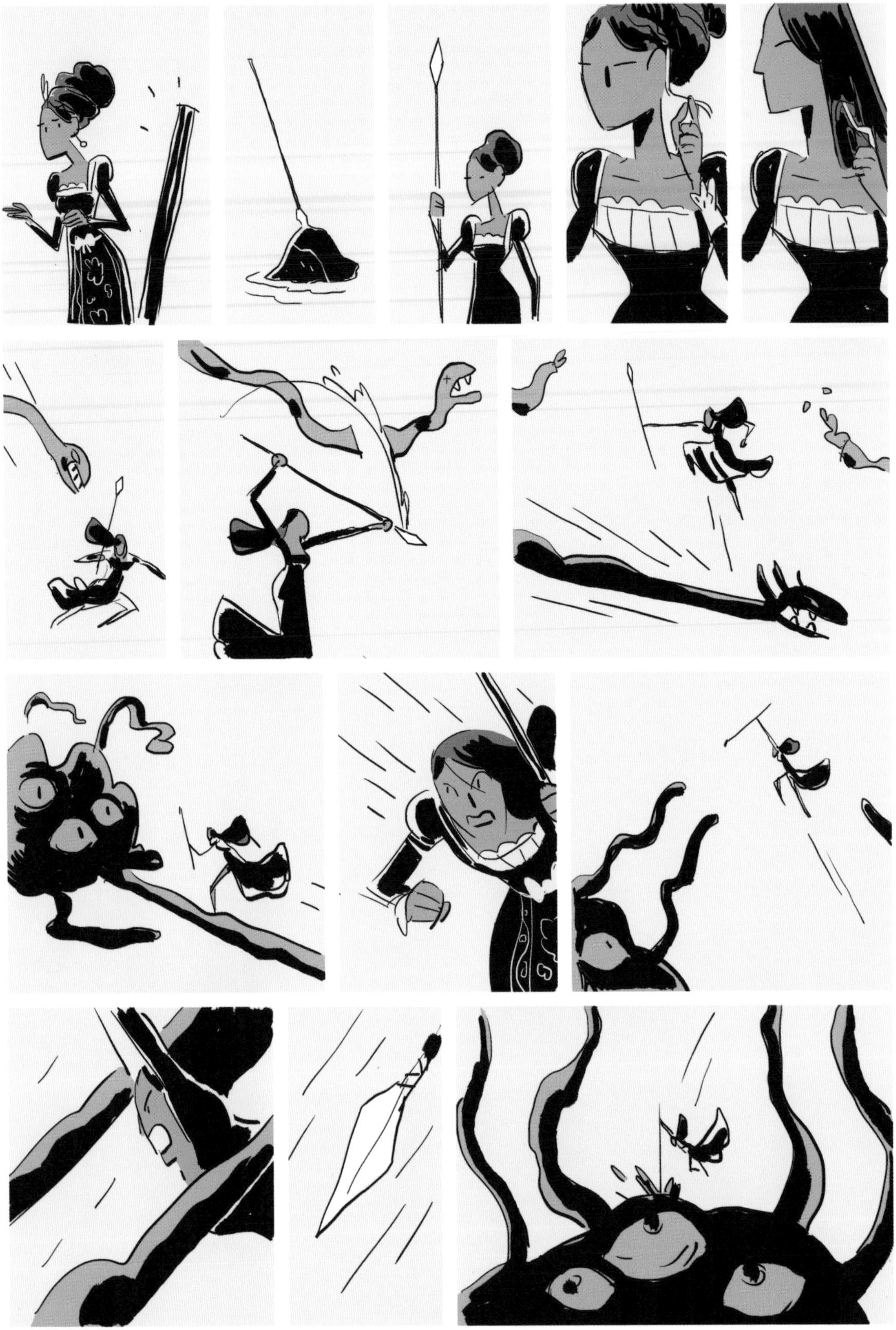

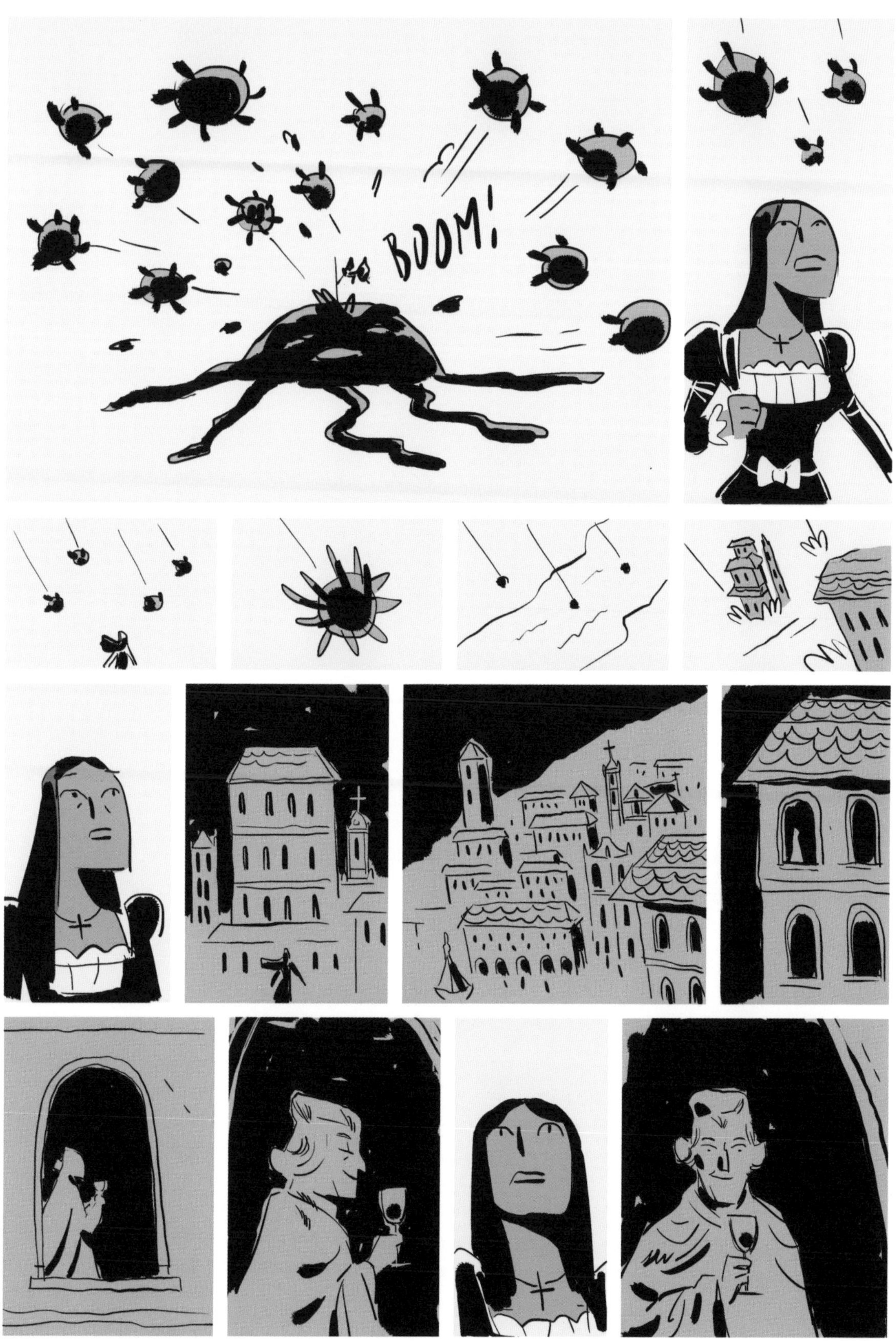
BOOM!

AVENGE OUR
PEOPLE.

GUARANI?!

AVENGE...

OUR PEOPLE.

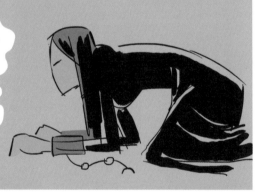

NEXT TIME YOU
HAVE A WHITE MAN
IN YOUR TARGET,

YOU
SHOOT!

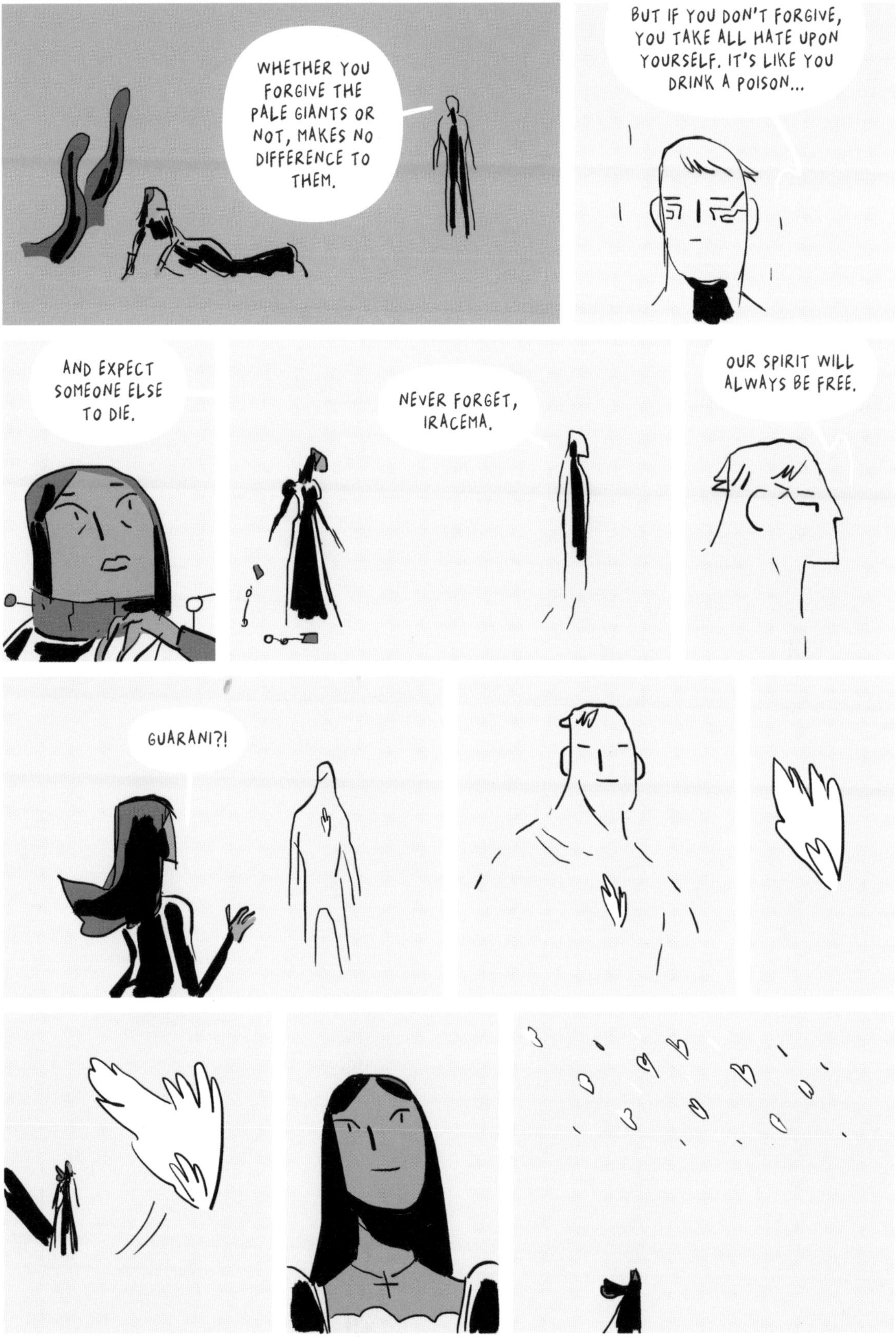
WHETHER YOU FORGIVE THE PALE GIANTS OR NOT, MAKES NO DIFFERENCE TO THEM.
BUT IF YOU DON'T FORGIVE, YOU TAKE ALL HATE UPON YOURSELF. IT'S LIKE YOU DRINK A POISON...
AND EXPECT SOMEONE ELSE TO DIE.
NEVER FORGET, IRACEMA.
OUR SPIRIT WILL ALWAYS BE FREE.
GUARANI?!

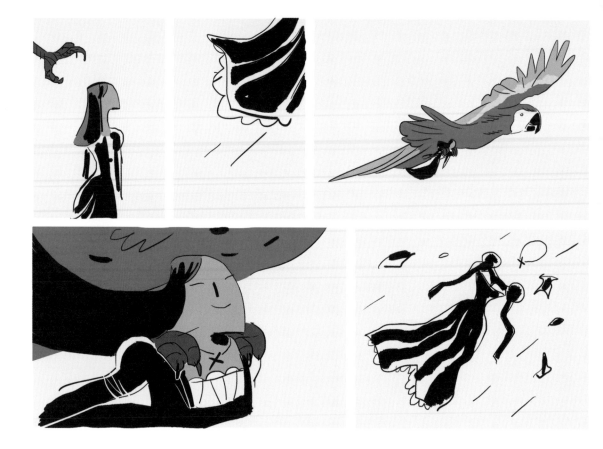

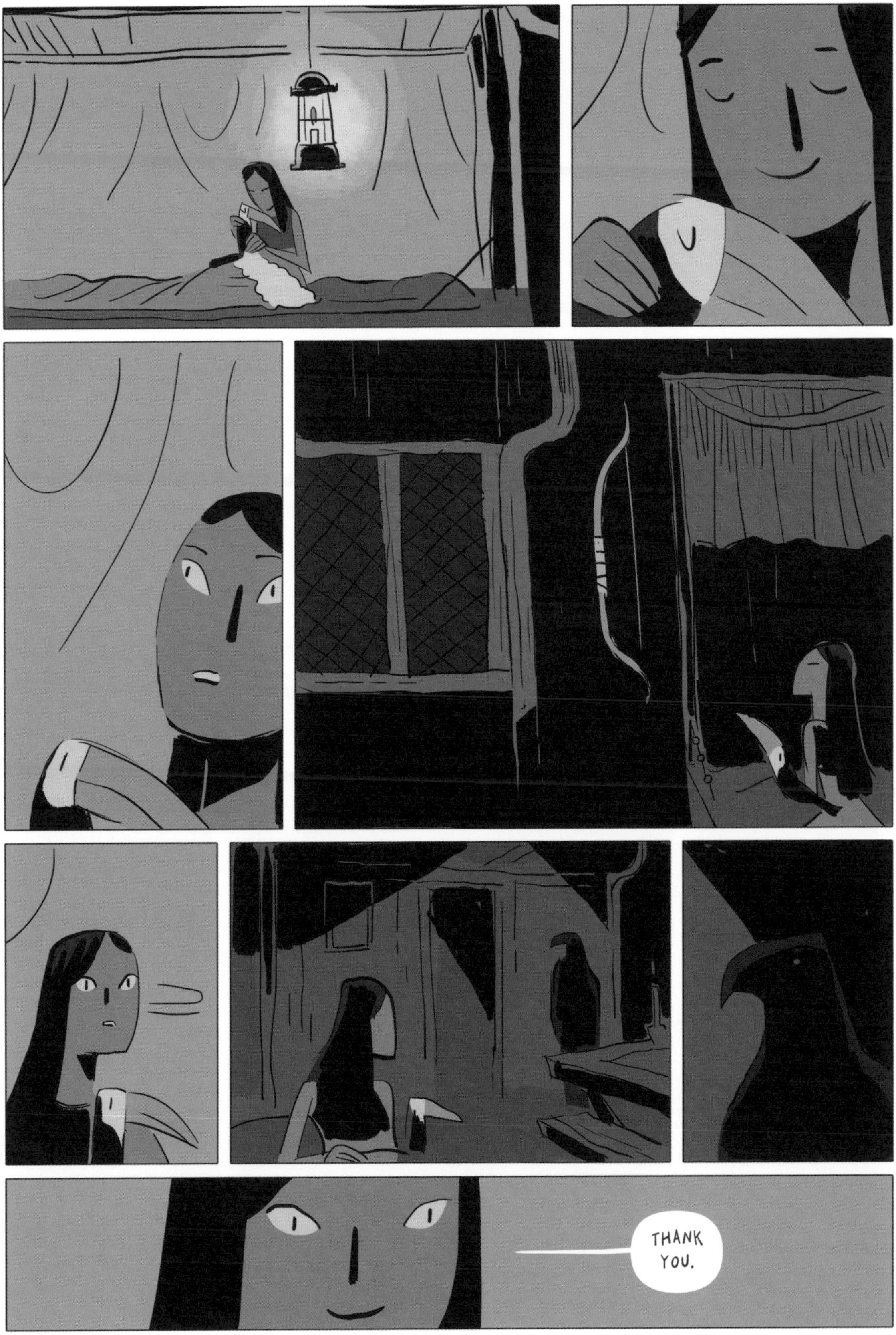
THANK YOU.

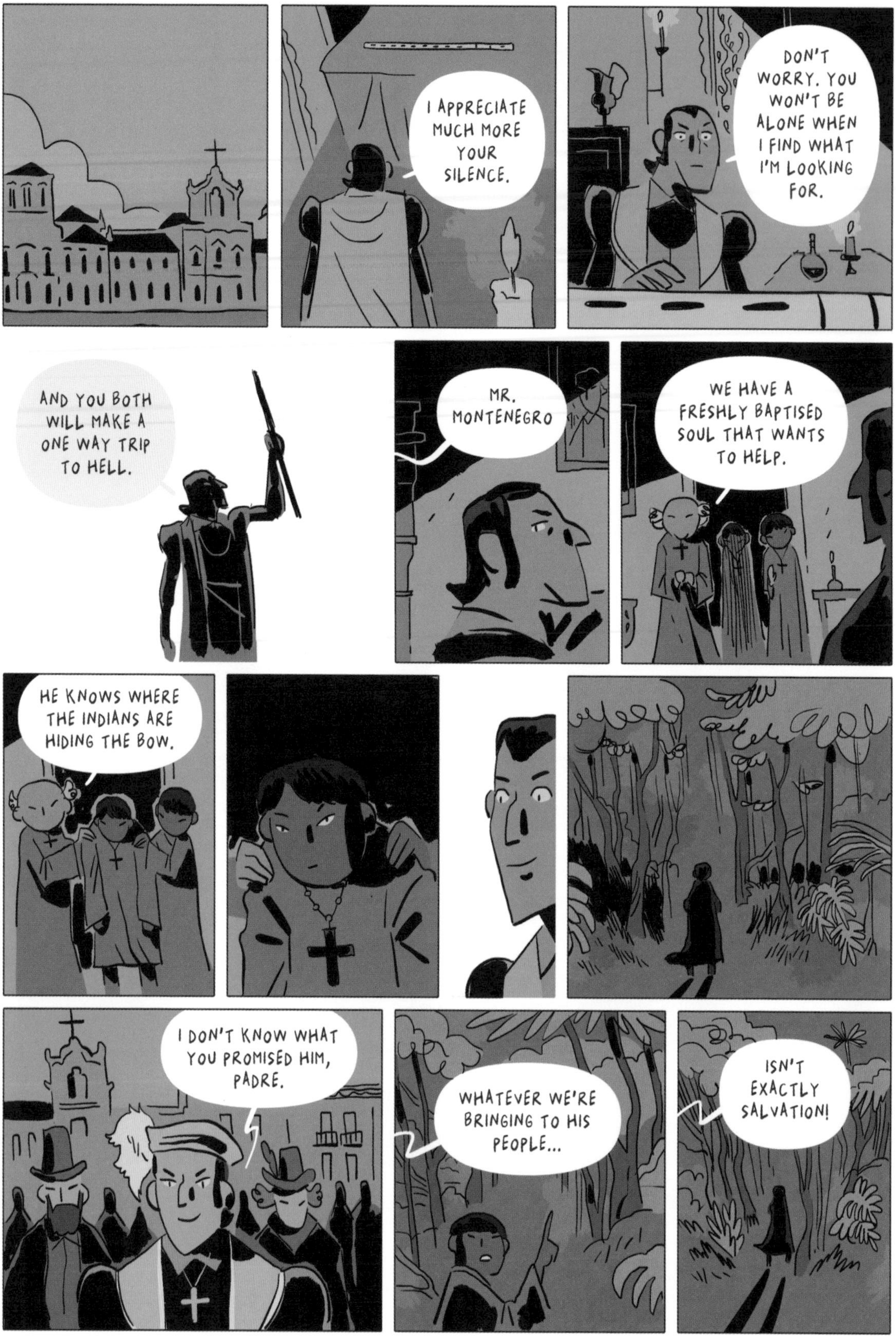
I APPRECIATE MUCH MORE YOUR SILENCE.
DON'T WORRY. YOU WON'T BE ALONE WHEN I FIND WHAT I'M LOOKING FOR.
AND YOU BOTH WILL MAKE A ONE WAY TRIP TO HELL.
MR. MONTENEGRO
WE HAVE A FRESHLY BAPTISED SOUL THAT WANTS TO HELP.
HE KNOWS WHERE THE INDIANS ARE HIDING THE BOW.
I DON'T KNOW WHAT YOU PROMISED HIM, PADRE.
WHATEVER WE'RE BRINGING TO HIS PEOPLE...
ISN'T EXACTLY SALVATION!

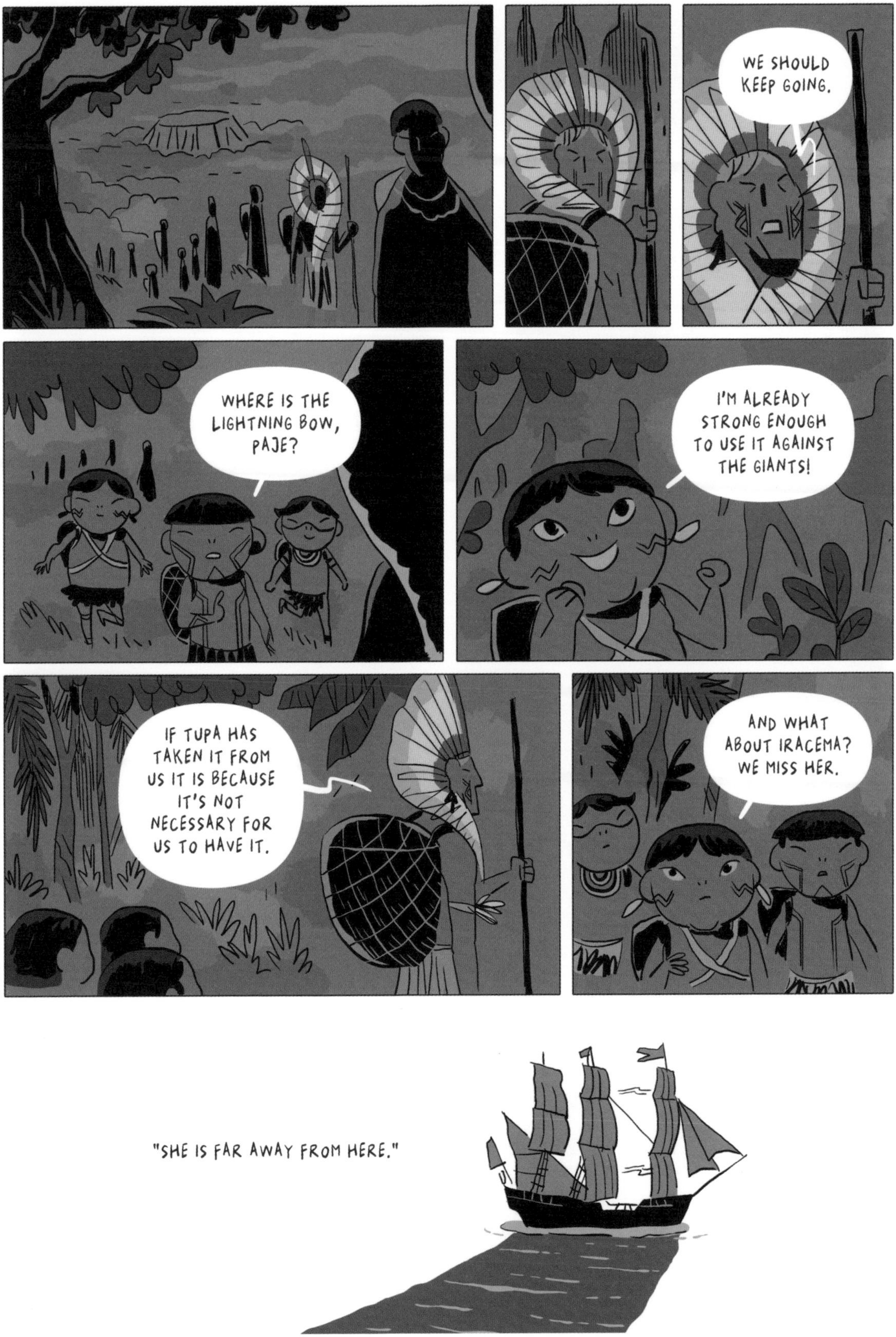
WE SHOULD KEEP GOING.
WHERE IS THE LIGHTNING BOW, PAJE?
I'M ALREADY STRONG ENOUGH TO USE IT AGAINST THE GIANTS!
IF TUPA HAS TAKEN IT FROM US IT IS BECAUSE IT'S NOT NECESSARY FOR US TO HAVE IT.
AND WHAT ABOUT IRACEMA? WE MISS HER.
"SHE IS FAR AWAY FROM HERE."

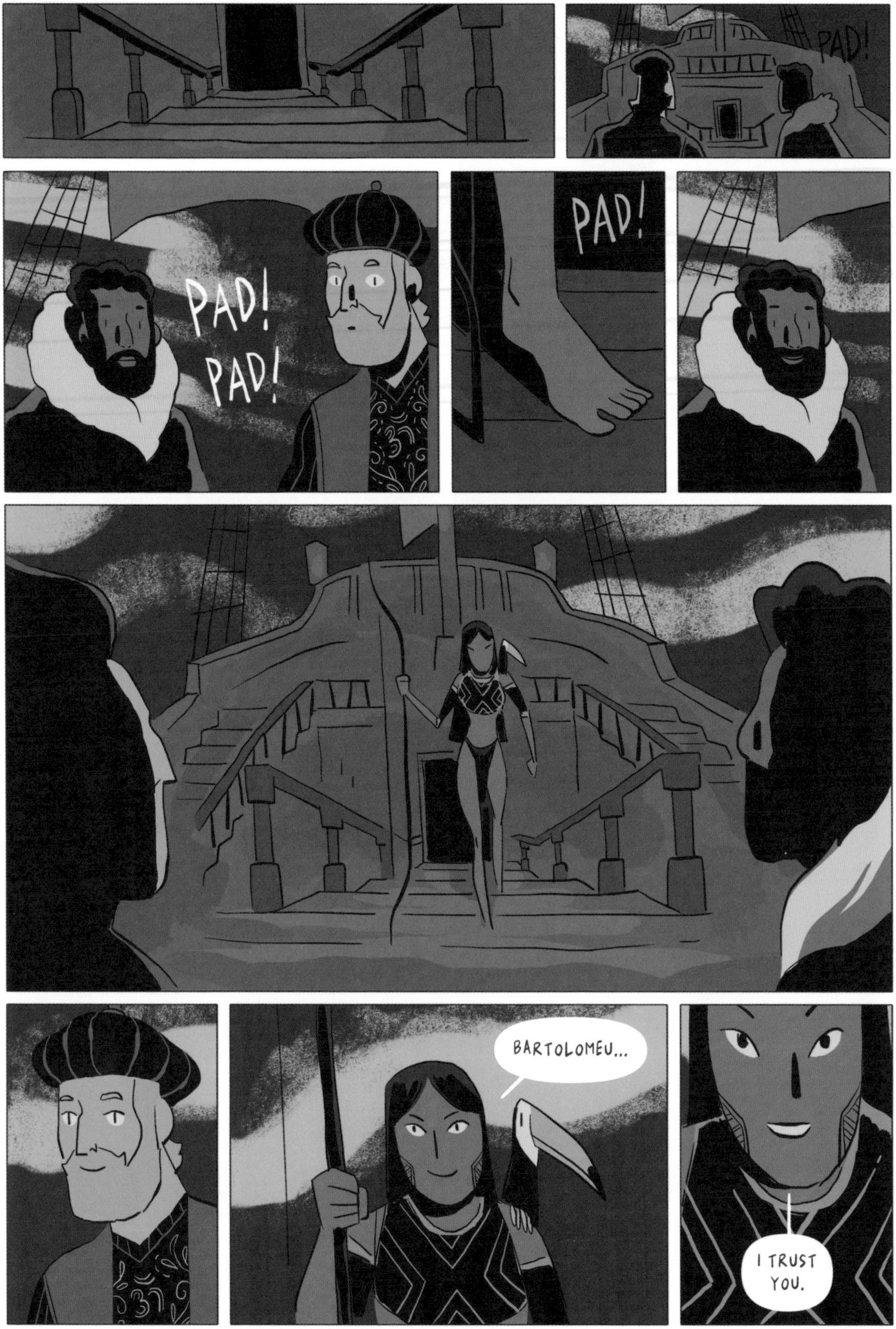
PAD!
PAD!
PAD!
PAD!
BARTOLOMEU...
I TRUST YOU.

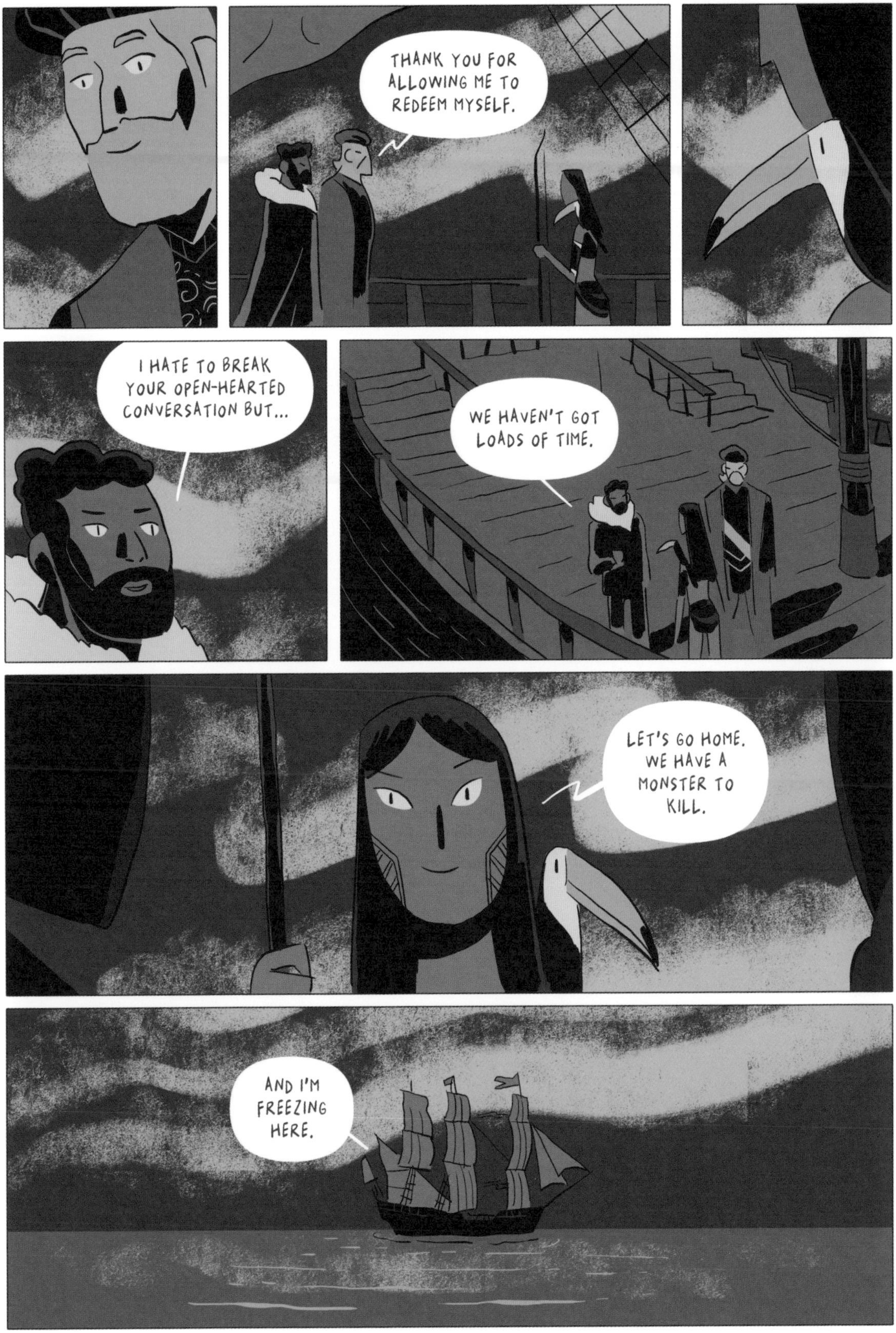
THANK YOU FOR ALLOWING ME TO REDEEM MYSELF.
I HATE TO BREAK YOUR OPEN-HEARTED CONVERSATION BUT...
WE HAVEN'T GOT LOADS OF TIME.
LET'S GO HOME. WE HAVE A MONSTER TO KILL.
AND I'M FREEZING HERE.

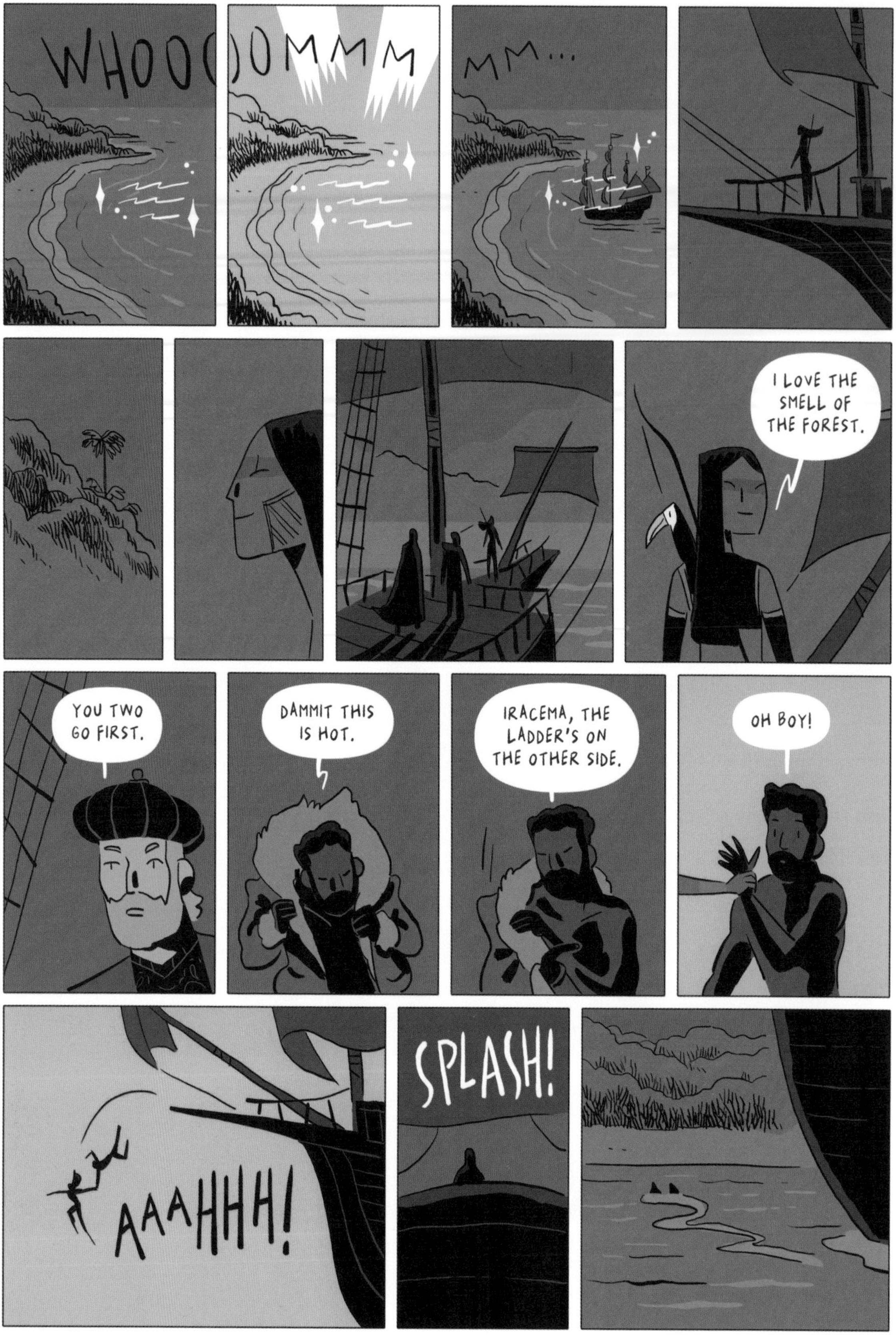
WHOOOOMMMMM...
I LOVE THE SMELL OF THE FOREST.
YOU TWO GO FIRST.
DAMMIT THIS IS HOT.
IRACEMA, THE LADDER'S ON THE OTHER SIDE.
OH BOY!
AAAHHH!
SPLASH!

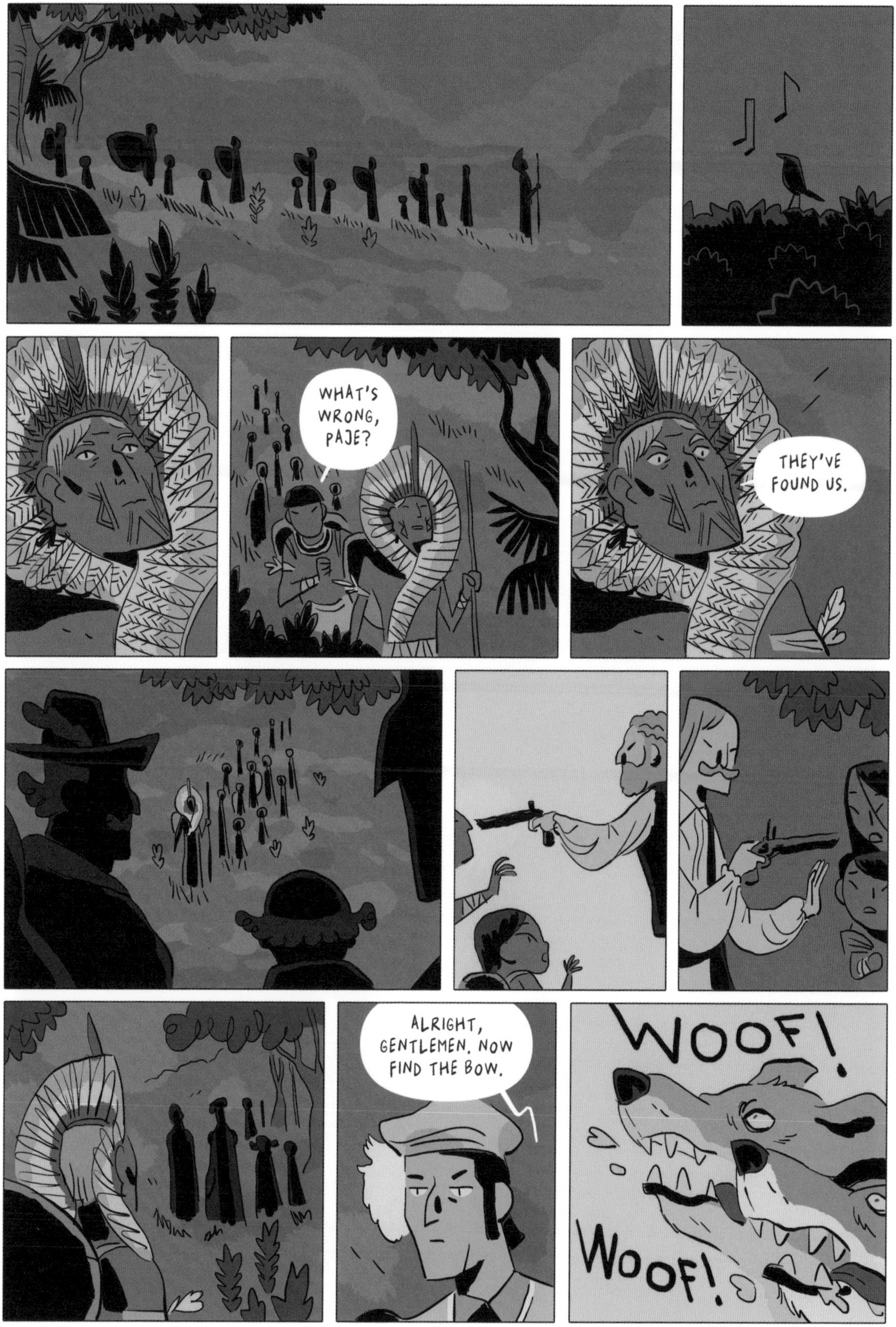
WHAT'S WRONG, PAJE?
THEY'VE FOUND US.
ALRIGHT, GENTLEMEN. NOW FIND THE BOW.
WOOF!
WOOF!

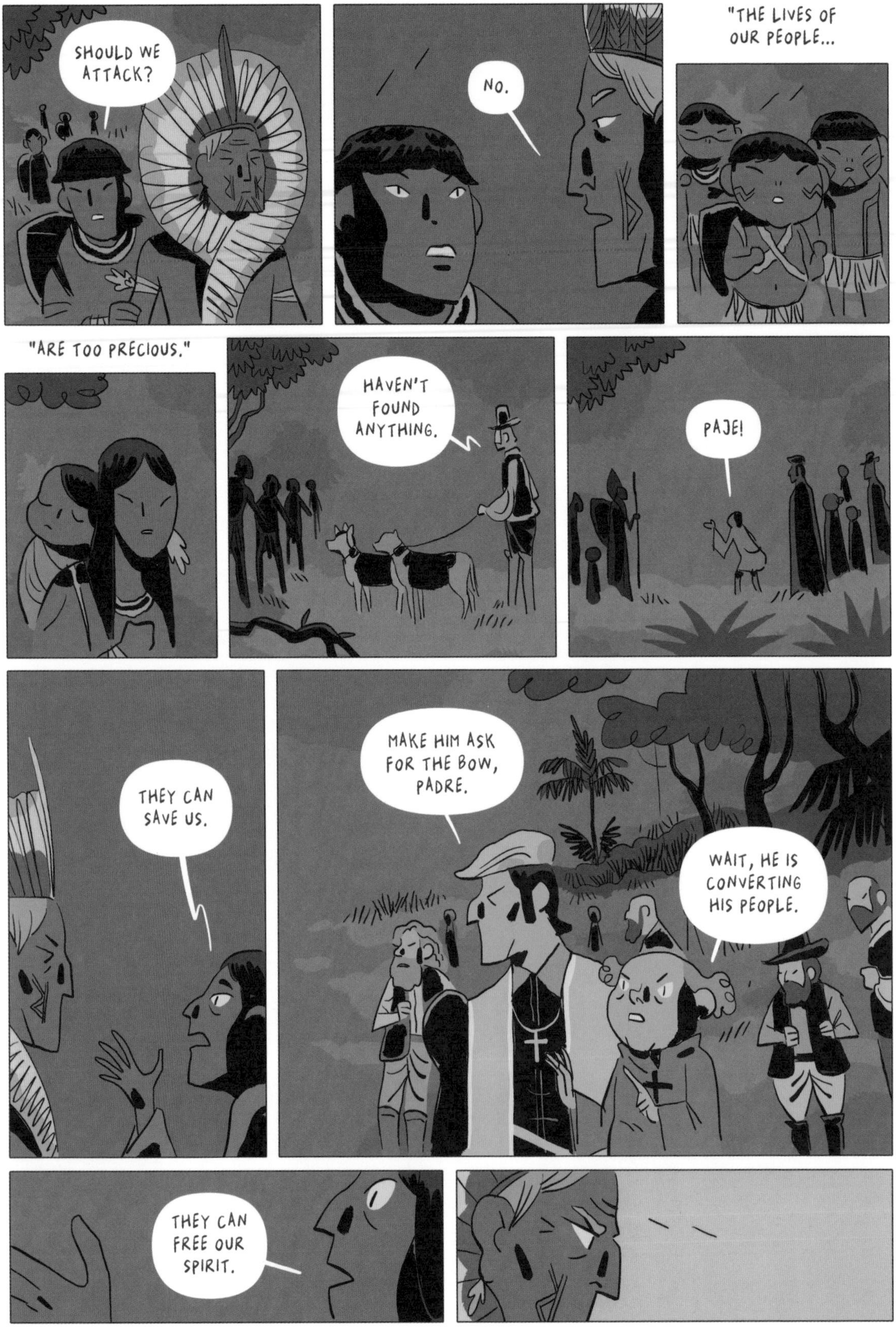
SHOULD WE ATTACK?
NO.
"THE LIVES OF OUR PEOPLE...
"ARE TOO PRECIOUS."
HAVEN'T FOUND ANYTHING.
PAJE!
THEY CAN SAVE US.
MAKE HIM ASK FOR THE BOW, PADRE.
WAIT, HE IS CONVERTING HIS PEOPLE.
THEY CAN FREE OUR SPIRIT.

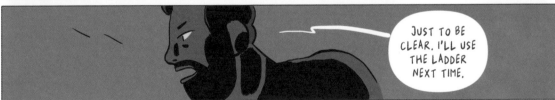

JUST TO BE CLEAR. I'LL USE THE LADDER NEXT TIME.

PAJE, ARE YOU LISTENING TO...

EXCUSE ME, SON.

I WANT THE BOW.

NOW!

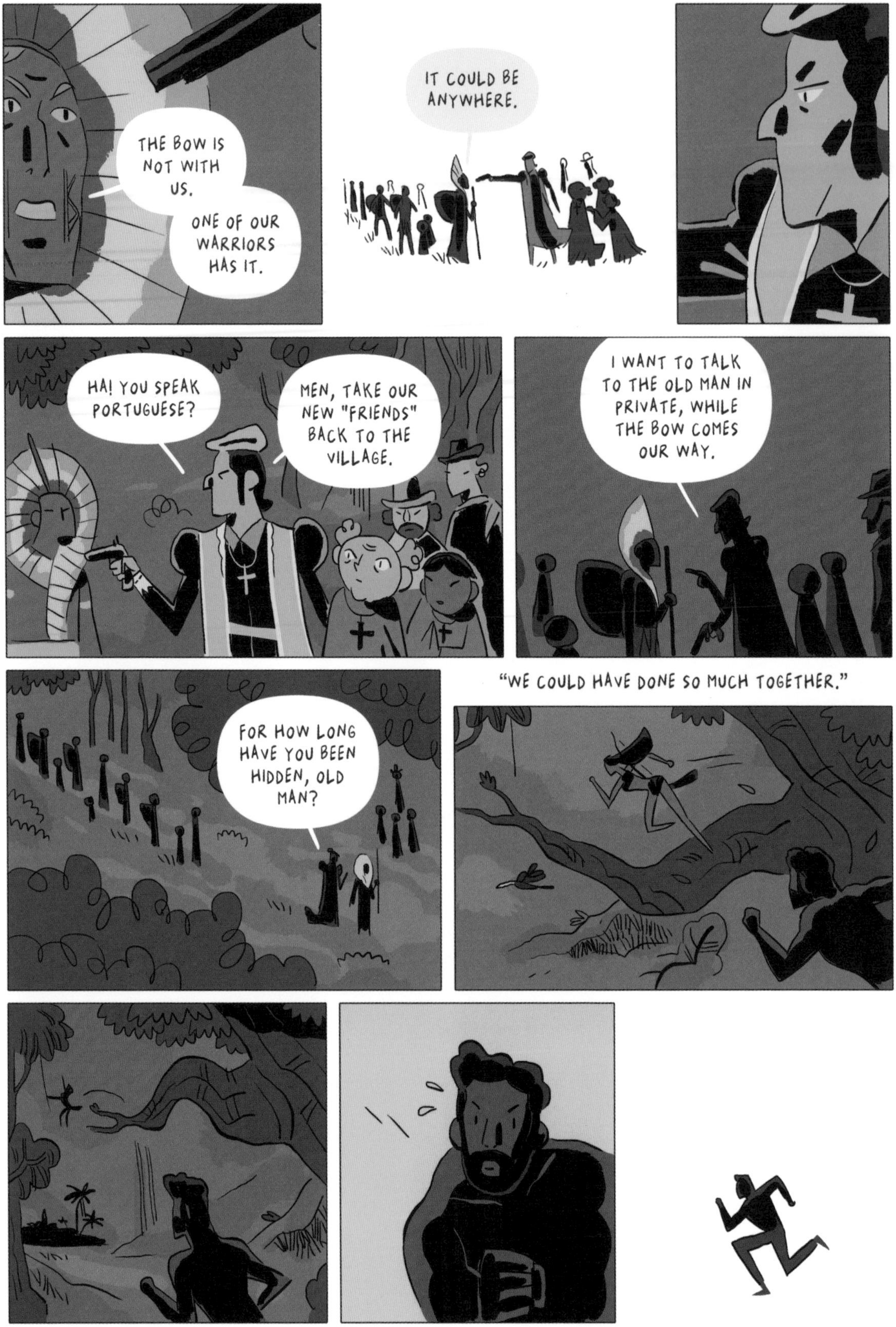
THE BOW IS NOT WITH US.
ONE OF OUR WARRIORS HAS IT.
IT COULD BE ANYWHERE.
HA! YOU SPEAK PORTUGUESE?
MEN, TAKE OUR NEW "FRIENDS" BACK TO THE VILLAGE.
I WANT TO TALK TO THE OLD MAN IN PRIVATE, WHILE THE BOW COMES OUR WAY.
FOR HOW LONG HAVE YOU BEEN HIDDEN, OLD MAN?
"WE COULD HAVE DONE SO MUCH TOGETHER."

IT WON'T TAKE LONG, MY FRIEND.

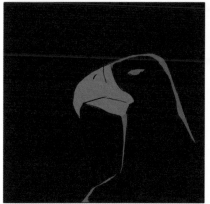

I JUST HOPE THERE AREN'T TOO MANY MOSQUITOS.

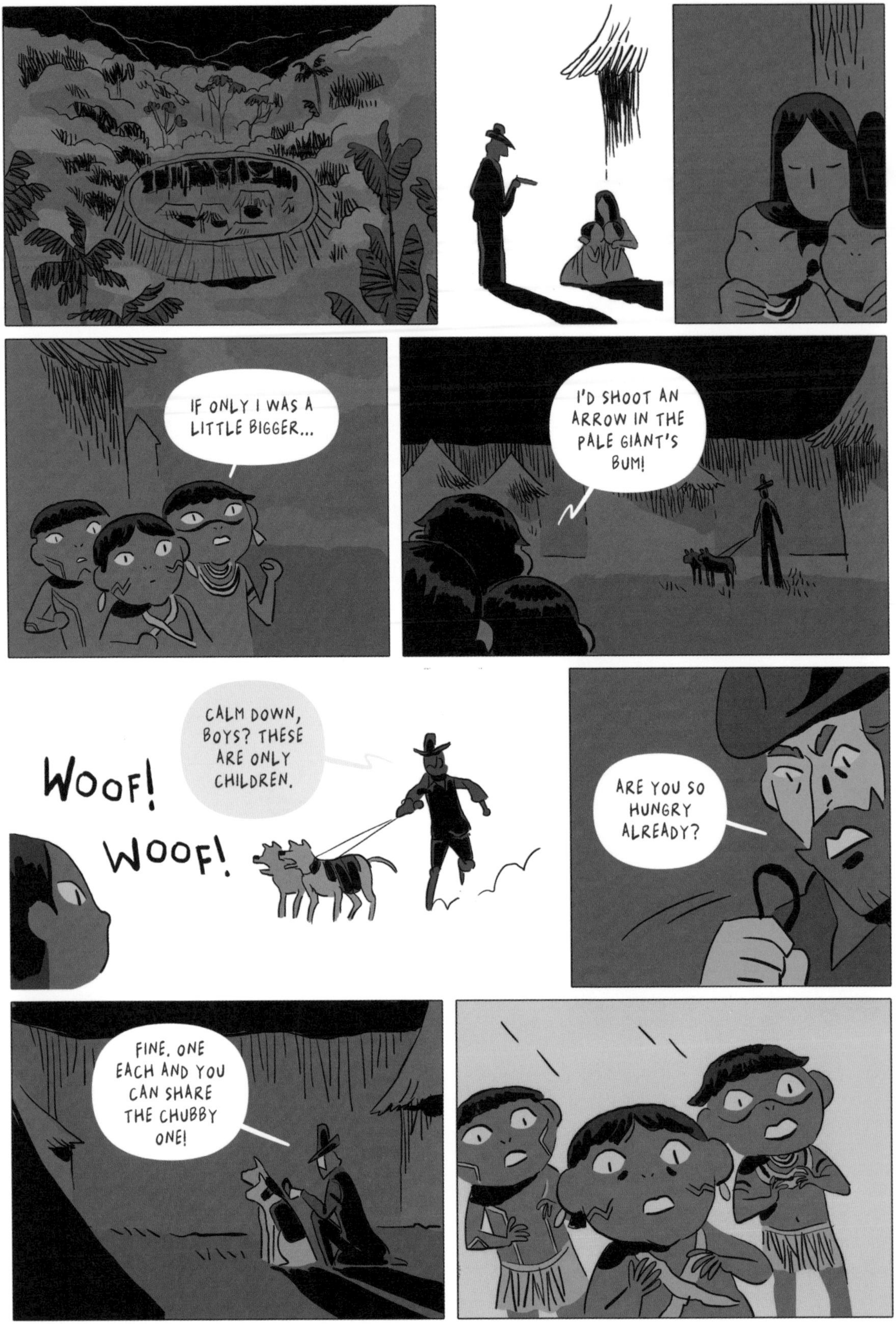
IF ONLY I WAS A LITTLE BIGGER...
I'D SHOOT AN ARROW IN THE PALE GIANT'S BUM!
WOOF! WOOF!
CALM DOWN, BOYS? THESE ARE ONLY CHILDREN.
ARE YOU SO HUNGRY ALREADY?
FINE. ONE EACH AND YOU CAN SHARE THE CHUBBY ONE!

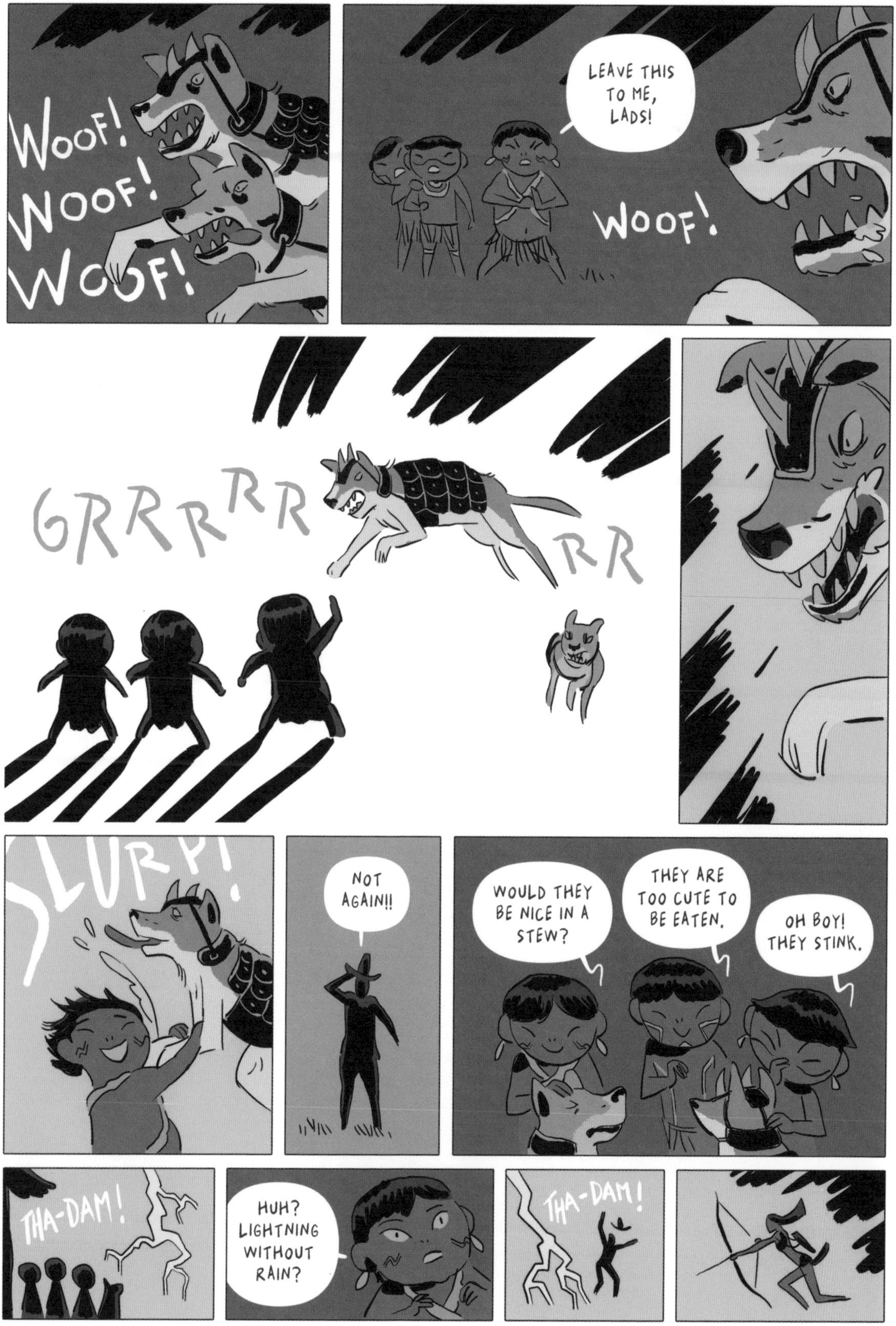
WOOF! WOOF! WOOF!
LEAVE THIS TO ME, LADS!
WOOF!
GRRRRRRRR
SLURP!
NOT AGAIN!!
WOULD THEY BE NICE IN A STEW?
THEY ARE TOO CUTE TO BE EATEN.
OH BOY! THEY STINK.
THA-DAM!
HUH? LIGHTNING WITHOUT RAIN?
THA-DAM!

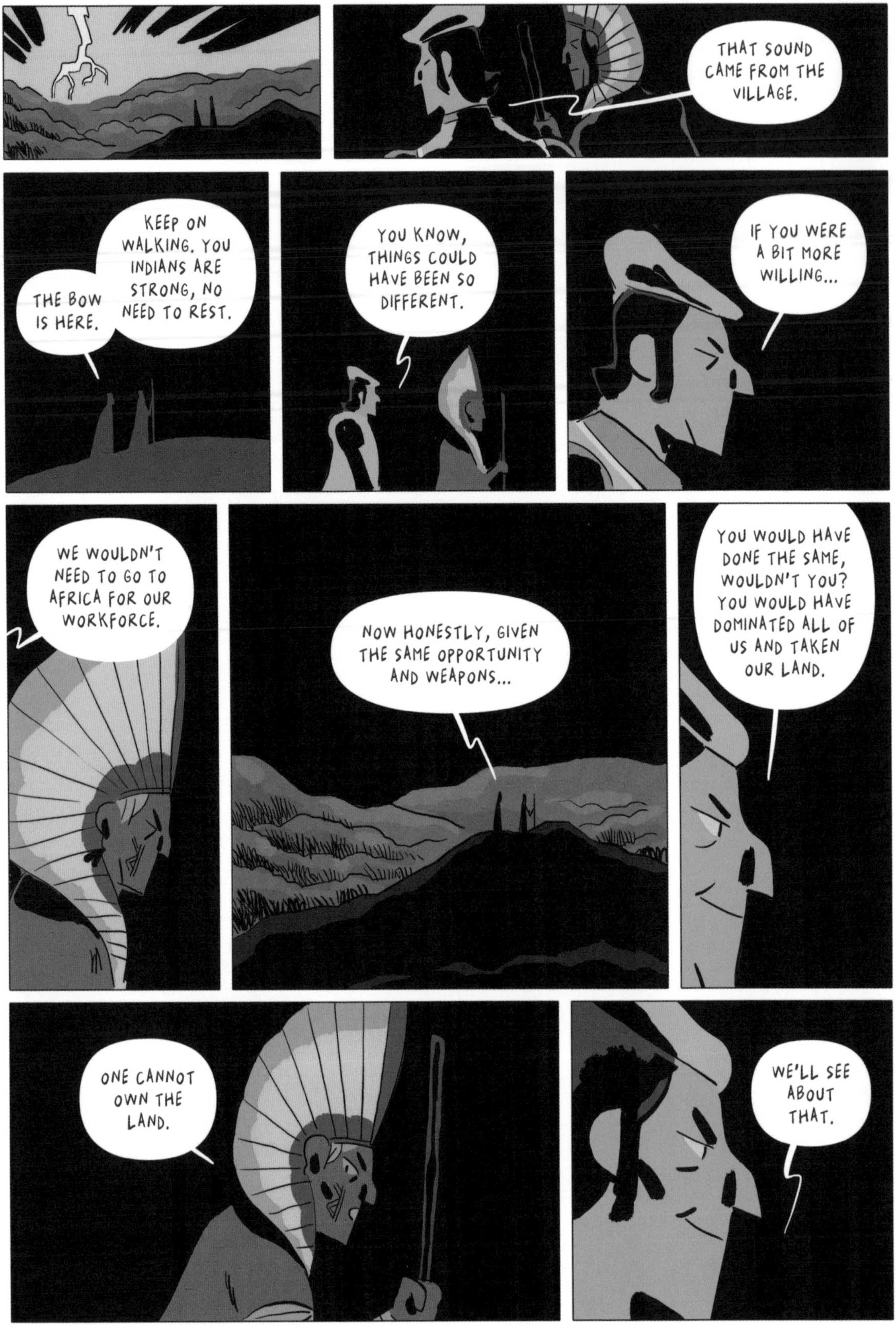
THAT SOUND CAME FROM THE VILLAGE.
KEEP ON WALKING. YOU INDIANS ARE STRONG, NO NEED TO REST.
THE BOW IS HERE.
YOU KNOW, THINGS COULD HAVE BEEN SO DIFFERENT.
IF YOU WERE A BIT MORE WILLING...
WE WOULDN'T NEED TO GO TO AFRICA FOR OUR WORKFORCE.
NOW HONESTLY, GIVEN THE SAME OPPORTUNITY AND WEAPONS...
YOU WOULD HAVE DONE THE SAME, WOULDN'T YOU? YOU WOULD HAVE DOMINATED ALL OF US AND TAKEN OUR LAND.
ONE CANNOT OWN THE LAND.
WE'LL SEE ABOUT THAT.

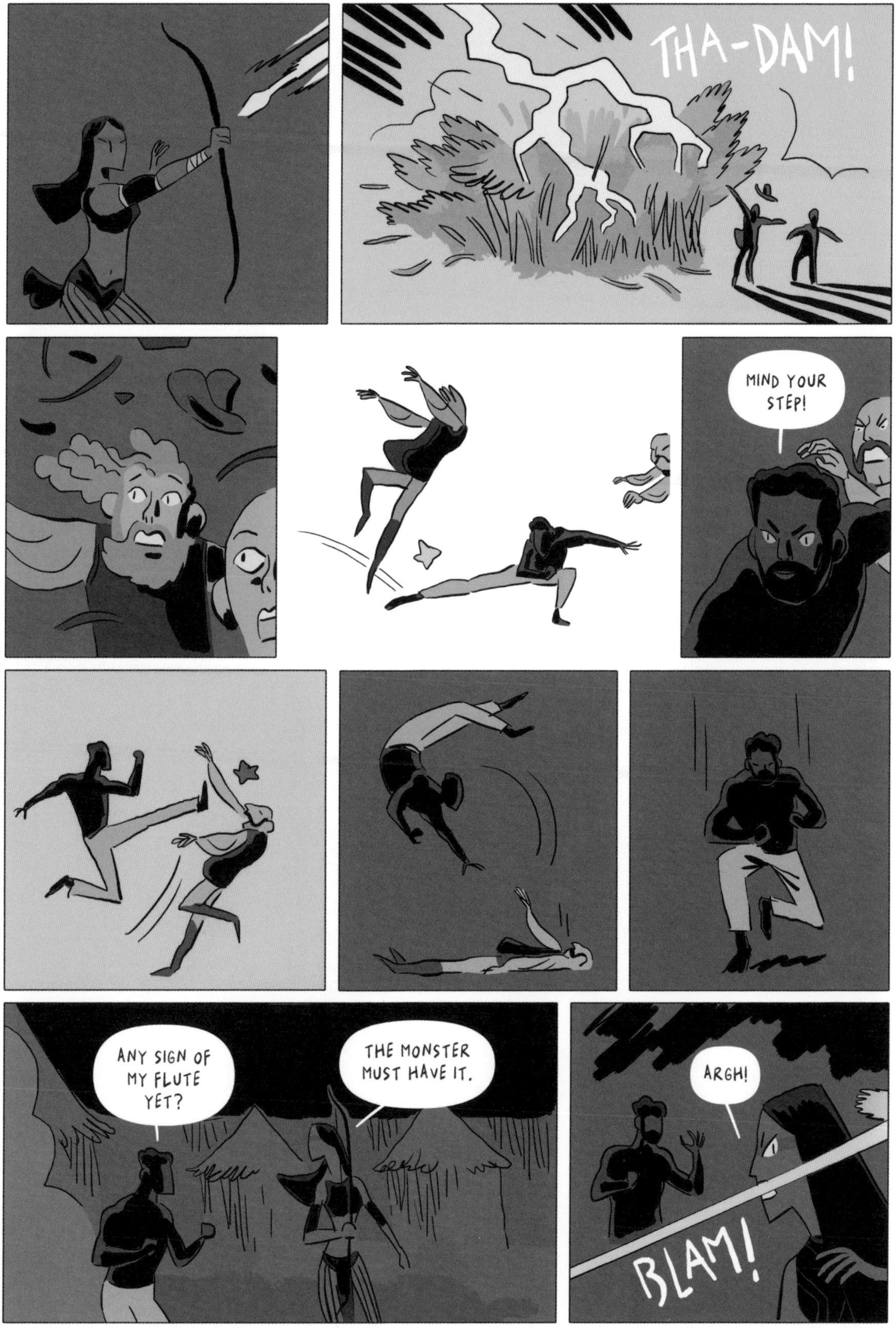
THA-DAM!
MIND YOUR STEP!
ANY SIGN OF MY FLUTE YET?
THE MONSTER MUST HAVE IT.
ARGH!
BLAM!

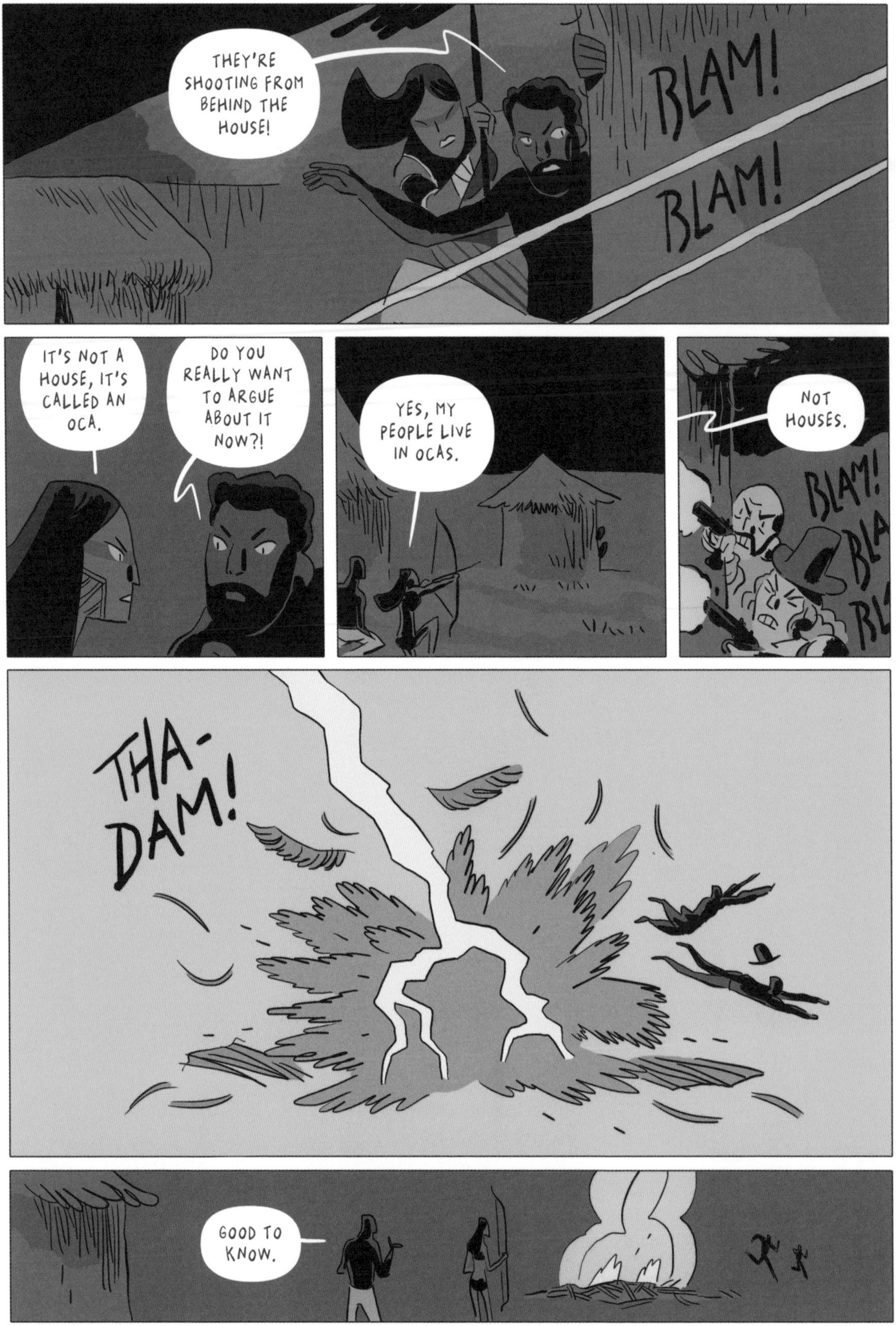
THEY'RE SHOOTING FROM BEHIND THE HOUSE!
BLAM!
BLAM!
IT'S NOT A HOUSE, IT'S CALLED AN OCA.
DO YOU REALLY WANT TO ARGUE ABOUT IT NOW?!
YES, MY PEOPLE LIVE IN OCAS.
NOT HOUSES.
BLAM!
THA-DAM!
GOOD TO KNOW.

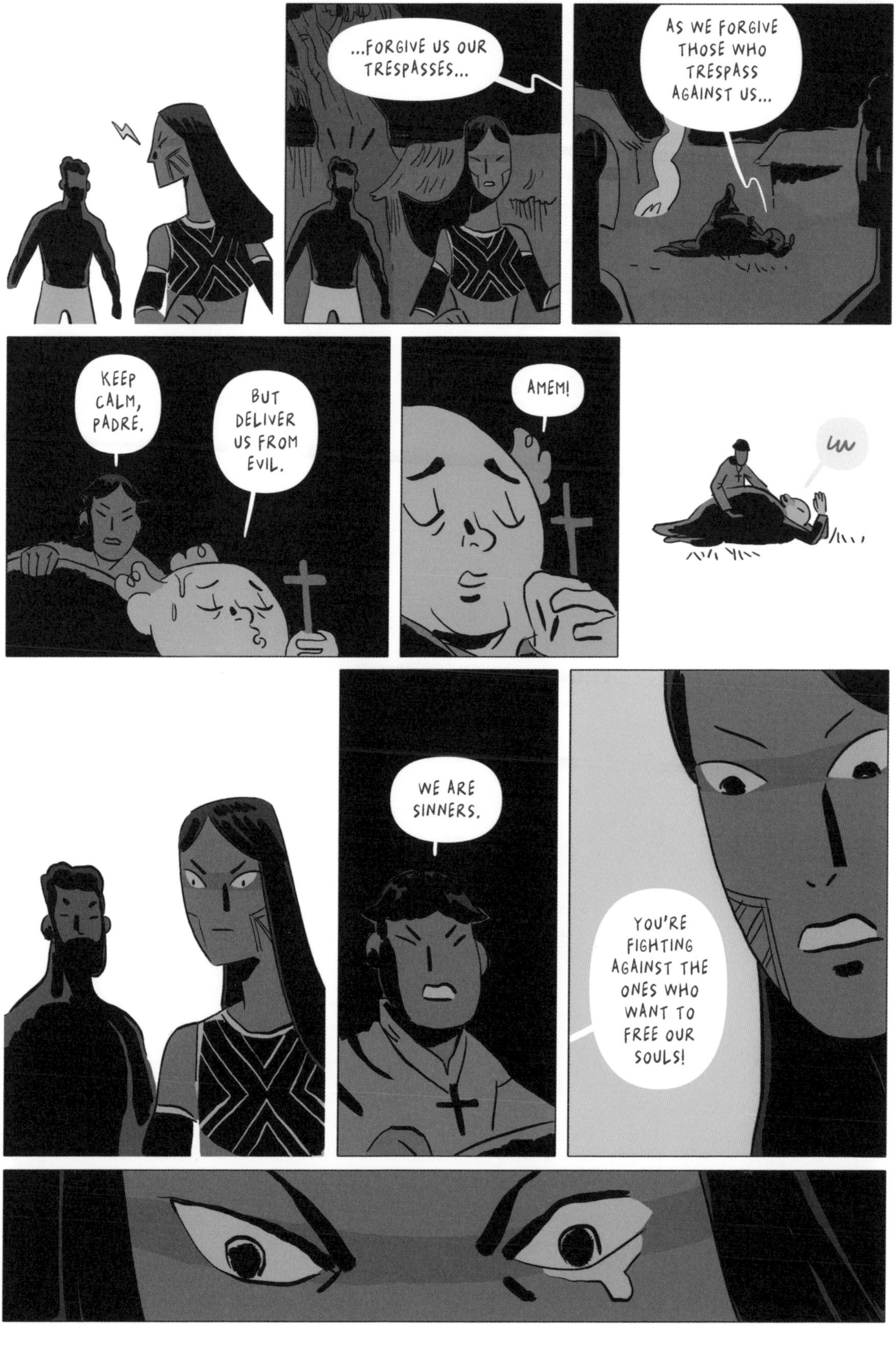
...FORGIVE US OUR TRESPASSES...
AS WE FORGIVE THOSE WHO TRESPASS AGAINST US...
KEEP CALM, PADRE.
BUT DELIVER US FROM EVIL.
AMEM!
WE ARE SINNERS.
YOU'RE FIGHTING AGAINST THE ONES WHO WANT TO FREE OUR SOULS!

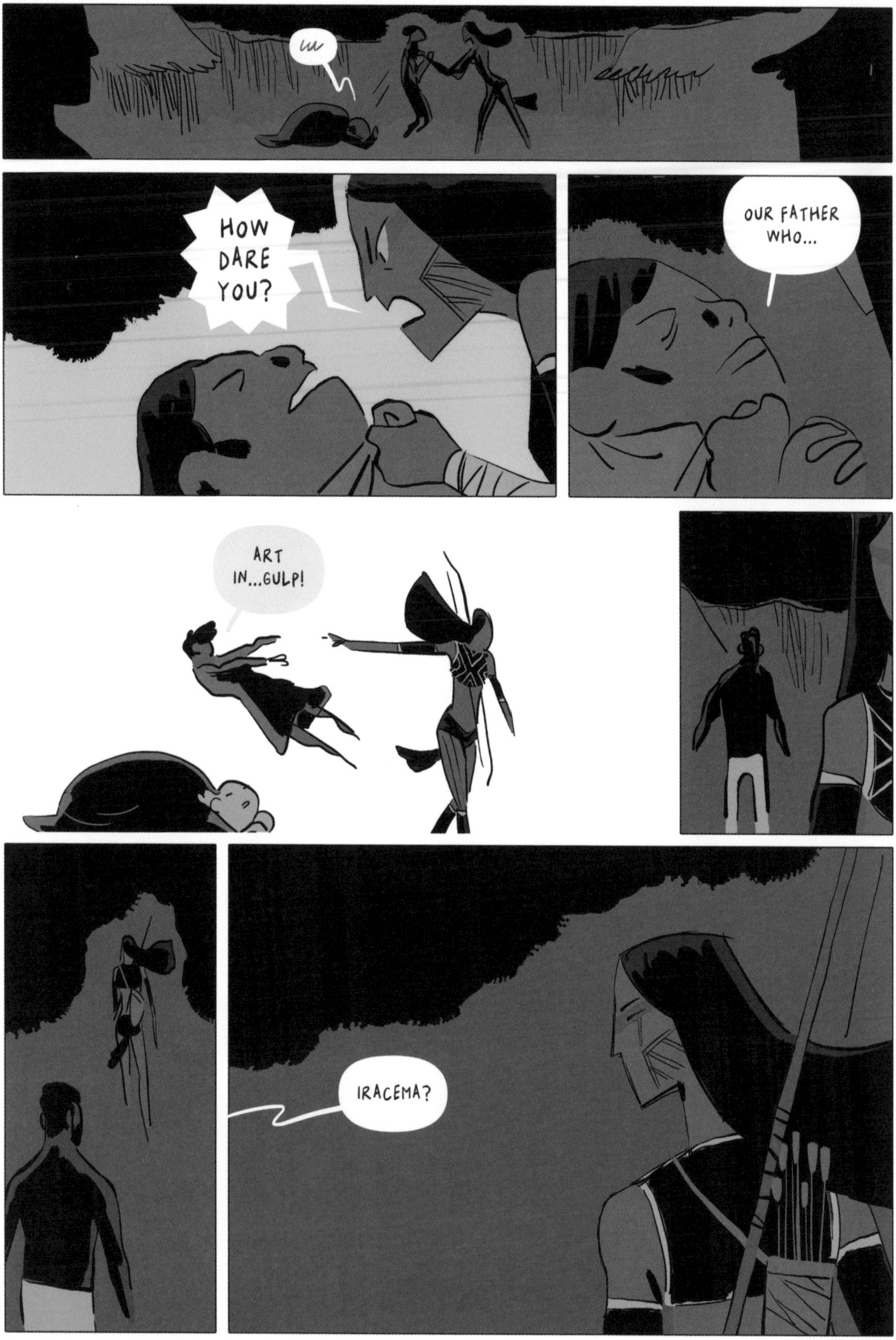

HOW DARE YOU?
OUR FATHER WHO...
ART IN...GULP!
IRACEMA?

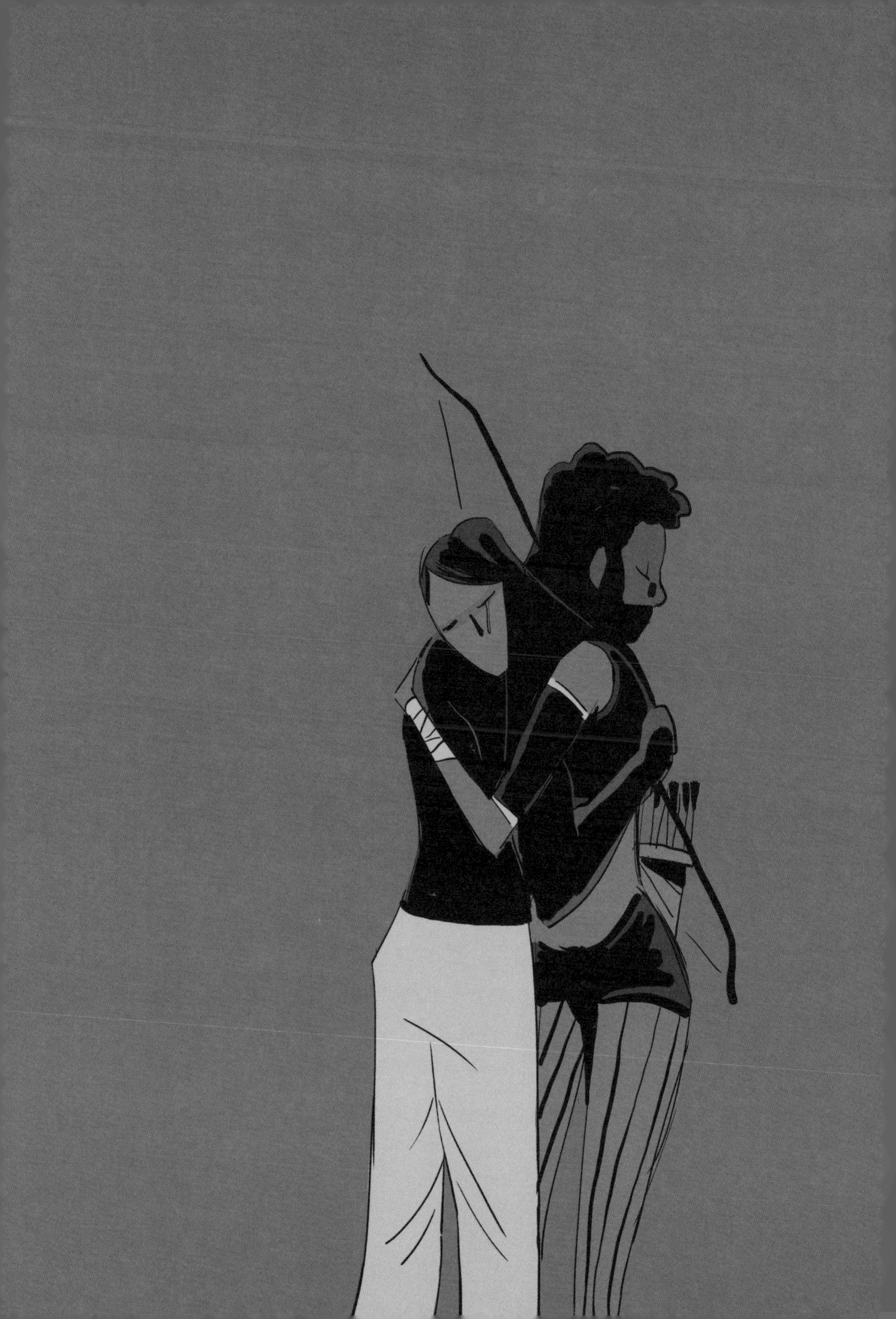

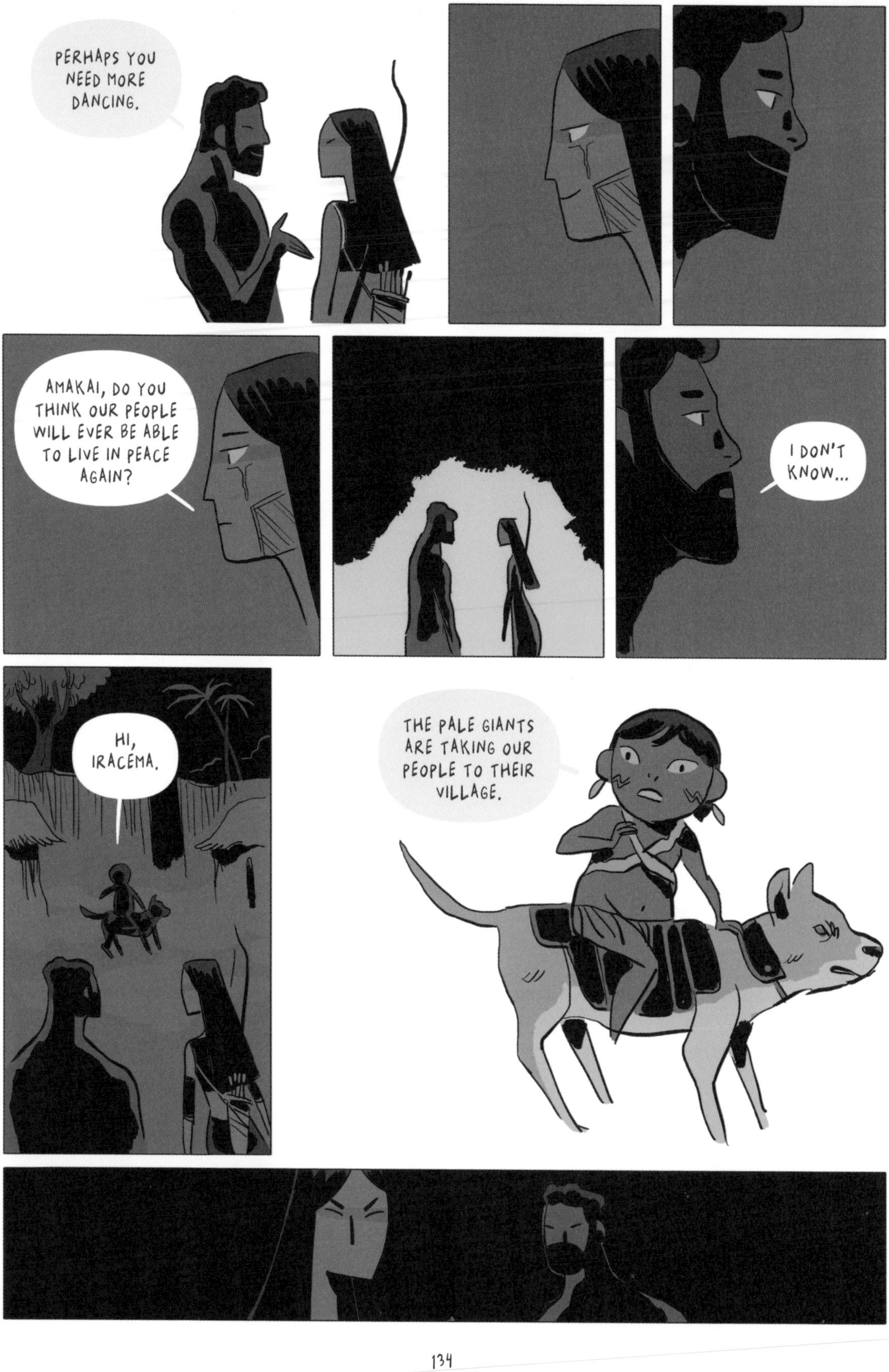
PERHAPS YOU NEED MORE DANCING.
AMAKAI, DO YOU THINK OUR PEOPLE WILL EVER BE ABLE TO LIVE IN PEACE AGAIN?
I DON'T KNOW...
HI, IRACEMA.
THE PALE GIANTS ARE TAKING OUR PEOPLE TO THEIR VILLAGE.

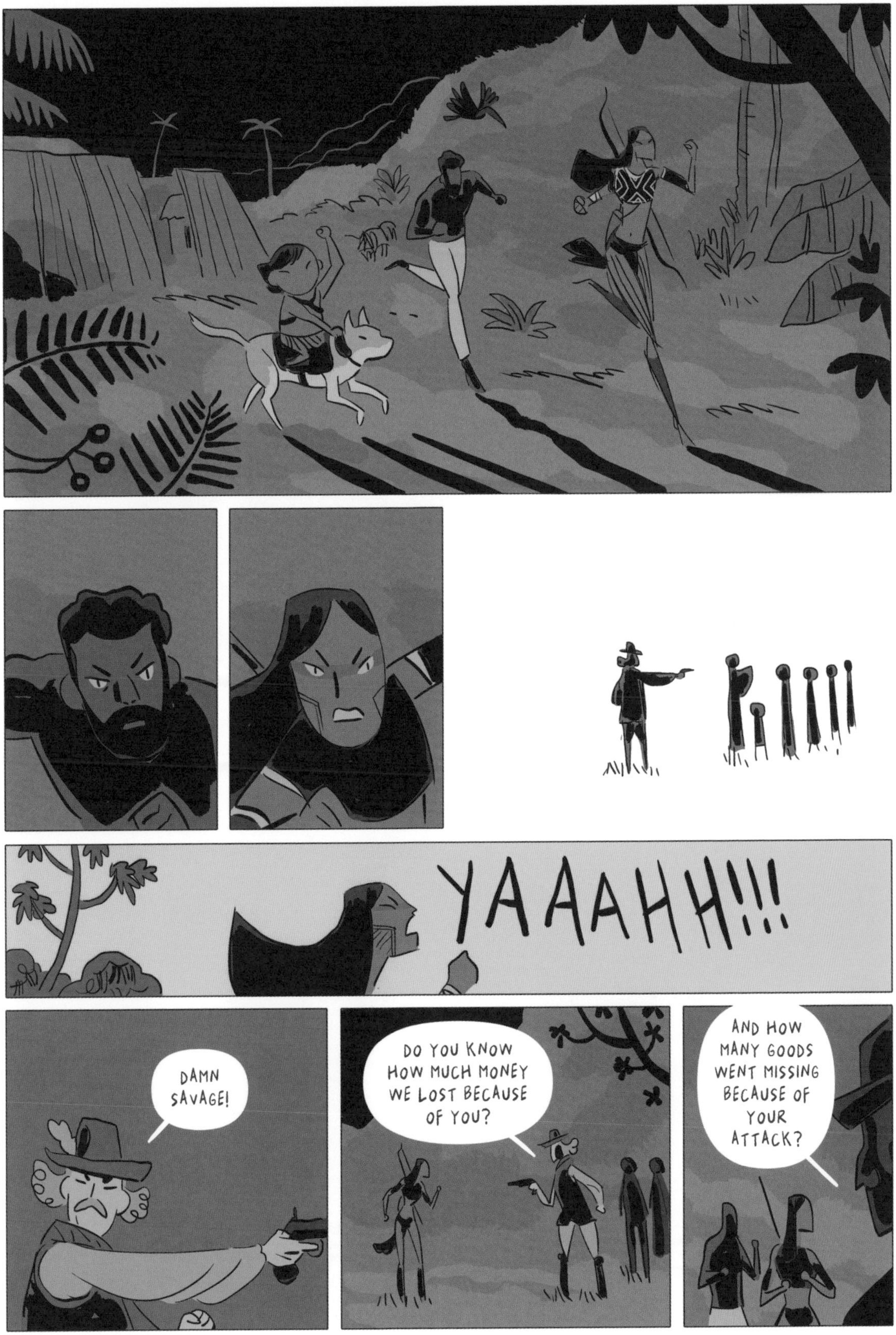
YAAAHH!!!
DAMN SAVAGE!
DO YOU KNOW HOW MUCH MONEY WE LOST BECAUSE OF YOU?
AND HOW MANY GOODS WENT MISSING BECAUSE OF YOUR ATTACK?

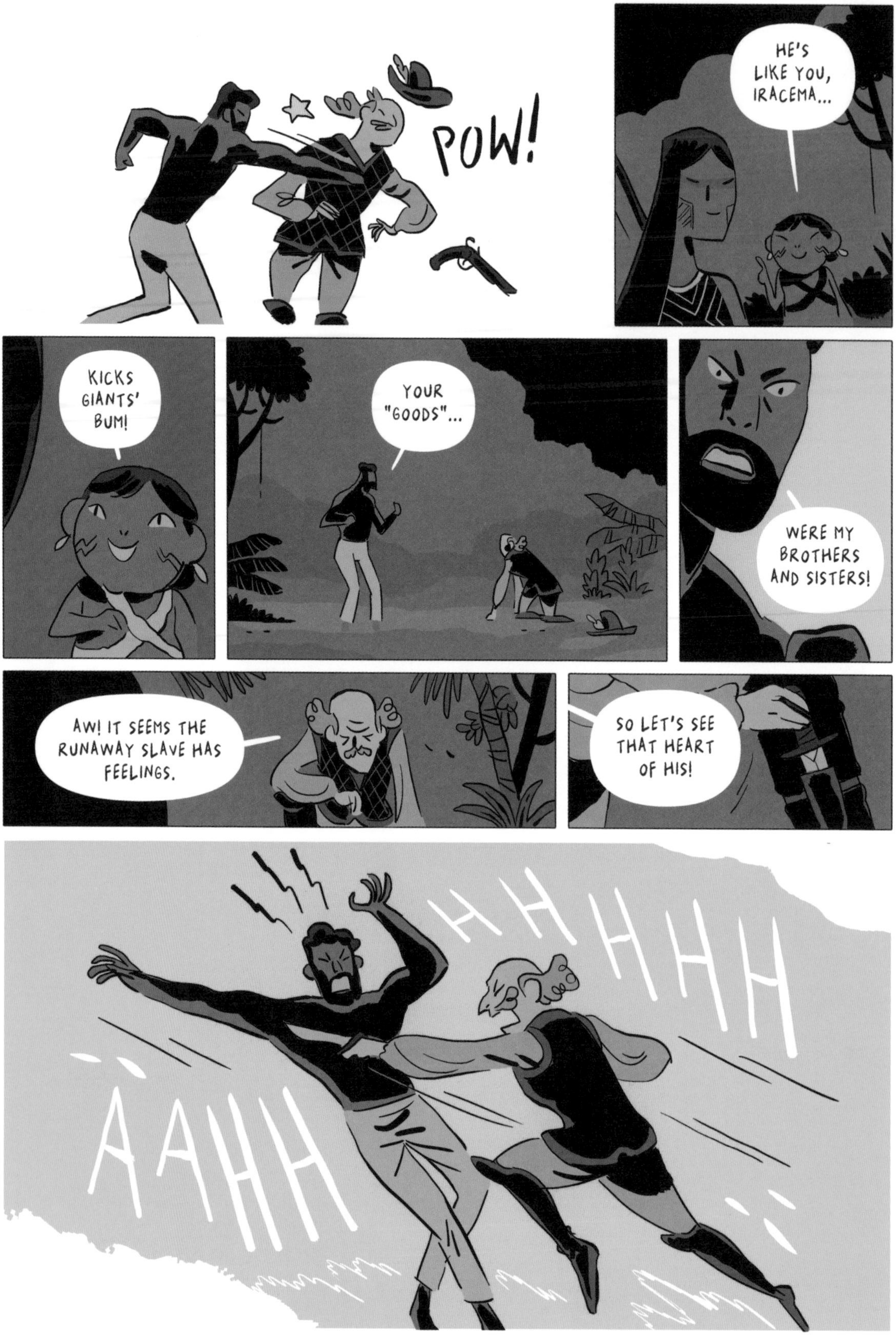
POW!
HE'S LIKE YOU, IRACEMA...
KICKS GIANTS' BUM!
YOUR "GOODS"...
WERE MY BROTHERS AND SISTERS!
AW! IT SEEMS THE RUNAWAY SLAVE HAS FEELINGS.
SO LET'S SEE THAT HEART OF HIS!
HHHHHH
AAHH

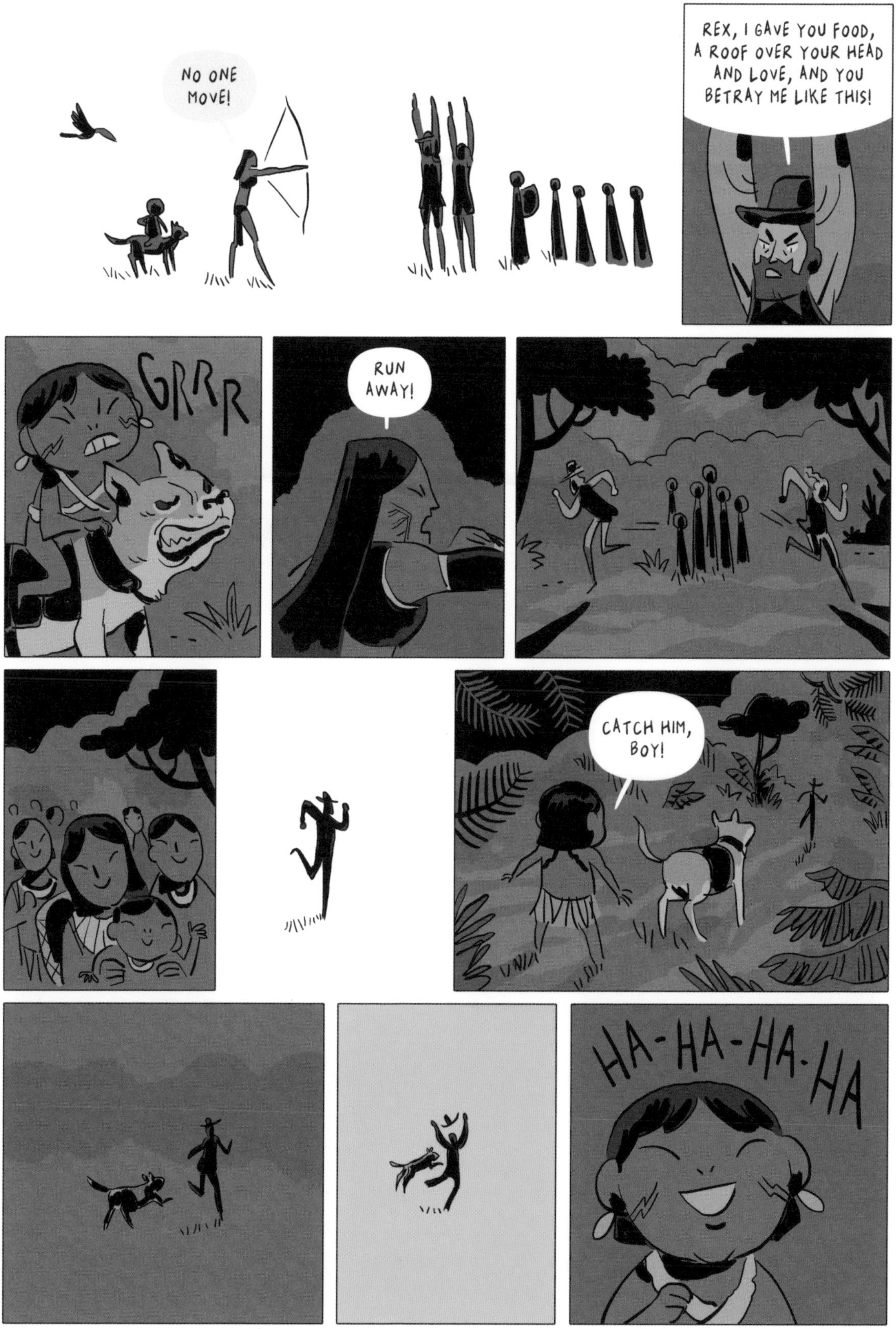
NO ONE MOVE!
REX, I GAVE YOU FOOD, A ROOF OVER YOUR HEAD AND LOVE, AND YOU BETRAY ME LIKE THIS!
GRRR
RUN AWAY!
CATCH HIM, BOY!
HA-HA-HA-HA

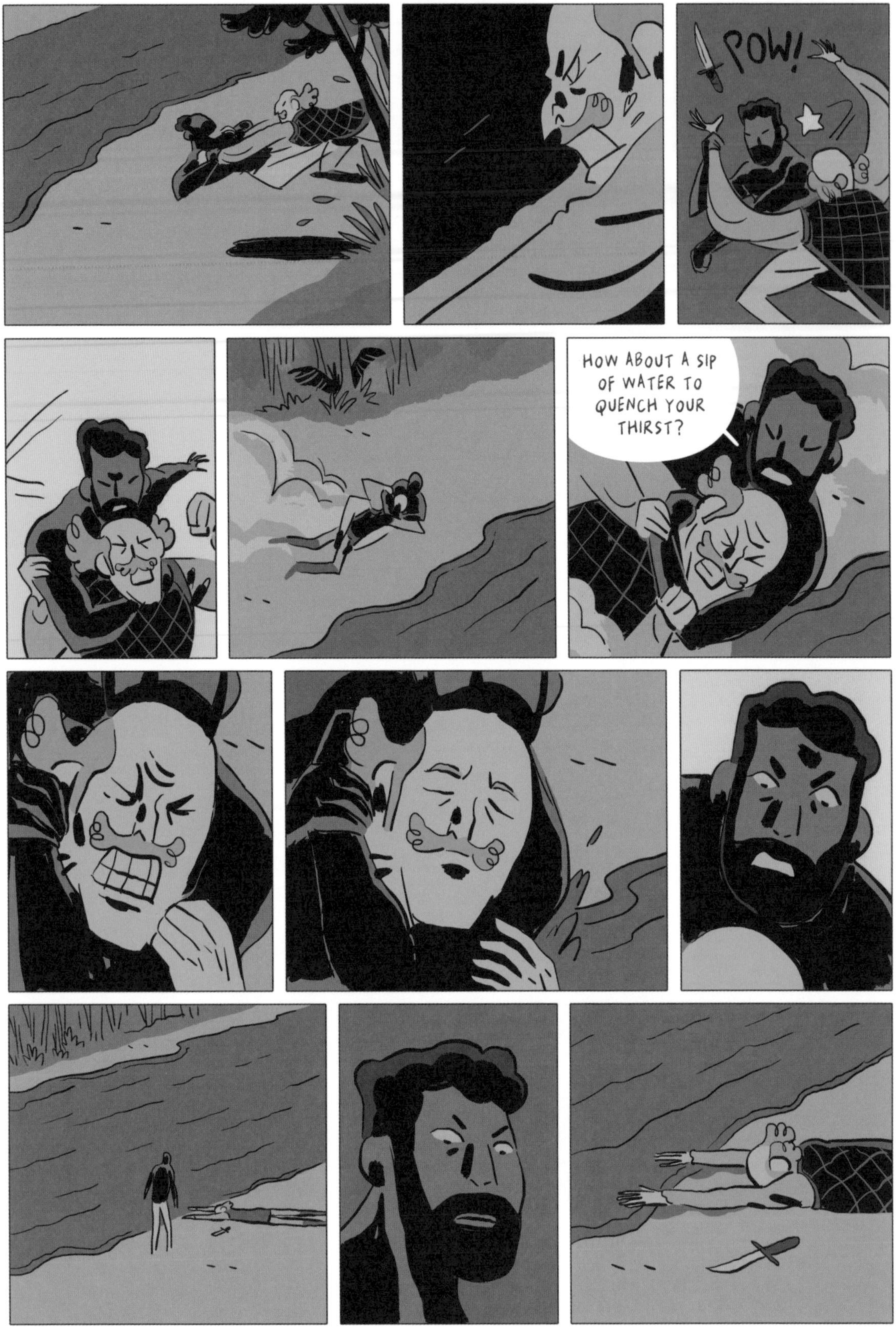
POW!
HOW ABOUT A SIP OF WATER TO QUENCH YOUR THIRST?

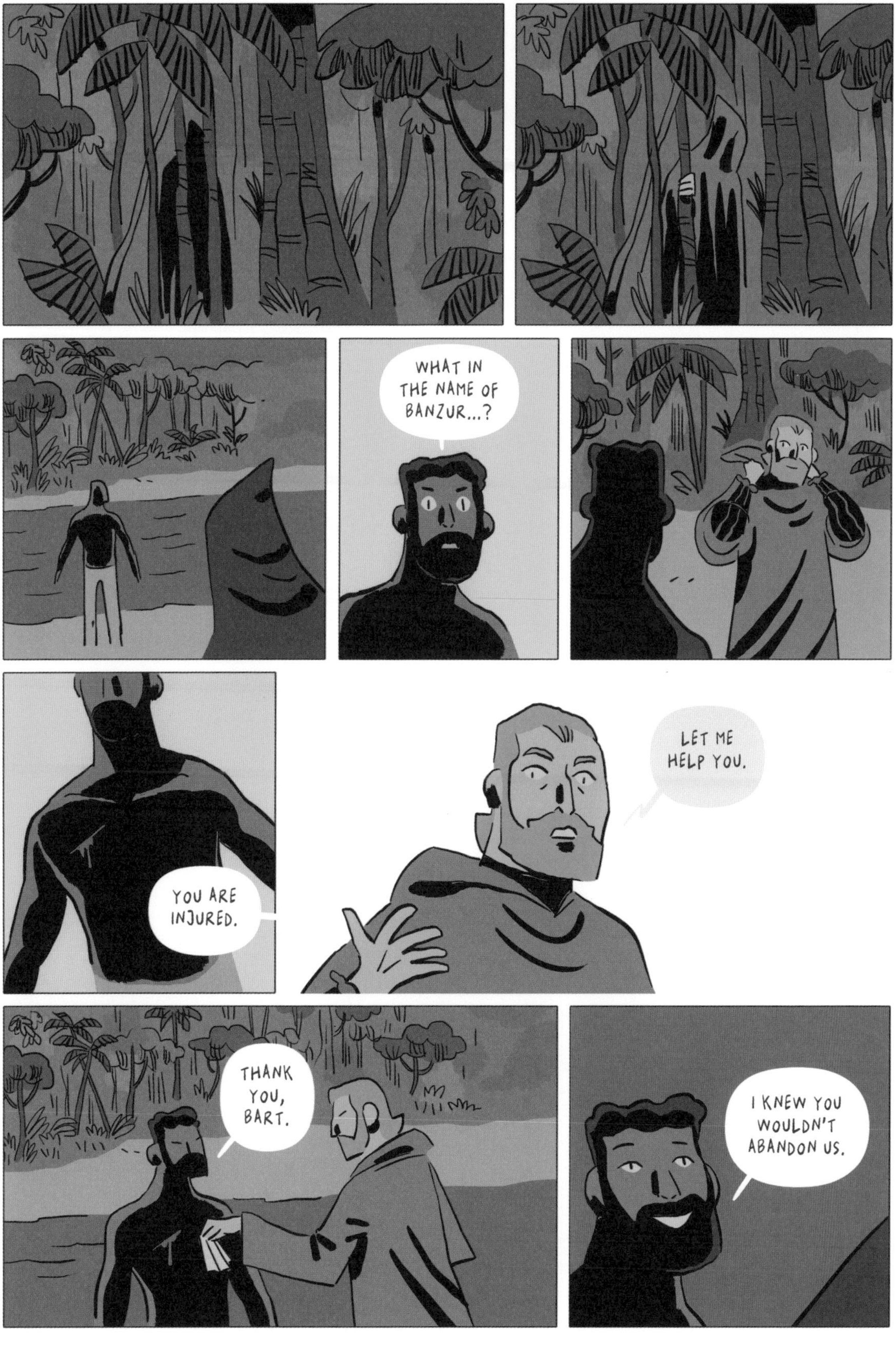
WHAT IN THE NAME OF BANZUR...?
YOU ARE INJURED.
LET ME HELP YOU.
THANK YOU, BART.
I KNEW YOU WOULDN'T ABANDON US.

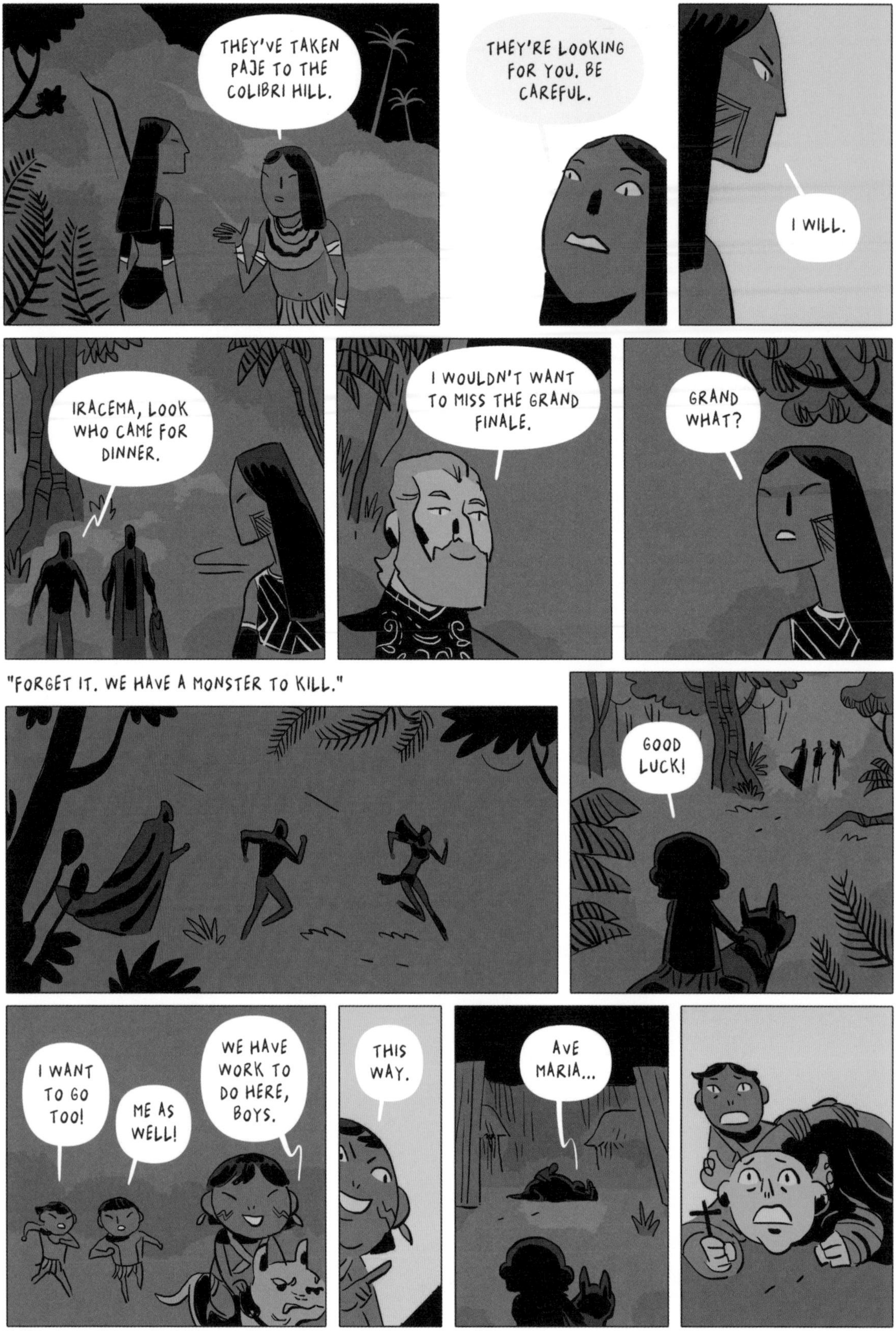
THEY'VE TAKEN PAJE TO THE COLIBRI HILL.
THEY'RE LOOKING FOR YOU. BE CAREFUL.
I WILL.
IRACEMA, LOOK WHO CAME FOR DINNER.
I WOULDN'T WANT TO MISS THE GRAND FINALE.
GRAND WHAT?
"FORGET IT. WE HAVE A MONSTER TO KILL."
GOOD LUCK!
I WANT TO GO TOO!
ME AS WELL!
WE HAVE WORK TO DO HERE, BOYS.
THIS WAY.
AVE MARIA...

PLEASE, STOP PLAYING IT.

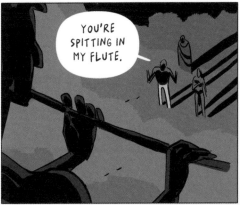

YOU'RE SPITTING IN MY FLUTE.

DISGUSTING!

WHERE IS PAJE?

THE OLD MAN?

I'VE FOUND HIM A SAFE SPOT.

PAJE!

LET ME TAKE YOU OUT OF THERE.

IRACEMA, DON'T WORRY ABOUT ME. DO WHAT YOU HAVE TO DO.

I THINK THIS FLUTE IS NO GOOD AFTER ALL.

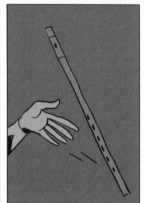

IT'S ALL YOURS!

COME ON, PLAY YOUR SWEET SONG AND SHOW THEM WHO I TRULY AM.

AND YOU, INDIAN GIRL.

PREPARE YOUR BOW.

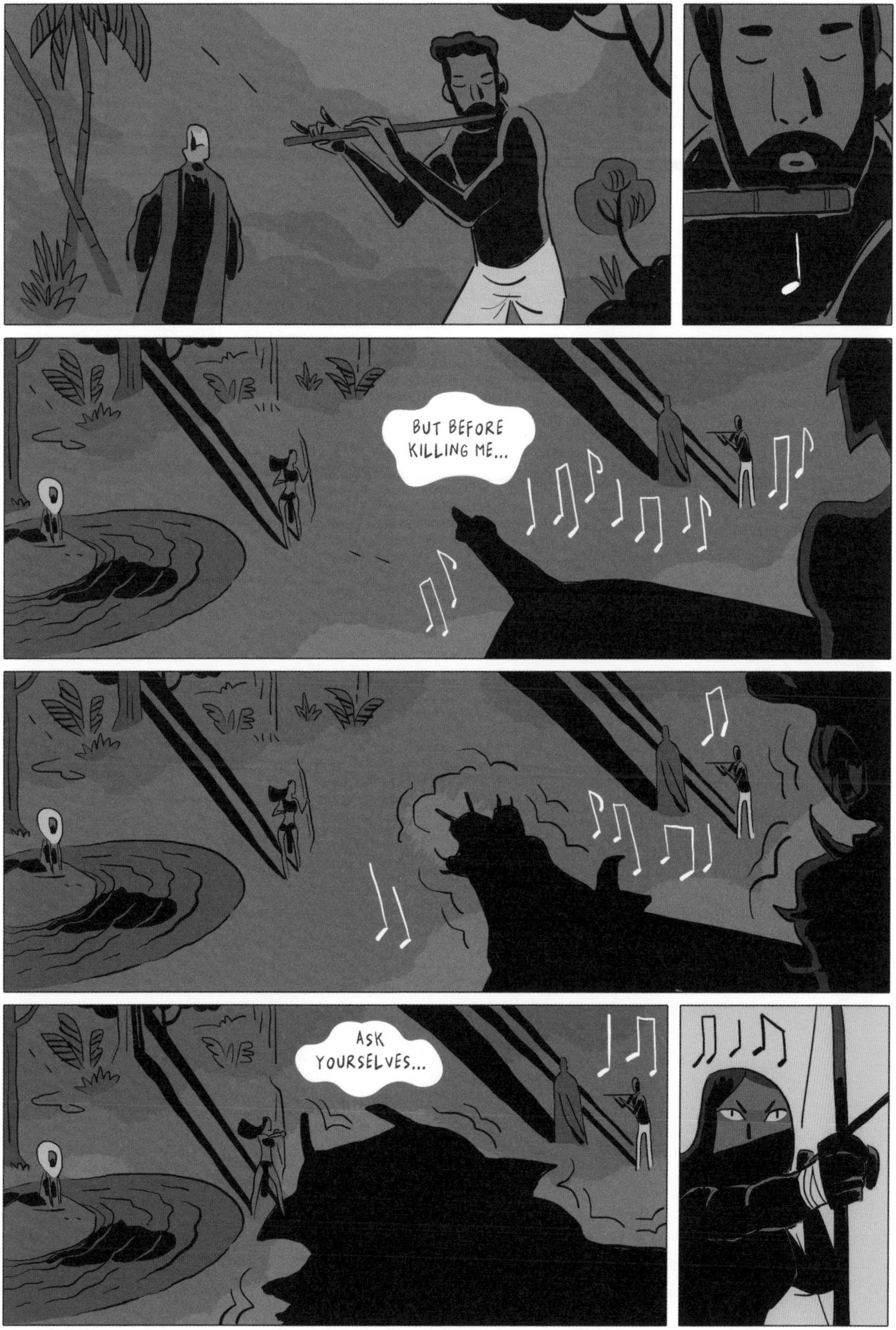
BUT BEFORE KILLING ME...
ASK YOURSELVES...

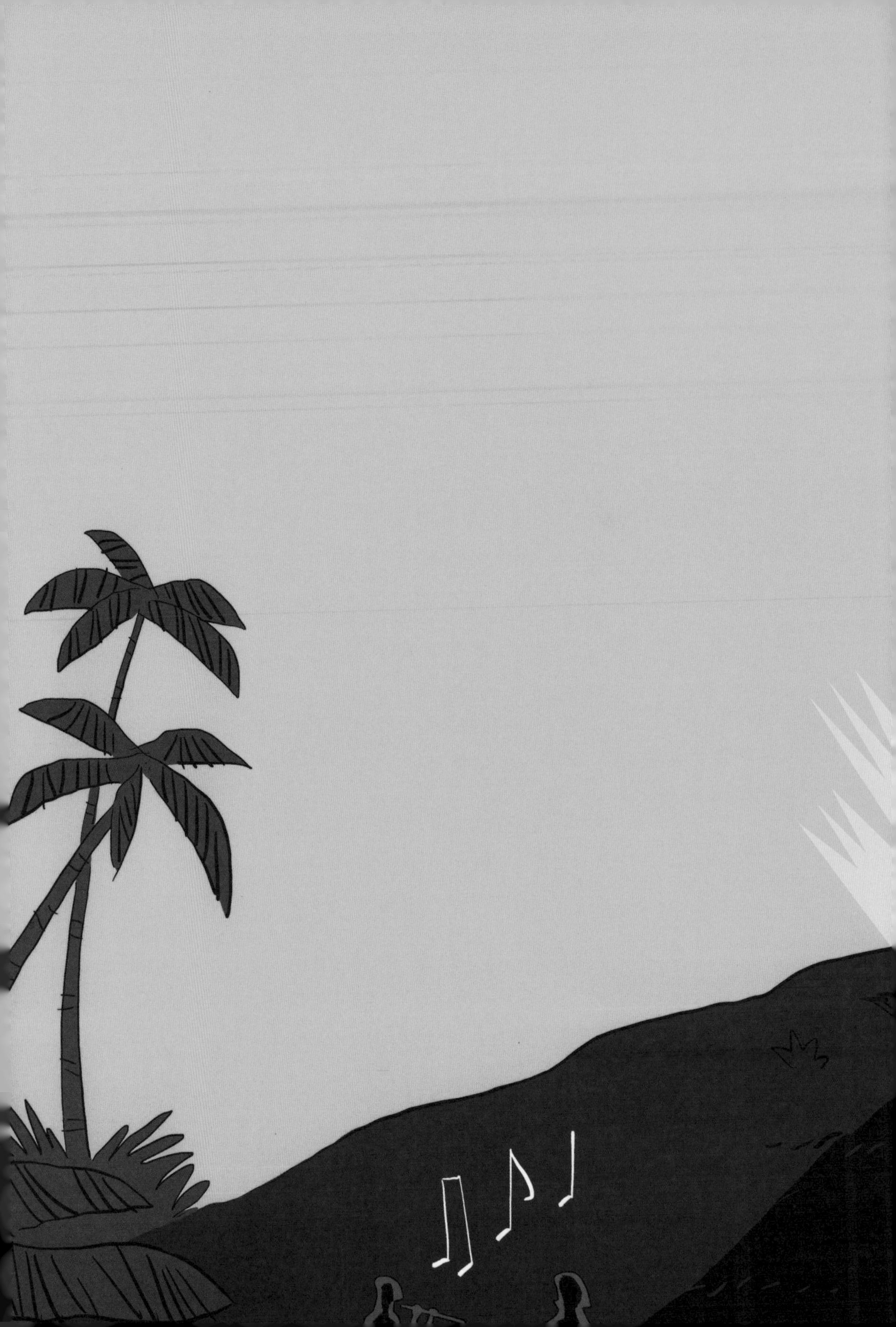

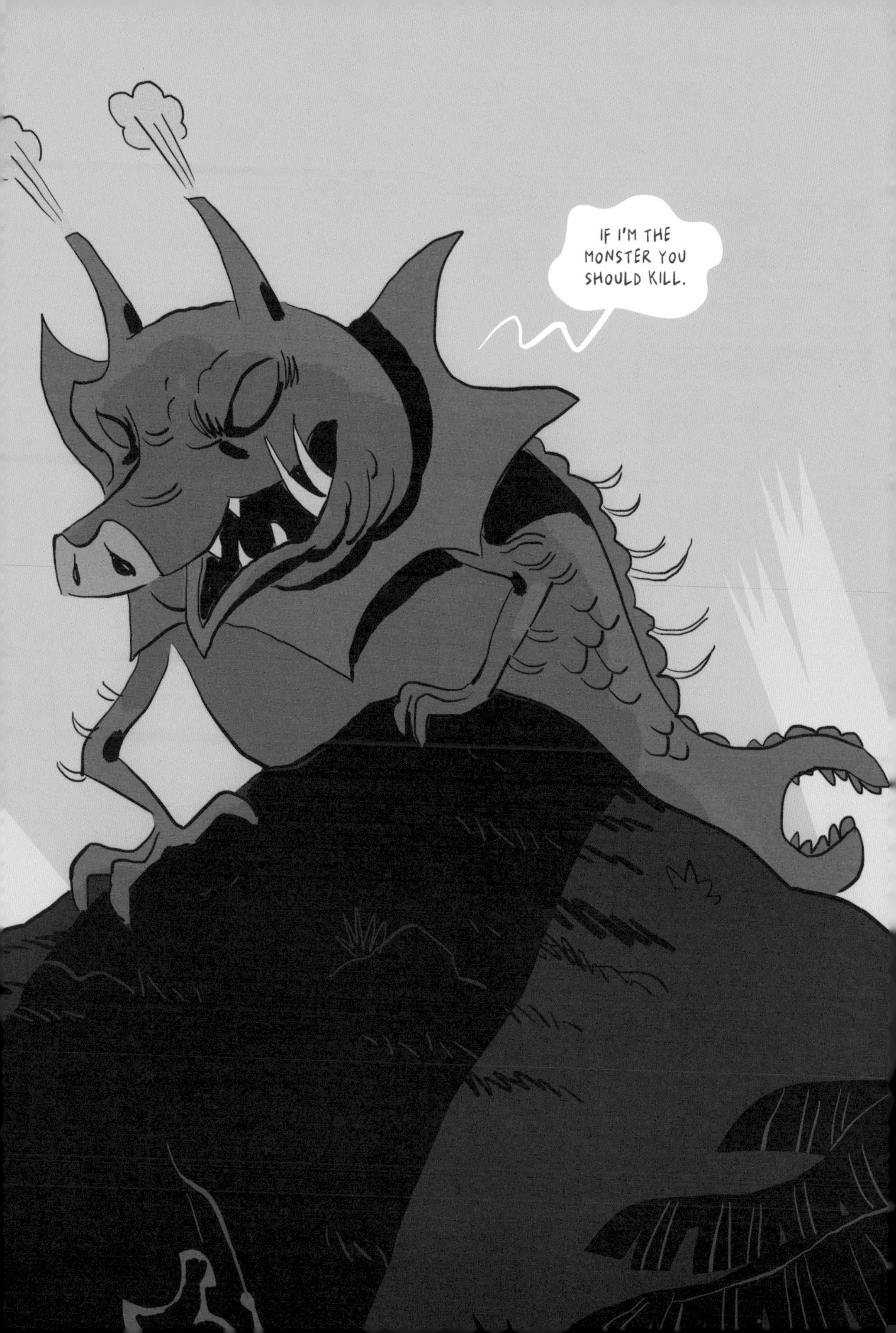
IF I'M THE MONSTER YOU SHOULD KILL.

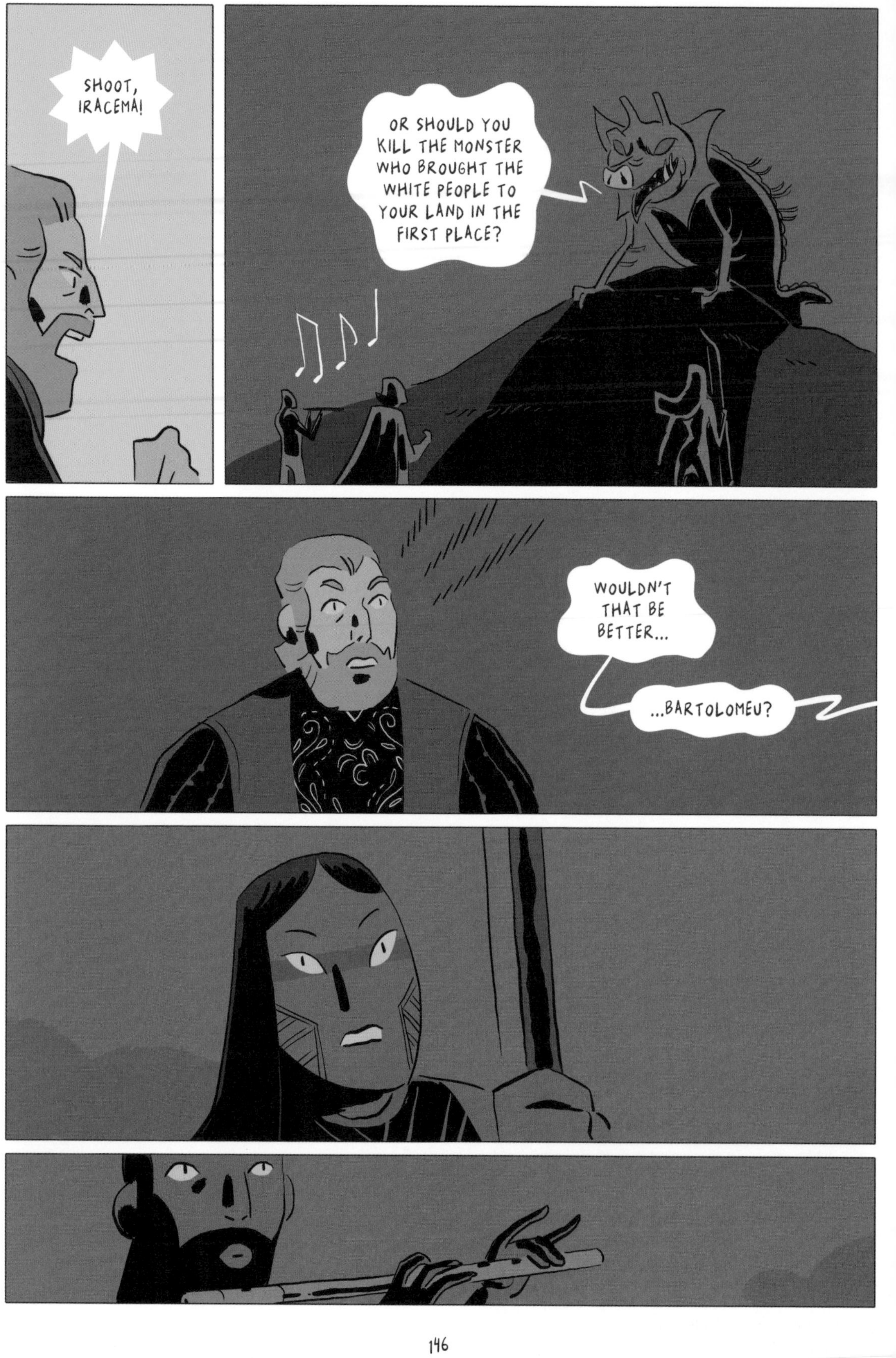
SHOOT, IRACEMA!
OR SHOULD YOU KILL THE MONSTER WHO BROUGHT THE WHITE PEOPLE TO YOUR LAND IN THE FIRST PLACE?
WOULDN'T THAT BE BETTER...
...BARTOLOMEU?

IT WAS YOU WHO SPREAD RUMORS...

...ABOUT THE IMMENSE WEALTH OF THIS LAND.

"YOUR STORIES ABOUT MOUNTAINS OF GOLD IN A PLACE CALLED ELDORADO...

"MADE THEM FEVERISH WITH THE DESIRE...

"OF GLORY AND RICHES."

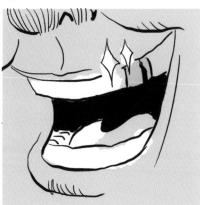

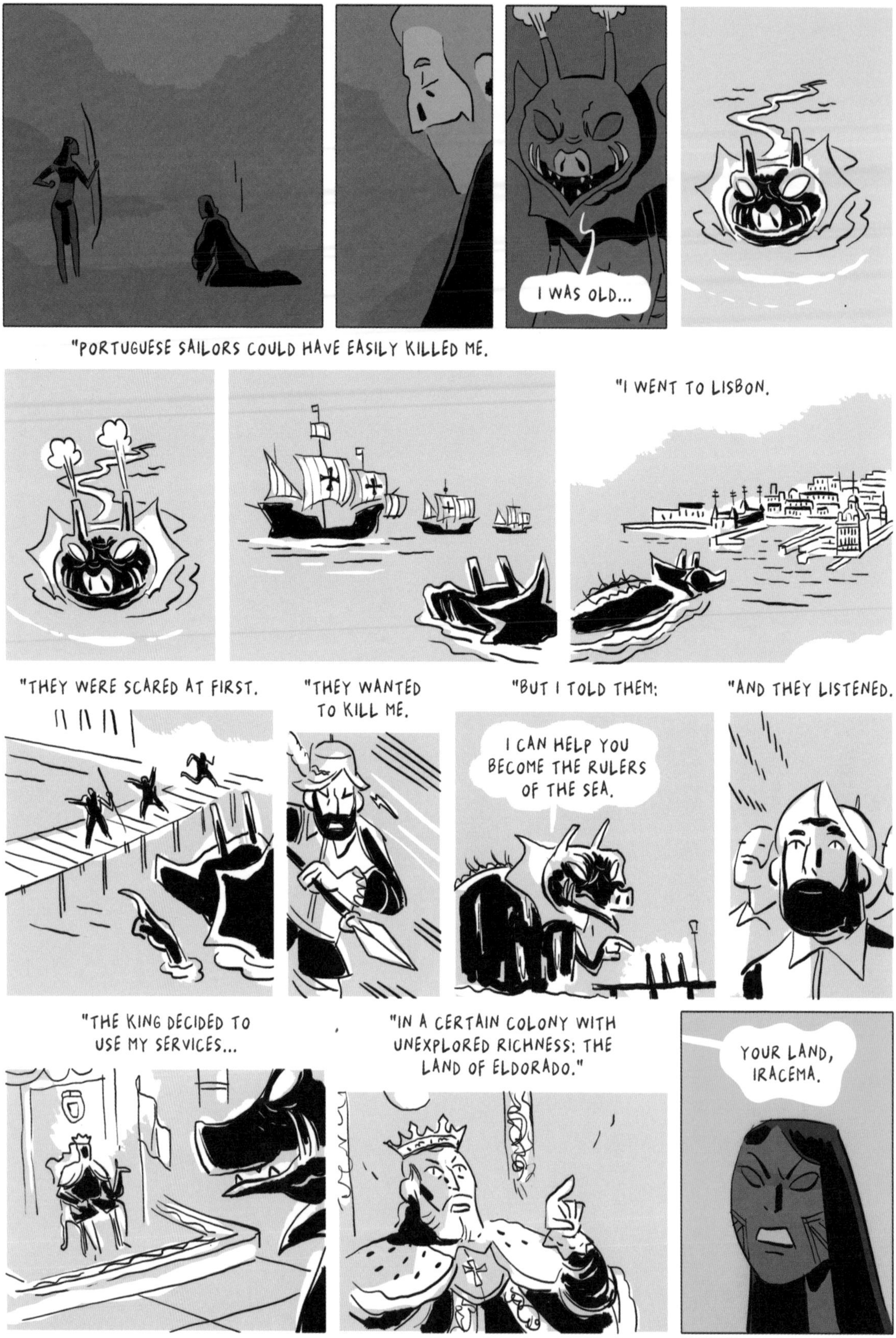
I WAS OLD...
"PORTUGUESE SAILORS COULD HAVE EASILY KILLED ME.
"I WENT TO LISBON.
"THEY WERE SCARED AT FIRST.
"THEY WANTED TO KILL ME.
"BUT I TOLD THEM:
I CAN HELP YOU BECOME THE RULERS OF THE SEA.
"AND THEY LISTENED.
"THE KING DECIDED TO USE MY SERVICES...
"IN A CERTAIN COLONY WITH UNEXPLORED RICHNESS: THE LAND OF ELDORADO."
YOUR LAND, IRACEMA.

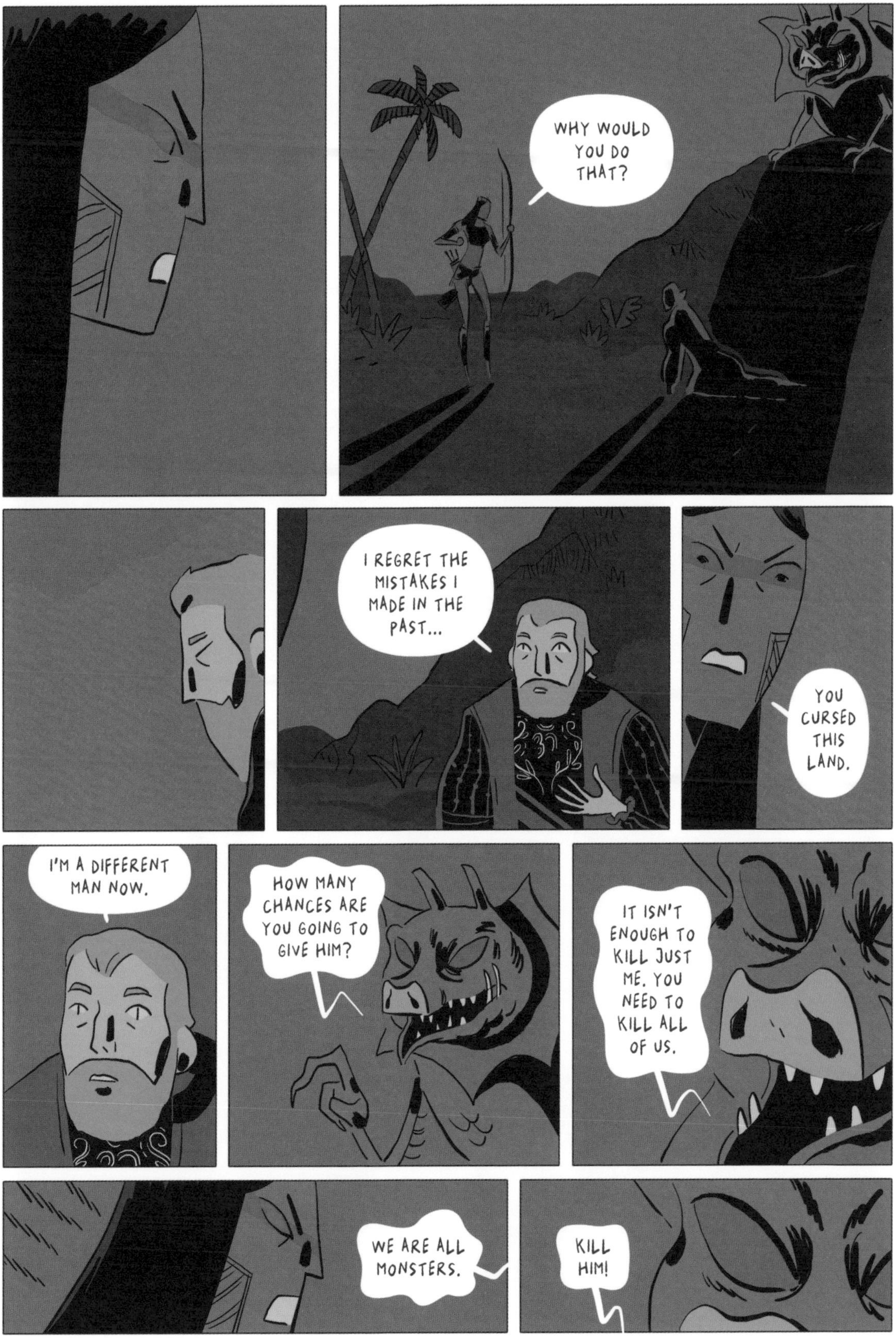
WHY WOULD YOU DO THAT?
I REGRET THE MISTAKES I MADE IN THE PAST...
YOU CURSED THIS LAND.
I'M A DIFFERENT MAN NOW.
HOW MANY CHANCES ARE YOU GOING TO GIVE HIM?
IT ISN'T ENOUGH TO KILL JUST ME. YOU NEED TO KILL ALL OF US.
WE ARE ALL MONSTERS.
KILL HIM!

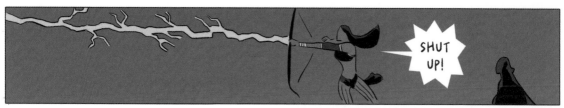

SHUT UP!

THA-DAM!

BOOM!

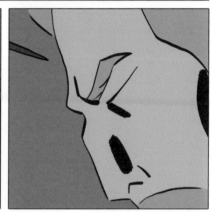

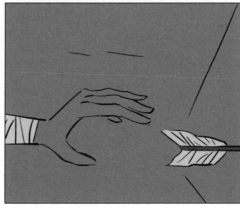

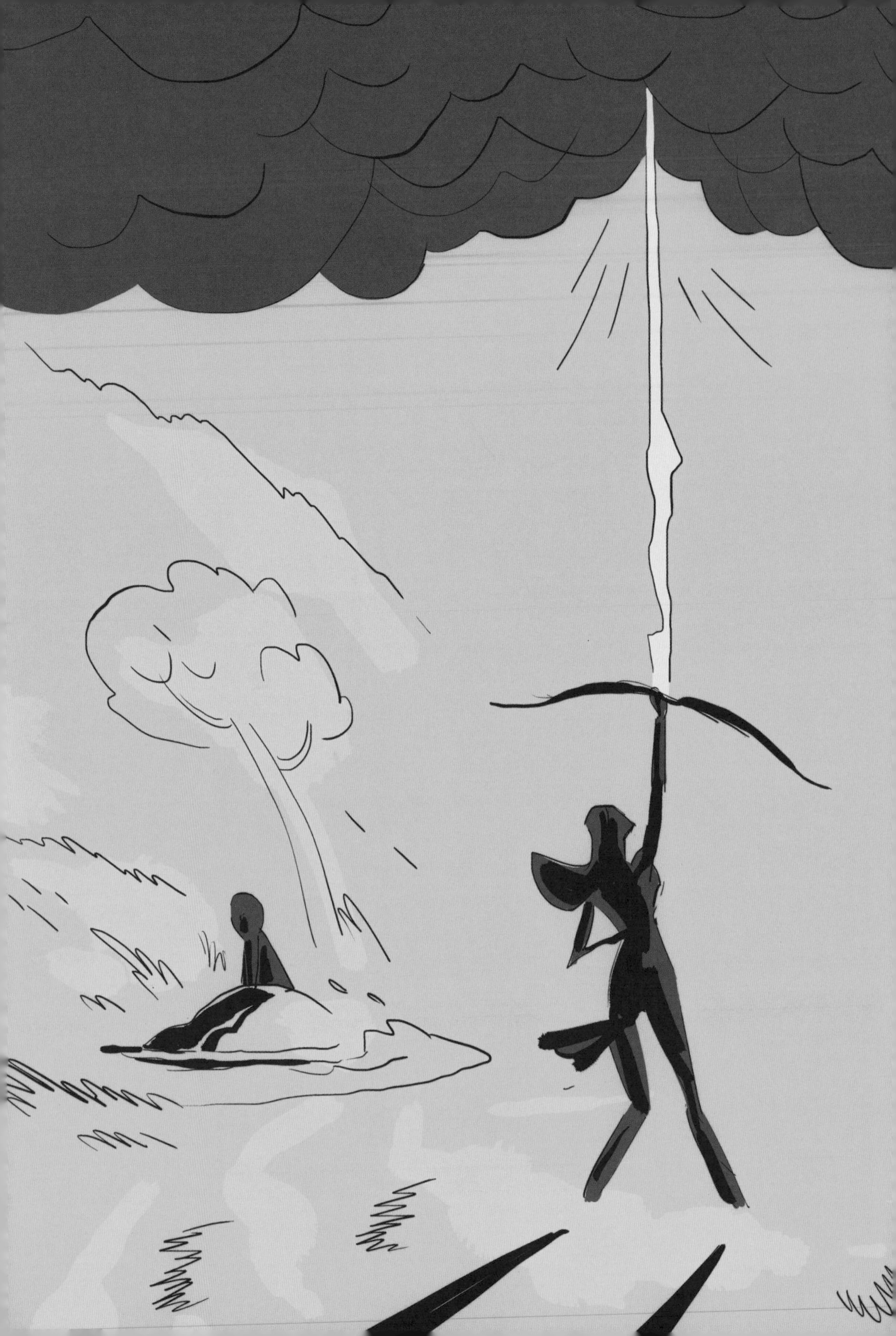

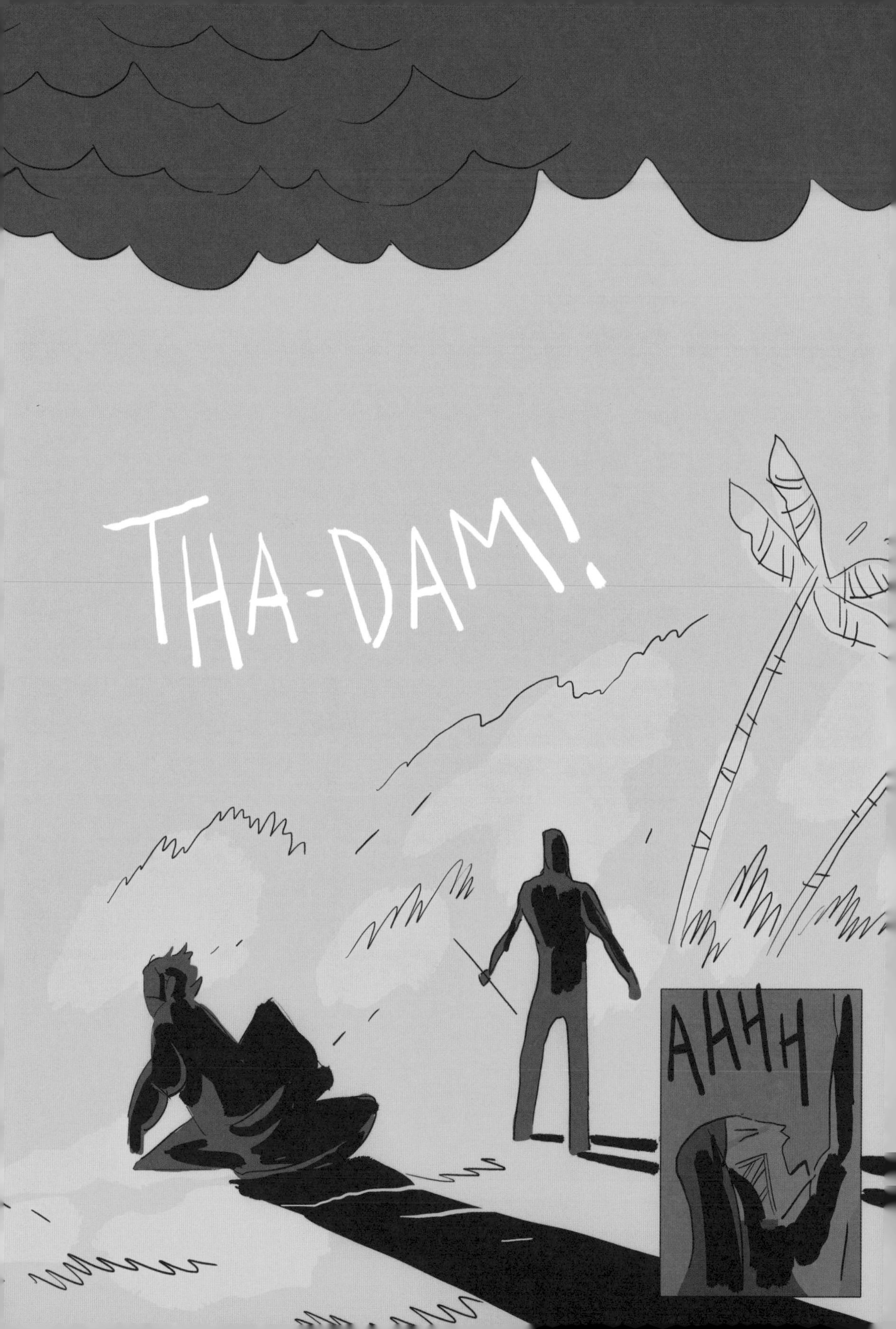
THA-DAM!
AHHH

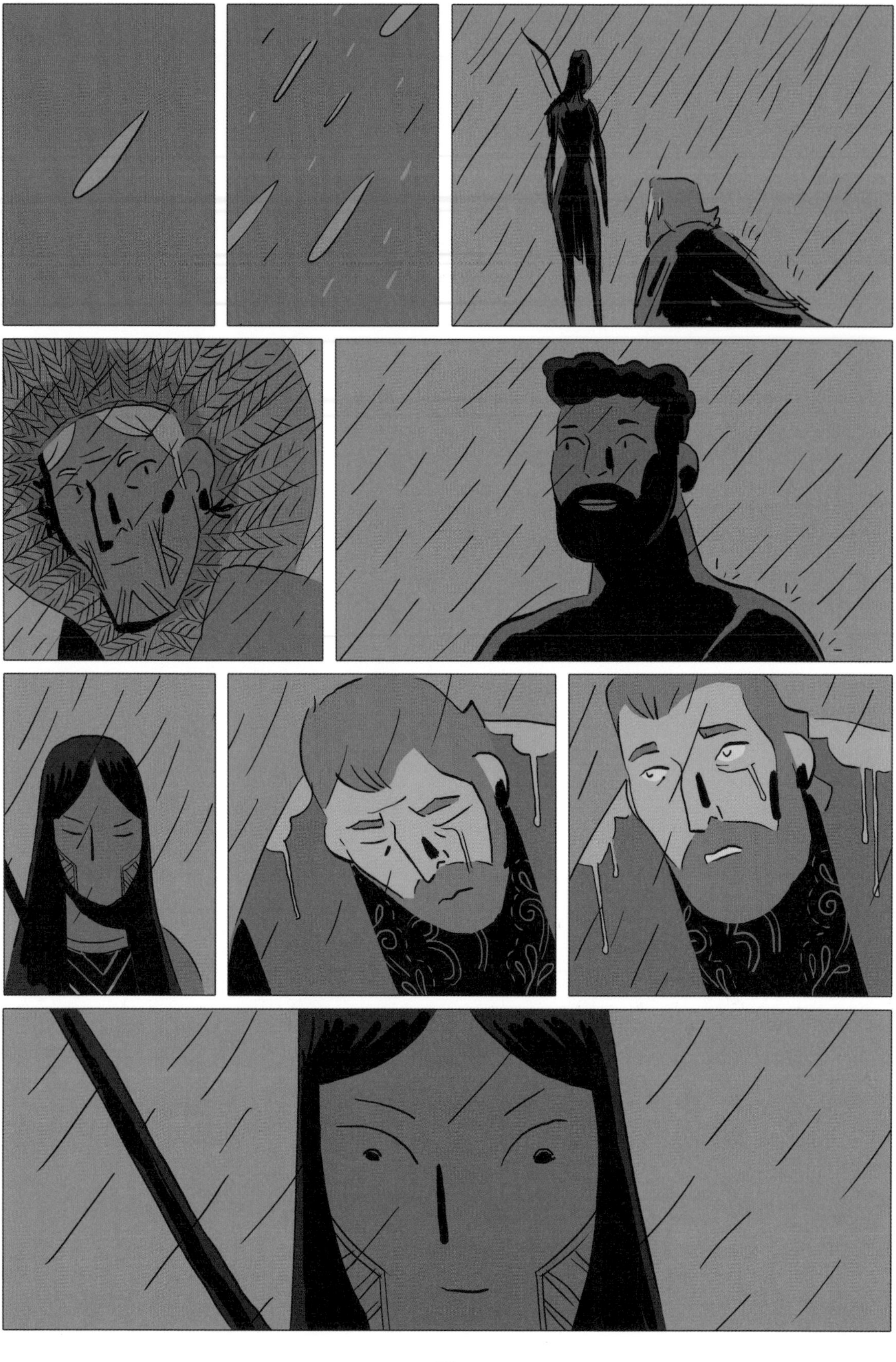

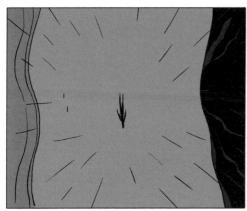

I SEE SHE WAS SOFT ON YOU, BARTOLOMEU.

I'M DYING. WELL DONE. BUT YOU THINK YOU SAVED YOUR LAND?

WE'LL TAKE IT FROM YOU.

WE'LL SPREAD OURSELVES ALL OVER IT.

NO ONE WILL EVER REMEMBER WE WERE MONSTERS.

NO.

WE WON'T LET THEM FORGET.

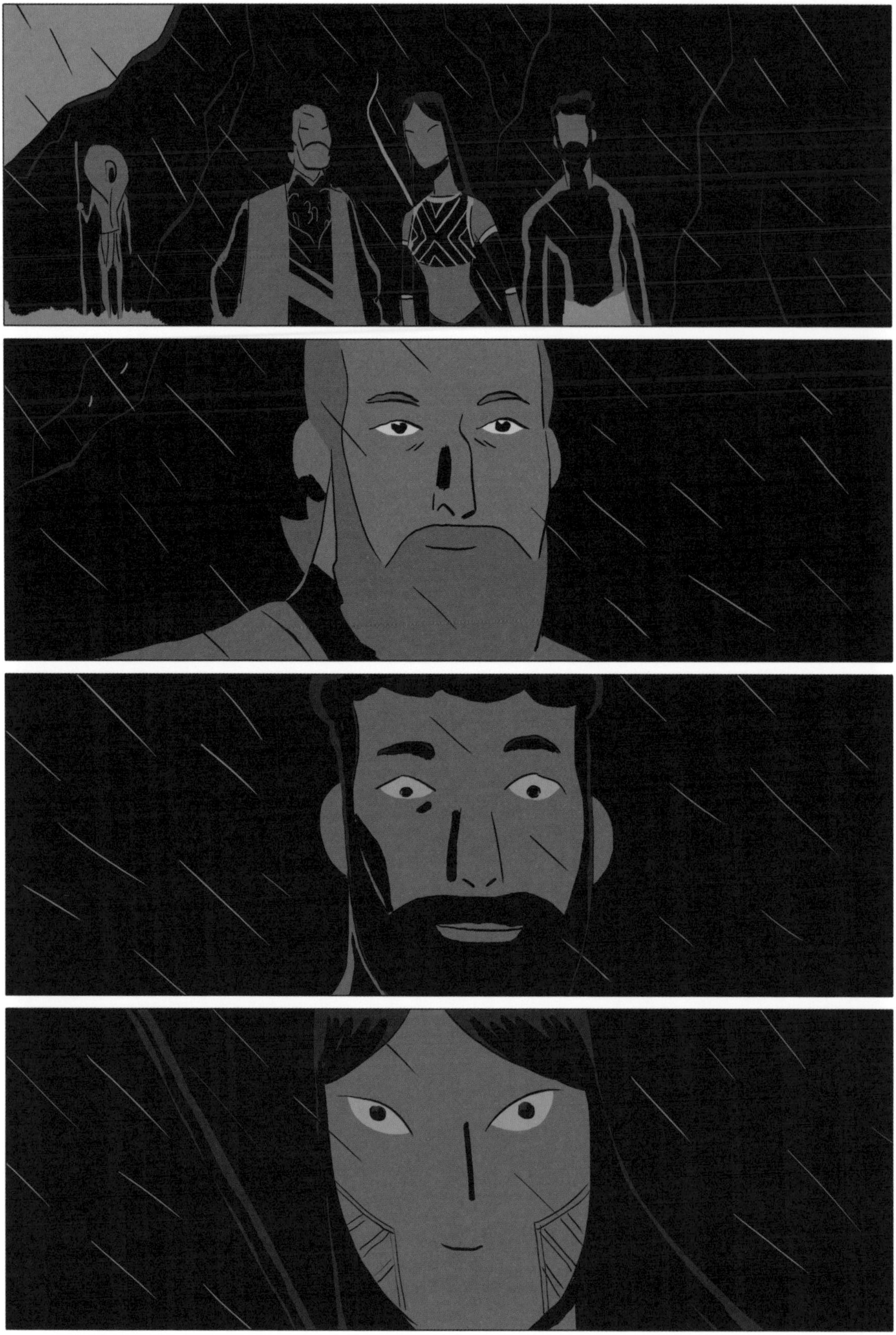

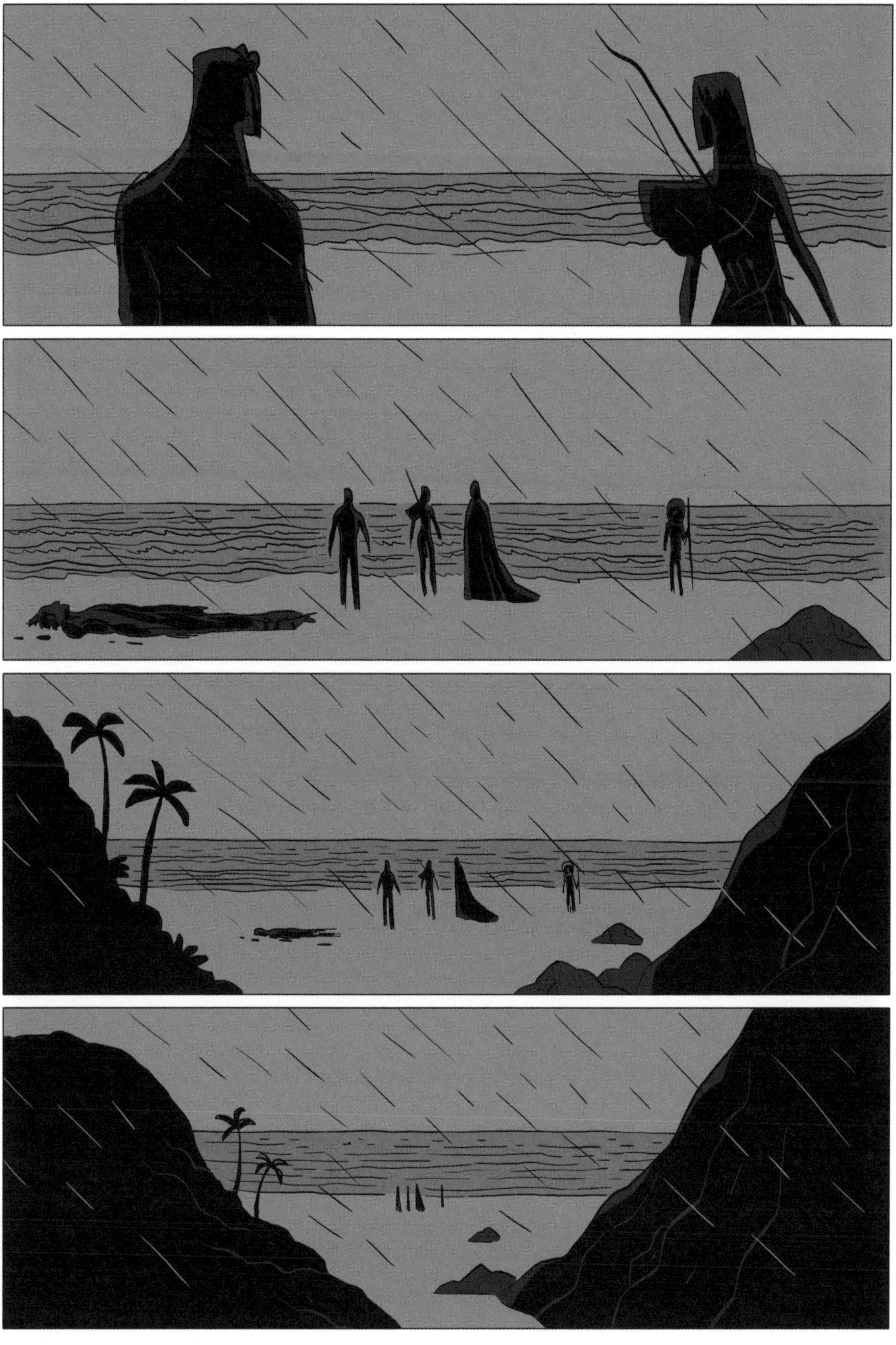

ALSO AVAILABLE FROM DAVID JESUS VIGNOLLI AND **ARCHAIA**

"*A Girl in the Himalayas* is a wonderful fable about learning the value of this incredibly magical world
we live in, which we can so easily forget, and how sometimes we must protect this world from the
dangerous illusion we create and come to believe."

—FÁBIO MOON *(TWO BROTHERS, DAYTRIPPER)*

A GIRL IN THE HIMALAYAS™

DAVID JESUS VIGNOLLI

ARCHAIA. **DISCOVER** YOURS

IN STORES
NOW

IN THE HIMALAYAS is ™ & © 2019 David Jesus Vignolli de Mello. All rights reserved.

WWW.**BOOM-STUDIOS**.COM

DISCOVER
GROUNDBREAKING TITLES

ASAF HANUKA
THE REALIST

LONG WALK TO VALHALLA
ADAM SMITH · MATTHEW FOX

THE MARCH OF THE CRABS
THE CRABBY CONDITION
ARTHUR DE PINS

Jane
ALINE BROSH McKENNA
RAMÓN K. PÉREZ

ROYDEN LEPP
RUST
VOLUME ONE
VISITOR IN THE FIELD

MOUSE GUARD
THE BLACK AXE
DAVID PETERSEN

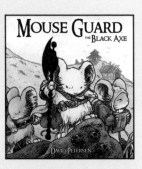

ARCHAIA

AVAILABLE AT YOUR LOCAL COMICS SHOP AND BOOKSTORE

To find a comics shop in your area, visit www.comicshoplocator.com

WWW.**BOOM-STUDIOS**.COM

The Realist
Asaf Hanuka
ISBN: 978-1-60886-688-5 | $24.99 US

The Realist: Plug and Play
Asaf Hanuka
ISBN: 978-1-60886-953-4 | $24.99 US

Long Walk to Valhalla
Adam Smith, Matt Fox
ISBN: 978-1-60886-692-2 | $24.99 US

The March of The Crabs
Arthur De Pins
Volume 1: The Crabby Condition
ISBN: 978-1-60886-689-2 | $19.99 US
Volume 2: The Empire of the Crabs
ISBN: 978-1-68415-014-4 | $19.99 US

Jane
Aline Brosh McKenna, Ramón K. Pérez
ISBN: 978-1-60886-981-7 | $24.99 US

Rust
Royden Lepp
Volume 0: The Boy Soldier
ISBN: 978-1-60886-806-3 | $10.99 US
Volume 1: Visitor in the Field
ISBN: 978-1-60886-894-0 | $14.99 US
Volume 2: Secrets of the Cell
ISBN: 978-1-60886-895-7 | $14.99 US

Mouse Guard
David Petersen
Mouse Guard: Fall 1152
ISBN: 978-1-93238-657-8 | $24.95 US
Mouse Guard: Winter 1152
ISBN: 978-1-93238-674-5 | $24.95 US
Mouse Guard: The Black Axe
ISBN: 978-1-93639-306-0 | $24.95 US

The Cloud
K.I. Zachopoulos, Vincenzo Balzano
ISBN: 978-1-60886-725-7 | $24.99 US

Cursed Pirate Girl Coloring Book
Jeremy A. Bastian
ISBN: 978-1-60886-947-3 | $16.99 US